# IN SEARCH OF A NEW
# WORLD ECONOMIC ORDER

# IN SEARCH OF
# A NEW
# WORLD ECONOMIC
# ORDER

EDITED BY

## HUGH CORBET
*Director, Trade Policy Research Centre, London*

AND

## ROBERT JACKSON
*Fellow, All Souls College, University of Oxford*

A HALSTED PRESS BOOK

## JOHN WILEY & SONS
New York          Toronto

Published in the USA, Canada and
Latin America by Halsted Press,
a Division of John Wiley & Sons, Inc., New York

ISBN 0-470-17221-5
Library of Congress Catalog Card No: 73-22724

Printed in Great Britain

# Trade Policy Research Centre

The Trade Policy Research Centre, London, was established in 1968 to promote independent analysis and public discussion of commercial and other international economic policy issues. It is privately sponsored and is essentially an entrepreneurial research centre.

Intense international competition, technological advances in industry and agriculture and new and expanding markets, together with large-scale capital flows, are having profound and continuing effects on international production and trading patterns. With the increasing integration of the world economy there is thus a growing necessity to increase public understanding of the problems now being posed and of the kind of solutions that will be required to overcome them.

The Centre is managed by a Council, which is headed by Mr Frank McFadzean, Chairman of the Shell Transport and Trading Company. Professor Harry G. Johnson, of the London School of Economics and the University of Chicago, is in charge of the Centre's research activities, while the director is Mr Hugh Corbet. Listed below are the members of the Council.

The principal function of the Centre is the sponsorship of research programmes. Specialists in universities and private firms are commissioned to carry out the research, the results of which are published and circulated in academic, business and government circles throughout the European Community and in other countries. Seminars and meetings are also held from time to time.

Activities of the Centre are financed by foundations, corporate donations and membership subscriptions.

Publications are presented as professionally competent studies worthy of public consideration. The interpretations and conclusions in them are those of their authors and do not purport to represent the views of the Council or others associated with the Centre.

# *The Round Table*

*The Round Table*, the Commonwealth journal of international affairs, is published in London four times a year. Since its foundation in 1910 it has been a completely independent journal supported by Round Table groups in many parts of the Commonwealth.

Articles in the journal range from developments in specific Commonwealth countries to broad issues in international relations extending beyond the Commonwealth as such. Sometimes a whole number of *The Round Table* is devoted to a particular theme and symposia are also arranged.

The editor of the journal is Mr Robert Jackson, a Fellow of All Souls College at the University of Oxford, and the editorial board, with the overseas members set out separately, is as follows:

Contributions to *The Round Table* are abstracted and indexed in *Historical Abstracts* and/or *America: History and Life*. Enquiries about subscription rates, the airmail edition, back numbers, contributions and so on should be addressed to the Secretary, *The Round Table*, 18 Northumberland Avenue, London WC2 6BX, United Kingdom.

# Contents

# *Preface*

This collection of essays has been compiled as a contribution to public discussion on what needs to be done about the crisis in international economic relations that has necessitated the reform of the international system of trade and payments. In order to contain the uncertainties which have been developing in the world economy there is a need for governments to express a political will to solve common problems in an international framework of co-operation. In 1972-73, two fora were established to broach the most important issues: the Committee of Twenty, within the framework of the International Monetary Fund, for a negotiated reform of the international monetary system; and the Tokyo Round negotiations, within the framework of the General Agreement on Tariffs and Trade (GATT), for a reform of the international commercial system.

Since the essays first went to press, however, there have been dramatic increases in crude oil prices, which have engendered great uncertainties about the likely *loci* of balance-of-payments deficits and surpluses in the next few years. As a result the Committee of Twenty decided in January 1974 to draw their deliberations to a close, accepting floating exchange rates as a fact of current economic life, and leaving unresolved the fundamental issues facing the international monetary system. But the question of reform is likely to be raised again once the problems of oil payments have been overcome. It is therefore important not to lose sight of the degree of understanding that has been achieved in the Committee of Twenty.

The present volume therefore focusses on the reform of the international commercial system that is to be pursued in the context of the further liberalisation of world trade. But there have been great uncertainties hanging over the Tokyo Round negotiations which have had to wait on the passage of the Trade Reform Act through the United States Congress. Not that the United States Administration requires Congressional authority to negotiate. But the trading partners of the United States prefer to be reassured in advance that the United States can implement whatever agreements are reached. Similarly the European Community needs to be able to reassure its partners that it can keep its side of a bargain. With tariffs and para-tariff barriers there is no difficulty. But many non-tariff barriers are instruments of industrial policy and in the European Community industrial policy remains the prerogative of national governments.

Underscoring the inter-relationship of economic and politico-strategic issues, the prospects for the Tokyo Round negotiations will depend, in the end, on developments in American relations with the countries of Western Europe both as members of the European Community and as members of the North Atlantic Alliance. Unless steps are taken to repair matters, the serious deterioration in Atlantic relations, which came to light as a result of the Middle East war of October 1973, could produce a general concensus that trade negotiations and economic co-operation between the United States and the European Community are becoming less and less relevant. After all, the spirit of the American mandate, as proposed to Congress, has been based on the economic and political interdependence of the industrialised countries of the world. If that underlying assumption is called in question the Tokyo Round would lose its force and logic.

While the timetable of international negotiations is therefore plagued by uncertainties, and the faces of governments are always changing, the issues confronting the international economic order remain the same. In compiling the present volume it has not been our intention to develop a particular theme. There is, though, a certain coherence about the papers. In the first part are two introductory papers which deal with the nature of the crisis in international commercial relations. The second part of the volume covers issues which are affecting the climate of the Tokyo Round negotiations. Significant issues not actually on the GATT agenda are discussed in the third part. It is in the fourth part that the specific issues to be addressed in the negotiations are reviewed and analysed.

The essays evolved from a symposium of five articles on the preparations for the Tokyo Round negotiations that were published, with the assistance of the Trade Policy Research Centre, in the April and July 1973 numbers of *The Round Table*. These articles, revised to varying degrees, have been supplemented here by papers commissioned by the Centre, while some are reproduced by kind permission of other sources.

Editing a collection of essays is no easy task. In compiling this collection we are grateful for the advice of a number of senior officials in Geneva, Brussels and London, while Janet Strachan and Judith Flynn, of the Trade Policy Research Centre, thoroughly earned the gratitude we owe them in organising the papers and preparing them for publication.

London
Spring 1974

HUGH CORBET
ROBERT JACKSON

# *Abbreviations*

| | |
|---|---|
| ASP | American Selling Price system of customs valuation |
| CAP | common agricultural policy of the European Community |
| CET | common external tariff of the European Community |
| c.i.f. | cost, insurance and freight |
| ECE | Economic Commission for Europe |
| EEC | European (Economic) Community |
| Euratom | European Atomic Energy Commission |
| FAO | Food and Agriculture Organisation |
| FEOGA | Fonds Europeen d'Orientation et de Garantie Agricole |
| f.o.b. | free on board |
| GATT | General Agreement on Tariffs and Trade |
| GNP | gross national product |
| IBRD | International Bank for Reconstruction and Development |
| IMF | International Monetary Fund |
| MFN | most favoured nation |
| MITI | Ministry of International Trade and Industry in the Japanese Government |
| NATO | North Atlantic Treaty Organisation |
| OECD | Organisation for Economic Co-operation and Development |
| OEEC | Organisation for European Economic Co-operation |
| OPEC | Organisation of Petroleum Exporting Countries |
| SITC | Standard International Tariff Classification |
| UNCTAD | United Nations Conference on Trade and Development |
| USDA | United States Department of Agriculture |

# Biographical Notes on Contributors

HUGH CORBET: Director of the Trade Policy Research Centre, London, since its inception in 1968; formerly a specialist writer on international economic affairs on *The Times*, London. Since 1965, Mr Corbet has been Secretary of the Foreign Affairs Club, also in London. He is the co-author of *Trade Strategy and the Asian-Pacific Region* (1971).

GERARD CURZON: Professor of International Economics, Institut Universitaire de Hautes Études Internationale, University of Geneva; also on the staff of the Centre d'Études Industrielles, Geneva. Professor Curzon is Editor, too, of *The Journal of World Trade Law*, London. His major study, *Multilateral Commercial Diplomacy*, was published in 1965.

RALF DAHRENDORF: Commissioner for Education and Science, Commission of the European Community, since 1973 having previously been Commissioner for External Affairs from 1970; earlier Parliamentary Secretary of State to the Minister of Foreign Affairs, Government of West Germany. Before entering politics Dr Dahrendorf was Professor of Sociology at the University of Constance. He is Director-designate of the London School of Economics.

GERHARD FELS: Director of Studies, Institut für Weltwirtschaft, University of Kiel, having been on the staff since 1969. Before then Dr Fels was on the research staff of the German Council of Economic Experts in Bonn. He is co-author of *Protektion und Branchenstruktur* (1973) and author of *Der Internationale Preiszusammenhang* (1969).

SIDNEY GOLT: economic consultant; formerly Deputy Secretary, Department of Trade and Industry in the British Government, 1970-71; earlier Adviser on Commercial Policy, Board of Trade (since superseded by the DTI). Mr Golt was chairman of the high-level group established by the Organisation for Economic Co-operation and Development to advise on tariff preferences for developing countries.

ROBERT JACKSON: Fellow of All Soul's College, University of Oxford, since 1969 and Editor of *The Round Table*, London, since 1970, during which time he has been a leader writer on *The Times*.

Mr Jackson was briefly Political Secretary to the Secretary of State for Employment in the Heath Government.

D. GALE JOHNSON: Professor of Economics, University of Chicago, since 1954; an authority on agricultural policy, often engaged to advise the Administration and Congressional enquiries in the United States. Professor Johnson was a key member of the Presidential Commission on Food and Fiber (1965-67) and was Agricultural Adviser to President Johnson's Special Representative to Trade Negotiations. He is the author of, among other works, *World Agriculture in Disarray* (1973).

HARRY G. JOHNSON: Professor of Economics, London School of Economics, since 1966, and at the University of Chicago since 1959; and also Vice-Chairman, and Director of Studies, Trade Policy Research Centre, London. He was previously Professor of Economic Theory, University of Manchester (1954-59), having earlier been a Fellow of King's College, University of Cambridge. Among his many works are *The World Economy at the Crossroads* (1965), *Comparative Cost and Commercial Policy Theory for a Developing World Economy* (1968), *Aspects of the Theory of Tariffs* (1971) and *Further Essays in Monetary Economics* (1973).

PETER LLOYD: Senior Fellow, Research School of Pacific Studies, Australian National University, Canberra; previously Assistant Professor and later Associate Professor of Economics at Michigan State University; and earlier a Senior Lecturer at Victoria University of Wellington in New Zealand. Dr Lloyd is the author of *Non-Tariff Barriers to Australian Imports* (1973).

HARALD B. MALMGREN: Deputy Special Representative for Trade Negotiations, Executive Office of the President of the United States, since May 1972; previously an economic consultant, and earlier a Senior Fellow at the Overseas Development Council, in Washington. Dr Malmgren's main publication is *International Economic Peace-keeping* (1972). He was Assistant Special Representative for Trade Negotiations in the Johnson Administration.

FRANK McFADZEAN: Chairman of the 'Shell' Transport and Trading Company since 1972, having been a Managing Director of the Royal Dutch-Shell Group of Companies since 1964. Mr McFadzean is Chairman of the Trade Policy Research Centre, London; Visiting Professor of Economics, University of Strathclyde; and Chairman, Strathclyde Division, Scottish Business School. In

1972 he was chairman of an advisory group of the Trade Policy Research Centre which produced the report, *Towards an Open World Economy.*

NOBUYOSHI NAMIKI: Director, Industrial Structure Division, Japanese Ministry of International Trade and Industry, having previously been director of the housing industry, overseas market and research divisions. Dr Namiki was earlier a Lecturer in Economics at the University of Tokyo and, before that, at the Chuo University. He is the author of *Japan in the Era of the Internationalized Economy* (1971).

DAVID ROBERTSON: Reader in International Economics, University of Reading; also a Consultant to the Trade Policy Research Centre, and a Lecturer at the Civil Service College, both in London; earlier an economist in the Secretariat of the European Free Trade Association, Geneva. Mr Robertson is the author of *International Trade Policy* (1972).

JAN TUMLIR: Director of Economic Research, Secretariat of the General Agreement on Tariffs and Trade, in Geneva, since 1967 having joined the Secretariat three years earlier when he worked in the Trade and Development Division. Dr Tumlir, who previously taught economics at Yale University, studied law at Charles University, Prague, leaving Czechoslovakia in 1949 for the United States.

*Part I*

INTRODUCTION

# CHAPTER 1

## Commercial Diplomacy in an Era of Confrontation

### HUGH CORBET

In public discussion a country's capacity to shape the course of world events tends to be judged in the context of the international security system where only great and super powers are thought to count. When it comes to the international system of trade and payments, however, small and middle powers can and do exert a considerable degree of influence, such is the growing interdependence of the world economy.[1]

This dichotomy has not been appreciated enough in the past to make a difference. But since the early 1960s there has been getting under way a redistribution of power among market-economy countries with the development of the European Community, the emergence of Japan and, partly as a result, the relative decline in strength of the United States, not to mention the growth to maturity of a number of smaller powers in the Southern Hemisphere.[2] There have also been changes taking place among the centrally-planned economies. These changes have contributed to the crisis in international economic relations that finally surfaced in the early 1970s and they pose deep problems in the search for a new international economic order. Together these changes and problems form the subject of the present volume. The nature of the economic crisis is discussed by Gerard Curzon in Chapter 2 and the political differences that have been emerging are analysed by Robert Jackson in Chapter 3.

No longer is the management of the international system of trade and payments the primary responsibility of the United States. That primary responsibility is being shared increasingly with the European Community and Japan. Neither though has developed an internal decision-making process that can readily respond to external events. The European Community has had difficulty in evolving a coherent approach to its external relationships which are reviewed by Ralf Dahrendorf in Chapter 4. And in becoming more intimately involved in the world economy Japan has had to make considerable internal adjustments of an industrial and socio-economic character; and these, and the prospects for further industrial adaptation, are dealt with in Chapter 5 by Nobuyoshi Namiki.

These shifts in power provide some scope, then, for other countries to make a difference in the international deliberations on the reform of the international trade and monetary system, which has served the free-enterprise world for a quarter of a century. What comprises the system?

Towards the end of World War II, governments were engaged on a new and challenging exercise, the deliberate planning of institutional arrangements that would together constitute a viable framework for the re-establishment of a liberal international system of trade and payments. The Bretton Woods negotiations, as they were called, after the location of the exercise in the United States, produced two institutions. The International Monetary Fund (IMF) was established as a means of improving the system of payments and currencies. In order to augment the flow of capital from rich to poor countries, there was also established the International Bank for Reconstruction and Development (IBRD), otherwise known as the World Bank. Almost concurrently, negotiations in Geneva produced, in place of the originally intended International Trade Organisation, the General Agreement on Tariffs and Trade (GATT) as an instrument for pursuing the liberalisation of world trade.[3]

Multilateral commercial diplomacy has thus largely been exercised during the postwar period through the GATT's institutional arrangements. Limited use has been made of the Commonwealth by its member countries and the European Community's spreading galaxy of preferential trade agreements has offered many developing countries an alternative focus for their commercial policy endeavours. But the United Nations Conference on Trade and Development (UNCTAD), established in 1964, has not become the market place for negotiations that some envisaged.[4]

As the membership of the GATT forum enlarged to eighty signatories, embracing more and more developing countries and extending to some of the centrally-planned economies, the leading advanced nations grew increasingly restless. The tedium of time-consuming set speeches from one delegation after another has only been part of the problem. Many issues between more developed countries are not of central concern to less developed ones. This is evident, for example, in the field of non-tariff barriers to trade: quantitative restrictions, public procurement policies, direct government subsidies, industrial standards and so on.[5] When closely analysed, these are found to be a complex of specific problems, relating to trades in specific goods between specific countries. As for the issues that are of central concern to the developing countries, the solutions to them, whether in the form of aid or trade or a combination of both, depend in the end upon agreement among the developed countries. (If the rich are falling out with one another they are likely to care even less for the poor.)

Several key capitals have accordingly come around to the view that the developed countries should use the Organisation for Economic Cooperation and Development (OECD) as the forum in which they decide, or at least clarify, their collective position on major issues confronting the world economy before taking them very far in a more universal setting. It was in the OECD, formed in 1961 to carry on the work of the Organisation for European Economic Cooperation (OEEC),[6] that the developed countries worked out how they would respond to the UNCTAD call for tariff preferences in favour of developing countries.[7] And it was in the OECD that they began to work out how to proceed with the next phase in the liberalisation of world trade. An understanding of what lay behind the OECD high-level group on 'trade and related problems', which reported in 1972,[8] would therefore seem essential to any understanding of what may lie ahead.

## European Frustration of American Initiative

After the Kennedy Round of GATT negotiations, which were successfully concluded in mid-1967, serious consideration on the question of maintaining the momentum of trade liberalisation was effectively thwarted at inter-governmental level by Britain's renewed application for membership of the European Community. In case there is any doubt about the question arising that early, it might be recalled that in the United States the first wave of Congressional demands for import quotas, following the Kennedy Round agreement was launched in August of the same year. By early November, 90 of the 100 Senators had sponsored, or co-sponsored, at least one legislative proposal for import quotas or some other restriction on foreign supplies.[9]

President Johnson anticipated the protectionist assault on the Congress of the United States. As soon as the Kennedy Round agreement was signed, he instructed William Roth, his Special Representative for Trade Negotiations, to prepare recommendations for another liberalising drive.[10] When the hue and cry for import quotas got under way, the White House set about mobilising resistance right across the country, operating through business and political connections of all kinds. On Washington's Capitol Hill, the Joint Economic Committee of Congress embarked on a series of studies and hearings on future American commercial policy,[11] while the Senate Finance Committee also took up the subject.

It was generally recognised, as it had been even before the Kennedy Round marathon was completed, that a fresh approach would have to be adopted in future multilateral trade negotiations.[12] It was acknowledged, too, that by the time the Kennedy Round agreement had been implemented in 1972, tariffs would be down to very low average levels. In fact, the average level of tariffs on manufactured and semi-manufactured goods, weighted by OECD trade, was then 8.3 per cent for the United States, 8.4 per cent for the European Community, 10.2 per cent for the United Kingdom (ignoring Commonwealth preferences) and 10.9 per cent for Japan. [13]

Harry G. Johnson and the present writer once attempted to put the situation in historical perspective in the following terms: The Kennedy Round negotiations, the sixth in the GATT series, marked the end of a liberalising phase in which *freer trade* could be the only realistic objective. After the Great Depression and World War II, the best that policy planners could envisage in the late 1940s and 1950s was a restoration of orderly conditions in international commerce and a reform, as well, of the autarkic and discriminatory policies which resulted from the protectionist excesses of the 1930s. With the tariff reductions and dramatic expansion of world trade that occurred in the 1960s it is now possible to regard *free trade* as not only a realistic goal but also a necessary one. [14]

Even so, as American attention began to focus on preparations for another major trade initiative, the British Government failed to perceive or, more charitably, chose to overlook the opportunity to obtain for the United Kingdom the benefits of Common Market membership by other means. Harold Wilson, the then Prime Minister, was contemptuous of non-official proposals at the time for the negotiation of a multilateral free trade association among developed countries. [15] On Britain's application for membership of the European Community, he expressed determination in November 1968, 'to be neither disheartened by obstruction nor distracted by plausible *soi-disant* alternatives or attractive and tempting blind alleys'. [16]

More than a decade before, when the Treaty of Rome was being negotiated and Britain held aloof, Jean Monnet observed that the British were incapable of grasping an idea; they can only get interested in something, he said, when they see it exists and can see it working. [17] On the coming into being of the European Community in 1958, the United Kingdom first tried to overcome the problems it posed for British interests by proposing an industrial free trade area between the members of the OEEC, thereby embracing the whole of Western Europe. The subsequent OEEC negotiations, the ministerial stage of which was conducted under the chairmanship of Reginald Maudling, as British Paymaster-General, came very close to success, but in the end the six Common Market countries, the inner Six, refused to compromise. Led by Britain, the outer Seven, not sharing the political objectives of the Six, thereupon formed in 1959 the European Free Trade Association (EFTA).[18] Two years later, however, the United Kingdom applied to join the European Community.

Britain's preoccupation with the pursuit of Common Market membership became more and more obsessive as the 1960s wore on. Indeed, by 1967 one of the most persuasive Whitehall arguments in favour of renewing the British application, following the breakdown at the end of 1962 of the negotiations on the first application, was the sober truth that 'the European issue' had to be settled, one way or the other, before any alternative course could be seriously considered. 'Getting into Europe', like winning the war, had become the be all and end all of everything.

While proponents of the Europeanist cause were fond of emphasising the need for change, they seemed most influenced themselves by changes that had taken place in the 1950s and even earlier, which might not be surprising in a movement that derived its impetus from World War II and the Iron Curtain period. They appeared oblivious, though, to the changes that were taking place in the world around them. This state of mind was reflected in the British Government's highly propagandist White Paper in 1971 on the Great Debate.[19] There the security arguments were wrapped up in mumbo-jumbo about 'Europe united' and 'Europe divided' that dated more from the 1930s than from current realities. Nowhere in the White Paper, or in the speeches of Government ministers, was it acknowledged — implicitly or otherwise — that since the 1940s international security has been a matter of global balance. Nor did official statements suggest an acquaintance with the degree of integration and interdependence that has been achieved in the world economy since the 1950s. In the past twenty years world trade has increased five-fold and in the 1960s was expanding twice as fast as world income.[20]

Strong commitments to achieving British membership of the Common Market were not confined to London or just the capitals of Western Europe. There were strong commitments in Washington as well and they were able, without much difficulty, to forestall any major trade initiative that might otherwise have been proposed. In a memorandum (later published as an article) prepared in March 1970, for circulation in Whitehall, following a visit to Washington, the present writer noted:

'There is emerging (in the United States Administration) a division of opinion, although by no means serious, over the timing of the next major trade initiative. The view of White House staff remains that new trade proposals should not be embarked upon while Britain, and the other EFTA countries, are negotiating with the European Community. But there is a widespread view to the contrary that that is precisely when the next major trade initiative should be launched. The former view is largely motivated by a desire not to appear to be interfering in European affairs, while the latter view is largely motivated by a desire to ensure that outward-looking policies, rather than inward-looking ones, are developed during the negotiations on the European Community's enlargement.' [21]

With the awful problems of 'limited warfare' in Indo-China and urban and communal troubles at home, President Nixon was not disposed to pay close heed to international economic issues, particularly when his most influential advice was that economic questions were not a central concern of foreign policy. Little attention was given, in the absence of positive action, to the negative course of resisting mounting protectionist pressures. On the contrary, priority was given to negotiating with Japan and other East Asian countries 'voluntary' restraints on their exports of non-cotton textiles to the United States, in order to fulfil one of President Nixon's election promises.

The initiation, however, towards the end of 1969, of another series of hearings and studies by the Joint Economic Committee of Congress and the establishment, soon after, of the Presidential Commission on International Trade and Investment Policy (the Williams Commission) served *inter alia* to bolster resistance to the demands of economic nationalism. It is easy to be cynical about government-appointed enquiries. But these two encouraged, at a time when American foreign economic policy was suffering from an obvious lack of direction, the devotion of business, bureaucratic and institutional resources to devising new ways of promoting the further liberalisation of international trade and capital movements and of overcoming the accompanying social and employment problems. By clarifying the issues and generating public interest, even if at an élitist level, the two enquiries also served to consolidate momentum behind a new move forward that could be expected to acquire eventually a momentum of its own.

Meanwhile, the lack of leadership and coordination in the conduct of foreign economic policy left the various economic departments in the Nixon Administration freer to express, in public as well as in inter-departmental exchanges, the growing disaffection of many powerful American interest groups with the policies being implemented by the European Community, not to mention those of

Japan and other countries. The waning though still influential 'Europe first' school in the State Department, which in the heyday of 'the Club' in the late 1950s and early 1960s had been responsible for inspiring American support for the cause of European unification, was able to hold off a major trade initiative that might have afforded Britain a way out of her European predicament. But the State Department could not hold off the criticism of the European Community that its prospective enlargement was serving to aggravate.

Among the grievances which have contributed to the grave deterioration in international commercial relations since the late 1960s has been the impact on agricultural trade of the Common Market's mercantilist farm-support policies. The full effects of the common agricultural policy of the European Community only began to be felt in 1966. In that year the rising trend of American shipments of farm produce to the Common Market was reversed, agricultural exports to the Six falling by nearly 20 per cent over the following three years, while those products subject to the variable import-levy system declined by over 40 per cent. For a time world grain shortages ameliorated these concerns. But access to the Common Market remains important to American agricultural exporters as it does to other efficient agricultural-producing countries. The parlous state of world trade in temperate-zone agricultural commodities is discussed by D. Gale Johnson in Chapter 12.

Another cause of alarm has been the proliferation of discriminatory trade agreements which the Community has been concluding over the years, beginning with the eighteen ex-colonies in Africa embraced by the Yaoundé Convention, followed by the Arusha Convention covering three East African countries; and Spain, Israel and some North African countries have been the most recent additions to a list that already included Greece and Turkey. What was more alarming was the prospect of the enlarged Common Market of ten countries negotiating free trade agreements with the six EFTA 'non-applicants' and, in addition, a round of preferential trade agreements designed to accommodate the Mediterranean, African and Caribbean members of the Commonwealth. The result could be a polarisation of the world economy around the two major trading entities.[22] The issue is taken up by the present writer, in Chapter 10 below, in the context of negotiations on industrial tariffs.

Thirdly, there has been increasing suspicion in the United States of the techniques by which West European governments are thought to enhance the ability of their products to penetrate the American market, either for their manufacture or for their export. These techniques, ranging from direct subsidies to tax allowances to public procurement policies, have produced the slogan that 'foreign trade is not fair trade'.[23] And the early efforts in the European Community to develop a common industrial policy have not been reassuring to those in the United States Administration who have supported European unification.[24] What are involved here are non-tariff distortions of international competition and how these might be broached is discussed by Peter Lloyd in Chapter 11.

Fourthly, there has been much heat generated in the United States over the operations of multinational enterprises, which have been seen by the labour unions as 'exporting jobs'. For many American-based firms have been investing in the production of labour-intensive products in developing countries. The importation of the low-cost products of those investments has then been seen as the cause of unemployment in the corresponding domestic industries. The issue was exacerbated by the balance-of-payments problems of the United States and by the feeling, by no means well-founded, that other countries — particularly in Western Europe — were not bearing their share of the 'burden' of developing-country exports. Much of the heat was taken out of the protectionist demands for import controls by the 1971 and 1973 *de facto* devaluations of the American dollar. But it is acknowledged (a) that greater export opportunities need to be provided for developing countries, (b) that more emphasis needs to be placed in developed countries on adjustment assistance to increased import competition and (c) that new provisions need to be made for emergency protection against sharp increases in imports. These three sets of problems are explored in the last three chapters below by Sidney Golt, Gerhard Fels and Jan Tumlir.

The above factors, though, have not been the only ones to affect the climate of international economic relations. Some of them are non-commercial. There has been the deepening resentment of the United States over the unwillingness of other countries to bear their share, too, of the cost of collective security arrangements. Americans have grown weary, as well, of European assumptions of superiority, not only in cultural matters but also in diplomacy and politics — especially when there is so little evidence in the present day and age to sustain such arrogance.

It is not as if, to digress awhile, the Americans are without blame for their economic woes. After all, it was on American insistence that farm-support measures were, for all intents and purposes, taken out of GATT negotiations in the early 1950s, when subsidies in the United States were stimulating huge agricultural surpluses. It was American support for European unification which allowed GATT rules to be waived so that the Common

Market could proceed with tariff preferences for its associated overseas territories. Moreover, it was American use of defence procurement to support technologically advanced industries which, at least to some extent, induced West European governments to resort to similar policies in an attempt to close 'the technological gap'.[25]

Finer points such as these are by the way in an American context. Whereas once upon a time the European bureau in the State Department could effectively resist 'for political reasons' the pressures which other government departments wanted 'for economic reasons' to exert on the European Community, from the late 1960s onwards it found it increasingly difficult to do so; its position was weakened still more by the running down of the momentum towards European unification, the need for which was in any case being overtaken by other developments in international relations.[26] On the handling of United States policy towards the European Community, the mistrust of American business was summed up in the quip: 'We oughta get rid of that State Department and get one of our own.'

With the economic bureau in the State Department playing a larger role, a number of efforts were nevertheless made, even before President Johnson left office, to engage the European Community in discussions on further multilateral trade negotiations. Every time though there were reasons for delay. First there was the need to digest the Kennedy Round agreement. Then it was stressed that the 'enlargement' negotiations would first have to be completed. In due course the necessity to consolidate the enlarged Community was emphasised. Always the Six expressed interest in negotiating with the rest of the world. But it was like waiting for Godot.

The sense of frustration which had been building up in the United States Administration, and which it has been one of the purposes of this essay to try to explain, was succinctly stated by Peter Peterson, as President Nixon's Assistant for International Economic Affairs, in a paper published in December 1971:

'It seemed to many Americans that the interests of those countries which had benefited most from American policies were increasingly concentrating on regional or nationalistic arrangements that were too often either restrictive or discriminatory or both. In response to mounting expressions of American concern and urgings to negotiate corrections to these trends, the reply was too often that internal needs or preoccupations precluded meaningful external adjustments. It boiled down to a response of negotiations later rather than sooner.'[27]

As Mr Peterson went on to indicate, when the so-called crisis of the American dollar blew up in mid-1971, the United States 'had to convince its partners that negotiations sooner were no longer just desirable — they were imperative'. Observers were slow to understand that, besides countering the immediate symptoms, the measures taken by President Nixon on 15 August 'were designed to encourage the initiation of basic reforms in the international monetary and trading systems'.[28] Yet there had been plenty of prior indications — dating from the institution seven months before of the Council on International Economic Policy,[29] to correct the lack of co-ordination referred to earlier, to a spate of Cabinet speeches just before the annual meeting in June of the OECD Ministerial Council[30] — of the posture that the United States has since adopted in its relations with the European Community, Japan and Canada.

## Renewed Momentum of Trade Liberalisation

Believing that further multilateral trade negotiations would have to be initiated on the basis of agreement between the enlarged European Community, Japan and the United States,[31] the Nixon Administration achieved an important first step in that direction when the OECD Ministerial Council agreed to the setting up of a high-level study group to prepare recommendations.[32] The manoeuvre represented an American attempt to get the other industrialised countries to focus on the fundamental problems confronting the international trading system. Unfortunately there was a tendency in Europe to dismiss the exercise as an American attempt to contain domestic protectionist pressures. It took the imposition by the United States of a temporary import surcharge, together with other measures, properly to awaken the free-enterprise world to the dangers of creeping protectionism. 'Instead of stagnation,' as Olivier Long, the GATT Director-General, later observed, 'there developed a certain dynamic movement. Complacency disappeared overnight.'[33]

All the same, governments still had to be jolted along, such was their continuing reluctance to take concerted international action — excused on a variety of persuasive grounds ranging from general unreadiness to continuing world monetary turmoil (discussed by Harry Johnson in Chapter 9). 'We have to reconsider the procedures by which the rules of world trade can be maintained and developed in the light of both the old principles and the new facts of life,' wrote Ralf Dahrendorf, as the European Community's Commissioner for External Trade, a fortnight after President Nixon announced his New Economic Policy. 'I am not at all sure,' the Commissioner added, 'that we are prepared for this, either politically or intellectually.'[34]

That may well be so. But some have been better prepared than others. Another fortnight later, on 14 September, the massive report of the Williams Commission was published.[35] It had been sent to the White House a month before the 15 August measures. It can be expected to influence the course of American foreign economic policy in the 1970s in much the same way as the report of the Randall Commission did in the 1950s. The main thrust of the Williams Report was the call for 'the progressive elimination of most tariffs over the next ten years' and for 'the elimination of all barriers to international trade and capital movements within the next twenty-five years'. [36]

The first public sign that the United States Administration was giving favourable consideration to the Williams Report proposals was a major policy statement in London by William Eberle, as President Nixon's Special Representative for Trade Negotiations, in the course of which he said:

'There are many alternative bases on which . . . wide-ranging negotiations might be started. One possible approach which has been proposed both in and out of government is an agreement covering:
(a) a formula and time-table for an across-the-board elimination of substantially all industrial tariffs;
(b) rules of competition relating to non-tariff barriers to trade, services and investment;
(c) specific commitments aimed at opening world markets for agricultural products and rationalising national farm policies; and
(d) non-reciprocal tariff preferences in favour of developing countries over the transition to tariff-free trade.
At the present time this particular set of propositions may seem very grand. However started, on whatever basis, the need for starting a continuous process of negotiation is increasingly evident.' [37]

Mr Eberle's London statement, like the Williams Report it reflected, was in line with a general consensus which had been emerging from the comprehensive reappraisal of international economic policy that began in the United States at the end of the Kennedy Round negotiations, and in which the prospective needs of the world economy figured large. [38]

For a start, there had surfaced in Washington an inclination to accept that the only constructive way of overcoming preferential trading arrangements, and of avoiding an economic 'cold war' between the enlarged European Community and the United States, was for the developed countries to enter into negotiations aimed at dismantling all, or substantially all, tariffs on industrial goods traded among them. There was the added argument that another multilateral effort would have to be motivated by an objective compelling enough to induce in the major trading entities a political commitment to its eventual success. Merely halving the tariffs that remain might not be deemed worth the effort.[39] In this connection, the GATT Director-General has urged that 'the experience of Europe, in the Common Market and EFTA, has shown the value, in getting rid of industrial tariffs, of the technique of progressive, linear and automatic reductions'. M. Long continued: 'If the Europeans have done this, cannot the other industrialised countries of the world do the same? The idea of achieving over a period of years full industrial free trade among developed countries is one which deserves serious consideration.'[40]

Another part of the general consensus was that the only constructive way of dealing with the problem of 'unfair trade practices', more academically described as non-tariff distortions of international competition, was by negotiating commitments by governments to codes of good conduct, which are later elaborated upon in further negotiations.[41] It was also commonly argued — as in the Williams Report — that, in order to provide as much scope as possible for agreement to be reached, the removal of extant tariffs, the solution to non-tariff methods of protection and the freeing of agricultural markets should be tackled in the same negotiations. In fact, it was clear that if the United States was to gain Congressional support for a worthwhile scheme of tariff preferences in favour of developing countries, the proposals should be put to the legislature in the framework of a broad trade strategy. And for the strategy to obtain enough political support it would have to include provisions for large-scale adjustment assistance to import competition.[42]

### Events Leading to the Tokyo Round Negotiations

The Nixon Administration did formulate a broad trade strategy along the lines recommended in the Williams Report. But getting the other parties around the negotiating table continued to be plagued with problems which in part reflected the uncertainties in the enlarged European Community about its outlook on the rest of the world. But in the Smithsonian Accord of December 1971 reached in Washington which settled the monetary crisis of that year, the United States obtained from the other major trading powers — in return for having agreed to devalue the dollar in terms of gold — an agreement to hold comprehensive multilateral talks beginning in 1973 on the fundamental issues within the GATT framework.

In February 1972, after two months of further monetary confrontation, the United States concluded specific agreements with Japan and then with the European Community which amounted to a joint initiative by all three to launch a new round of GATT negotiations. The Joint Declarations on International Trade Relations which were finally received by the GATT Secretariat on 10 February 1972, stated that the 'comprehensive review of international economic relations' should cover *inter alia* 'all elements of trade, including measures which impede or distort agricultural, raw material and industrial trade' and that special attention should be given to the problems of developing countries. For the rest of the year attention focussed on the reform of the monetary system and trade problems returned to their customary second-place in the schedule of priorities. As far as Britain and the European Community were concerned, the enlargement of the Common Market was of more immediate interest than the forthcoming talks on the reform of the international trading system. But the formal decision was taken at the GATT session in November to begin preparations for the talks.

In February 1973, in the wake of yet another monetary crisis, the United States devalued the dollar for a second time. Trade talks seemed further off then ever. In the following April, however, the United States Administration presented its draft Trade Reform Act of 1973 to Congress, designed to give the President unprecedented power in the field of commercial policy. The bill was designed to give the President much needed flexibility in trade talks which has in the past been found wanting in the American negotiating position. Before the Watergate affair it was thought that the bill might be passed by October 1973. Constitutionally the President does not require the support of Congress to initiate negotiations with other countries. It is the implementation of the results that usually requires additional legislation.

On the European side things also moved more slowly than planned. This has mainly been due to the fact that the European Community, like a boa constrictor, has proved unable to move after absorbing three slightly indigestible morsels. Not to be outdone, though, the Commission of the European Community produced for the Council on 4 April 1973, a memorandum entitled 'Development of an Overall Approach to Trade in View of the Coming Multilateral Negotiations in GATT'. Known as 'the Soames memorandum', it attracted violent criticism from the French Government. Michel Jobert, as France's Foreign Minister, called it an *'ebauche de compromis'* — that is, something which did not even begin to represent a compromise of member views. Even so, the other eight members raised no objection to the Soames memorandum and so the unknown question was to what extent France, acting alone, could get it modified. On 26 June 1973 the Council of Ministers agreed a statement on the European Community's bargaining position. But it did not amount to a negotiating mandate.

Nearly four months later the seventh round of GATT negotiations were ceremonially launched at a Ministerial meeting in Tokyo with a declaration agreed by governments.

## NOTES AND REFERENCES

1. The basis of this introductory chapter is Hugh Corbet, 'Australian Commercial Diplomacy in a New Era of Negotiation', *Australian Outlook*, Melbourne, April 1972.

2. The politico-strategic and economic implications of the greater involvement of Asian-Pacific countries in the world economy is explored in Corbet *et al.*, *Trade Strategy and the Asian-Pacific Region* (London: Allen & Unwin, 1970).

3. For authoritative accounts of the development of the post-war system of international trade and payments, see Richard N. Gardner, *Sterling-Dollar Diplomacy: Anglo-American Collaboration in the Reconstruction of Multilateral Trade* (Oxford: Clarendon Press, 1956) and Gerard Curzon, *Multilateral Commercial Diplomacy* (London: Michael Joseph, 1965).

Also see Karin Koch, *International Trade Policy and the GATT 1947-67* (Stockholm: Almqvist & Wiksell, 1969) and Kenneth W. Damn, *The GATT Law and International Economic Organisation* (Chicago and London: University of Chicago Press, 1970).

4. The manoeuvres of the developing countries in UNCTAD are briefly discussed by Sidney Golt in Chapter 13 below.

5. Quantitative restrictions bear heavily on the exports of developing countries, but they do not call for the same degree of policy harmonisation that is likely to be required in order to overcome other methods of non-tariff protection. Instead their elimination calls for the implementation of adjustment assistance programmes for the industries in developed countries that are adversely affected by competition from developing countries.

6. For an analysis of the OECD, see Henry G. Aubrey, *Atlantic Economic Co-operation: the Case of the OECD* (New York: Praeger, for the Council on Foreign Relations, 1967).

7. The response was disappointing. It demonstrated, in a negative way, how the solutions to the problems of the poor depend upon agreement among the rich. For the developed countries were obliged to give up the idea of a single UNCTAD preference scheme because of American hostility towards the reciprocal preferences which the Common Market insisted on retaining under its special preference arrangements with associated overseas territories.

8. High-level Group on Trade and Related Problems, *Policy Perspectives for International Trade and Economic Relations,* Rey Report, (Paris: OECD, 1972).

9. *Constructive Alternatives to Proposals for US Import Quotas* (Washington and Montreal: Canadian-American Committee, 1968), p.9.

10. The outcome of the Roth enquiry was published just before President Johnson left office: Special Representative for Trade Negotiations, *Future United States*

*Foreign Trade Policy*, Roth Report (Washington: US Government Printing Office, 1969).

11. See *The Future of US Foreign Trade Policy*, Hearings before the Subcommittee on Foreign Economic Policy (Washington: US Government Printing Office, for the Joint Economic Committee, United States Congress, 1967), together with the Report under the same title and *Issues and Objectives of US Foreign Trade Policy*, a compendium of studies prepared for the Subcommittee.

12. See the statement by the then Director-General of the GATT, Sir Eric Wyndham White, 'International Trade Policy; the Kennedy Round and Beyond', in an address to the Deutsche Gesellschaft für Auswartige Politik, Bad Godesberg, 27 October 1966.

13. *The United States in a Changing World Economy* (Washington: Council on International Economic Policy, Executive Office of the President, 1971), p. 25.

14. Harry G. Johnson and Hugh Corbet, 'Pacific Trade in an Open World', *Pacific Community*, Tokyo, April 1970.

15. The proposals were first put forward, in a post-Kennedy Round context, in *A New Trade Strategy for Canada and the United States* (Washington and Montreal: Canadian-American Committee, 1966). Since then a considerable literature on the subject has developed. The circumstances of, and the arguments for, the free trade treaty proposal are summarised in Corbet *et al.*, *Trade Strategy and the Asian-Pacific Region, op. cit.*

16. Speech at the Lord Mayor's Banquet, London, 11 November 1968. Britain had reapplied for membership of the European Community on 10 May 1967.

17. Quoted in Leonard Beaton, 'Are we making the same mistakes all over again?' *Evening Standard*, London; 2 April 1968.

18. The OEEC negotiations and the origins of EFTA are critically examined in Haruko Fukuda, 'First Decade of EFTA's Realisation', in Corbet and David Robertson (eds.), *Europe's Free Trade Area Experiment: EFTA and Economic Integration* (Oxford and New York: Pergamon Press, 1970).

19. *The United Kingdom and the European Communities* (London: Her Majesty's Stationery Office, 1971). For a critique of the White Paper see Anthony Harris, 'What the White Paper leaves unsaid', *The Guardian*, London, 8 July 1971.

20. For a brilliant discussion of the integration of the world economy, see Richard N. Cooper, *The Economics of Interdependence: Economic Policy in the Atlantic Community* (New York: McGraw-Hill, for the Council on Foreign Relations, 1968).

21. Corbet, 'Course of US Trade Policy in the 1970s', *Journal of World Trade Law*, London, September-October 1970.

22. Sir John McEwen, as Deputy Prime Minister of Australia, sounded a note of apprehension on this prospect in the House of Representatives, Canberra, on 20 August 1970. His statement was republished as 'European Negotiations: Need for a "Third Party" Initiative', *The Atlantic Community Quarterly*, Washington, Winter 1970-71.

23. Hubert Humphrey, 'Agriculture's Place in International Trade', Address to the Trade Policy Research Centre, London, 30 July 1971.

24. Cf. C. Fred Bergsten, 'Crisis in US Trade Policy', *Foreign Affairs*, New York, July 1971. Dr Bergsten was, until a short time before, Assistant to the President for International Economic Affairs on the senior staff of the National Security Council, Executive Office of the President, in the United States Administration.

25. In this connection, see Corbet, 'Political and Commercial Perspectives on Relations between Developed Countries', in *A Foreign Economic Policy in the 1970s*, Hearings before the Subcommittee on Foreign Economic Policy (Washington: US Government Printing Office, for the Joint Economic Committee, United States Congress, 1970), Part 2, pp. 180-90.

26. Theodore Geiger, 'Ending of an Era in Atlantic Policy', *The Atlantic Com-*

*munity Quarterly*, Spring 1967. Also see Geiger, *Transatlantic Relations in the Prospect of an Enlarged European Community* (London, Washington and Montreal: British-North American Committee, 1971).

27. Peter G. Peterson, *A Foreign Economic Perspective* (Washington: Council on International Economic Policy, Executive Office of the President, 1971), p. 5.

28. *Ibid.*, pp. 1 and 5. For a further discussion of the motives behind the 15 August measures, see Harald B. Malmgren, 'The New Posture in US Trade Policy', *The World Today*, London, December 1971.

29. The council was set up on the recommendation of President Nixon's Advisory Council on Executive Organisation as an economic counterpart in the White House to the National Security Council and Peter Peterson, as Assistant to the President for International Economic Affairs, was its first executive director.

30. Perhaps the most notable was the address by John B. Connally, as Secretary of the Treasury, to the international banking conference of the American Bankers Association, Munich, 28 May 1971.

31. For an analysis of the background to this belief, see Corbet, 'Global Challenge to Commercial Diplomacy', *Pacific Community*, October 1971.

32. Because Denmark wanted to be represented on the group, and unlike Australia refused to take 'no' for an answer, the enquiry could not be announced as directly responsible to the OECD council, where an unanimity rule prevails. When the membership was finally announced on 8 December 1971, it had to be said that the group had been called together by the OECD secretary-general. The group, under chairmanship of Jean Rey, the former President of the European Community's Commission in Brussels, had been meeting since October.

33. Olivier Long, 'Toward Better Trade Relations in the 70s', Address to the Trade Policy Research Centre and the Foreign Affairs Club, London, 24 January 1972.

34. Ralf Dahrendorf, 'Why Europe is Shocked', *The New York Times*, New York, 1 September 1971.

35. Presidential Commission on International Trade and Investment Policy, *United States International Economic Policy in an Interdependent World*, Williams Report (Washington: US Government Printing Office, 1971), together with two volumes of papers prepared for the Commission.

36. *Ibid.*, pp. 10 and 304.

37. William Eberle, 'Trade Issues in the 1970s', Address to the Trade Policy Research Centre, London, 23 November 1971.

38. Besides the Roth and Williams reports and the hearings of the Joint Economic Committee of the United States Congress, not to overlook a host of academic studies, attention might be drawn to two private reports: *US Foreign Economic Policy in the 1970s: a New Approach to New Realities* (Washington: National Planning Association, 1971); and *The United States and the European Community: Policies for a Changing World* (New York: Committee for Economic Development, 1971).

39. Optional negotiating techniques are discussed in Gerard and Victoria Curzon, 'Options After the Kennedy Round', in Johnson (ed.), *New Trade Strategy for the World Economy* (London: Allen & Unwin, 1969; and Toronto: University of Toronto Press, 1970). In addition, see Johnson and Corbet, *op. cit.*, and Johnson, 'World Trade Policy in the Post-Kennedy Round Era', *Economic Record*, Melbourne, June 1968. Also see Chapter 10 below.

40. Long, *op. cit.*

41. An early sign of American interest in this approach was in *Constructive Alternatives to Proposals for Import Quotas*, *op. cit.* Also see Robert E. Baldwin, *Nontariff Distortions of International Trade* (Washington, Brookings Institution, 1970) and Malmgren, 'Negotiating Nontariff Barriers: the Harmonisation of National Economic Policies', in *US Foreign Economic Policy in the 1970s*, *op. cit.*

For a discussion of EFTA's experience with rules of competition, see Curzon and

Curzon, *Hidden Barriers to International Trade*, Thames Essay (London: Trade Policy Research Centre, 1970), pp. 45-60.

42. David Wall, *Third World Challenge: Preferences for Development*, Atlantic Trade Study (London: Trade Policy Research Centre, 1968).

# CHAPTER 2

## Crisis in the International Trading System

### GERARD CURZON

The international trading system, though by no means forgotten, tends to take second place in public discussion, given the urgency and drama of the international monetary crises which have plagued the 1970s. While plans for monetary reform and analyses of the monetary situation abound, the reverse side of the coin — the crisis in the trading system — has been less well defined. Yet it should be the other way round.

It is forgotten that an orderly international monetary system is needed for no other reason than to form a firm basis upon which to build a rational system for the exchange of goods and services between nations. Perhaps the reason is that the world trading system lends itself much less readily to systematic analysis and model-building than does the international monetary system. Even so, the gold standard of pre-World War I times, the monetary chaos of the inter-war period, the benign dollar standard of the 1950s and 1960s, and the not-so-benign dollar standard of the 1970s all have their trade counterpart in the *systeme des traites'* the beggar-thy-neighbour policies of the inter-war period, the General Agreement on Tariffs and Trade (GATT) in the post-World War II era and the growing dissatisfaction with the established trading order since the end of the 1960s. [1]

Which comes first, the chicken or the egg, is difficult to say. A sound trading order cannot exist in times of monetary disarray. This much seems to be clear from the disastrous inter-war experience. But can monetary disarray lead to the destruction of an existing world trading order? There is very little doubt that the answer to this is in the affirmative. Not only trade, but also social and political orders have in the past been brought to a fall through disorders of an economic and, more strictly speaking, a monetary nature. The process, however, is not — in our day and age — inevitable. Inflation due to a sudden increase in the supply of money is not a matter of chance discoveries of new gold deposits as was the case, for instance, of Spain in the sixteenth century. It is a matter of conscious economic policy-making in the United States and, to a more limited extent, in the European Community and Japan. Co-operation between these three poles of economic activity is the only really essential prerequisite for the establishment and maintenance of a sound trade *and* monetary order, of whatever blend or variety may be chosen as corresponding to the needs of the times. [2] The trade and monetary systems, though, must be in harmony with each other and, in some respects, it can even be said that the type of monetary system chosen will have an effect on the type of trading system that can be established to support it.

## Trade Crisis in Historical Perspective

Take, for instance, the trade policy implications of the gold standard. The latter implied a rather brutal adjustment mechanism for absorbing balance-of-payments deficits via (a) the price level, (b) the rate of employment and (c) real incomes, to which nineteenth-century policy-makers were not totally indifferent, however unformalised their reactions may have been. Economic policy instruments were nevertheless in short supply and exchange rates were, by definition, fixed in terms of gold. To the extent that the government was able to influence trade, therefore, this was one policy instrument which had to be used to avoid the hard times that went with a loss of bullion. The logical prescription for this was to increase the stock of gold (by increasing exports over imports) or, at least, to cause no reduction (by balancing exports and imports over time). Since all trading countries were faced with the problem of maintaining balance-of-payments equilibrium, there was little chance for negotiating a trade agreement which would lead to an excess of exports over imports (since this meant that at least one country would end up with a deficit). Efforts concentrated on the negotiation of a *reciprocal* exchange of trade advantages; that is, a balanced exchange of export opportunities and import openings.

Reciprocity by itself was not enough to guarantee this balance in practice. Indeed only under state trading could this ever be the case. One of the elementary safeguards against the erosion of past concessions developed very early on in the history of commercial treaties was the principle of non-discrimination expressed in the most-favoured-nation (MFN) clause. This had become a standard instrument of trade policy from the Middle Ages onwards. It meant that negotiated trade advantages could not be undermined by subsequent agreements which one's trade partners might negotiate with other countries. The exigencies of the nineteenth-century gold standard with fixed exchange rates thus gave rise to a trading system based on reciprocity and non-discrimination which — with its legal basis, its decennial tariff bindings and its regular renegotiations — probably had a more formalised existence than its monetary counterpart.

It is interesting to reflect on the fact that the unsatisfactory experience of the two inter-war decades led to the re-establishment of a monetary system that, in the minds of some of its architects and in outward appearance at least, closely resembled the nineteenth-century gold standard. In the post-World War II system fixed exchange rates were again defined in terms of gold, with exchange-rate margins uncannily near to the 'gold point' mechanism which, in the last resort, would bring about adjustment under the nineteenth-century gold standard.

Needless to say, the trading system that was developed in due course under the auspices of this re-styled gold standard resembled the *systeme des traites* in its essential points — reciprocity and non-discrimination. It was a trading system designed to maintain equilibrium in the balance of payments in order to avoid both (a) domestic deflationary policies in case of deficits which were politically unacceptable and (b) devaluations which were frowned upon internationally. Once again trade concessions could only be exchanged between countries if they could be counted upon to increase the volume of trade without altering the balance of trade. Also needless to say the calculation was inaccurate and subjective. But in the multilateral form of tariff bargaining that developed under the GATT, which implied the negotiation of a large number of inter-locking bilateral agreements multilateralised via the MFN clause, there was not only a good chance that errors in the calculation of reciprocity would cancel each other out; there was even a margin for subjective optimism which left each participant with the impression of having gained more than he had conceded.

Besides the need for balanced negotiations in a fixed-exchange-rate world, reciprocity had the added advantage in the domestic context of widening the constituency for freer trade policies. Thus although tariff reductions could be counted upon to bring forth wails from the affected import-competing sectors, expanded trade opportunities abroad would elicit cheers from the export industries concerned. A government could consider its domestic equilibrium to be maintained if the wails were no stronger than the cheers. Indeed, in the 1950s and 1960s, the progress of trade liberalisation was such that one is tempted to believe that the cheers rather consistently drowned the wails, at least in Western Europe and Japan.

## Conflict of Views in GATT System

In the 1940s, however, when the system was established, Europeans were less confident in it than is generally supposed.[3] They had already realised that different domestic policies, different priorities and different objectives would lead to balance-of-payments 'difficulties' quite unrelated to their trade position. As has since been pointed out by the United States, the system assumed that the deficit countries would do the adjusting, thus releasing surplus countries from any obligation to act. The Europeans therefore sought to extricate themselves from the obligation to adjust to what appeared to be a situation of permanent and chronic balance-of-payments deficits.

The results of these efforts are to be seen scattered throughout the post-war economic treaties. They could be seen especially in the GATT where physical controls on trade were permitted 'for balance-of-payments reasons'. And domestic full-employment policies and economic reconstruction efforts could be protected from the rigours of balance-of-payments adjustment under fixed exchange rates. In a similar vein, the principle of non-discrimination underwent a certain amount of erosion by the fact that pre-existing preferential agreements were permitted to continue in existence and a standard exception was made for customs unions (and, in a less traditional spirit, free trade areas). To put the matter simply, the GATT for the Americans was Article 1; for the Europeans, it was Articles 12 and 24.

Therefore, at the very outset of the establishment of the new world trade order, there existed fundamentally conflicting views as to what type of trade order had actually been negotiated. Was it a non-discriminatory equilibrium trade system based on strict reciprocity, the natural corollary of a fixed exchange-rate system based on convertibility? Or was it a preferential system based on trade controls directed against 'strong' currencies?

## Divergencies Masked by American Policies

During the 1940s and 1950s this conflict of views over the nature of the GATT was masked by the fact that the United States, having negotiated this equilibrium trading system, proceeded to relax the rules of reciprocity and non-discrimination for their European partners. In fact the benign dollar standard was matched by a benign trade standard. An outstanding example of this willingness to accept an unbalanced trade bargain is the first round of tariff negotiations in Geneva and Annecy in 1947 and 1949. Here the United States, armed with an authorisation to reduce tariffs by 50 per cent, exchanged real tariff concessions for fake ones from the Europeans. The latter, in fact, had ceased to use tariffs to regulate trade, and instead imposed quantitative restrictions to limit imports. The tariff concessions offered by the Europeans were therefore meaningless, in that they could not lead to an increase in American exports.

Outside the trade field, a similar readiness to forego the benefits of strict reciprocity could be seen in the unprecedented generosity of the Marshall Aid programme. Even more surprising was the American attitude to non-discrimination. One of the conditions of access to Marshall Aid which the United States insisted upon was that European countries should liberalise trade amongst themselves. The Organisation for European Economic Co-operation (OEEC) was established for this purpose. Its members proceeded, often reluctantly, to apply the 'liberalisation code' to intra-European trade, thereby discriminating by implication against dollar trade. That the United States should have insisted upon being discriminated against — seen at the time as a matter of very enlightened self-interest — is all the more surprising if one considers that the whole tone of Atlantic negotiations from the Atlantic Charter to the ill-fated ITO Charter (International Trade Organisation) centred upon the importance of non-discrimination in trade relations.

In a similar vein must be put the American endeavours to encourage European integration via the European Defence Community, in the political field, and the European Economic Community (EEC) in the economic field. The United States even went so far, in 1958, as to accept the multilateralisation of colonial preferences within the nascent EEC, thus extending to Germany, Italy, Belgium and the Netherlands, the mutual preferences existing within the French colonial empire. By acquiescing in this extension of colonial trade preferences, the United States abandoned (at least for the time being) one of their most cherished post-war objectives, the gradual elimination of all preferential trading systems and the creation of a single and truly multilateral one. It ignored the strong British protestations that this was contra the GATT.[4] This was a case of original sin which was to cost the United States dearly later on. If the GATT could be ignored by its principal author for *raison d'etat* it was not difficult to predict that others would soon do likewise.

Yet the irrational American behaviour stemmed from the best of motives. The United States wished to accelerate the process of European convalescence in order that it might have an equal partner with which to co-operate, not only politically and strategically, but also economically. Once Western Europe was 'on its feet' again the trading system based on reciprocity and non-discrimination could be made to work. Despite American aid and trade efforts, however, the process took longer than had been anticipated. Instead of the three-to-five year transitional period which was frequently mentioned just after the war, it was not until 1958-59, or thirteen to fourteen years after the end of the war, that Western Europe became capable of playing the game of economic co-operation roughly according to the rules.

On 1 January 1959, most West European countries made their currencies convertible for non-residents on current account and, since quantitative restrictions were no longer justified on balance-of-payments grounds, these were gradually lifted upon the insistence of the United States. By the early 1960s quantitative restrictions on manufactured products in most West European countries were a thing of the past. This was no mean achievement, if one considers that the last time this was so was probably in the last half of the nineteenth century, not counting a short period in the 1920s. In any event, the important fact to remember is that the fake tariff concessions made by the Europeans in the late 1940s and 1950s came into their own; and one element in the unbalanced trading system was corrected.

Success in this area, though, was not matched by success in the area of non-discrimination. Whilst the Common Market had been accepted by the United States as being an expression of the European will to unite politically, it caused the United States considerable tariff discrimination. Nevertheless, the United States responded positively to the challenge of European integration. President Kennedy's Grand Design of equal partnership between the European Community and the United States is now forgotten. It was on the strength of this ideal that the United States Congress passed the revolutionary Trade Expansion Act of 1962 which opened the way to the first major trade negotiation between the European Community and the United States — the Kennedy Round negotiations in which, of course, other GATT countries also participated.

This is not the place to indulge in an analysis of the achievements of the Kennedy Round. [5] It is enough to recall that it was the first truly reciprocal trade negotiation under the GATT system and that, as it drew to a close, the impression was one of immense achievement. For the first time since World War II the United States could say that the Bretton Woods-GATT system had actually worked. It had taken twenty years for the United States to achieve what they felt was an equilibrium in a balanced trade system.

### Divergencies Unmasked by European Policies

However, scarcely was the ink dry on the schedules of concession than the pendulum began to swing the other way. Already during the Kennedy Round negotiations some intractible problems had begun to cast a shadow over American-European relations. The Community, the embarrassed recipient of numerous requests for trade agreements and caught in its own logic, found that it could not offer trade advantages to some African countries and refuse them to others.

Similarly, in the Mediterranean, if Greece and Turkey had the right to access to the Common Market under special terms, why should other Mediterranean countries be treated differently? The only logical answer was to extend the preferences in question to those with a reasonable claim to equal treatment. Thus negotiations were begun with Nigeria and with the East African Common Market on the grounds that they were African countries of the type given preferences under the Yaoundé Convention. Talks were held with Spain, Israel and some North African countries on the grounds that they were Mediterranean countries like Greece and Turkey.

The Community's so-called 'Mediterranean-policy' was the unwanted result of an ill-planned 'association' policy, conceived at the outset of the Community's existence when it wished to avoid, at all costs, the accusation of being inward-looking. Instead of admitting the mistake, however, the Community plunged deeper and soon claimed that the Mediterranean was a European sphere of influence, further rationalising its right to extend its network of preferential agreements.

The United States no longer felt as generous as it had about the Community's 'special links' the extension of which could no longer be justified by *raison d'etat* since they were by no means essential for the strengthening of the effort towards European integration. Furthermore, instead of involving American trade interests in a very minor way (the pragmatic argument of the Community in favour of its original preferential agreement having been that the volume of United States trade effected was insignificant), some fairly vociferous American trading interests were directly affected by the extension of the Community's preferences in the Mediterranean — particularly the Florida and California citrus-fruit producers. Whether or not the Community's preferential arrangements were in conformity with the GATT was in practice irrelevant. They may or may not be free trade areas within the terms of Article 24. The point is that the United States considered that they were an abuse of this exception to the GATT's principle of non-discrimination. The United States, patrolling the Mediterranean with the Sixth Fleet, was unmoved by the Community's claim that the preferential agreements struck a blow for freedom and the West and would save the region from Soviet influence. In short, the difference of opinion on this issue was total and complete. Perhaps for the first time since World War II the United States found that it could no longer influence the course of policy-making in Western Europe.

As if this was not enough, the sense of American frustration was soon to be compounded by a problem far more important in trade terms than the European Community preference issue. The United States had known, ever since the Treaty of Rome was signed, that the common agricultural policy (CAP) would hurt American agricultural trade interests. Like the association of overseas territories, it was part of the price that had to be paid for French participation, it was therefore accepted with the resignation due to the inevitable. What was not foreseeable at the time was that the Community caught, as in the case of preferences, in a game of political give-and-take, found that it had fixed the price of wheat and butter so high that it not only became self-sufficient but became a net exporter as well.

The operation was an extremely expensive one for the Community, which first had to pay European farmers at a high price and then had to pay European exporters to sell at a low price. It was also bitterly resented by the United States which, with Canada and Australia, had organised the world wheat market and was managing it more or less satisfactorily under the auspices of the International Wheat Agreement, when suddenly the Community's grain surpluses were dumped on the world market. The disturbance caused by this auction was such that it caused the collapse of the International Wheat Agreement, and when it came up for renewal in 1969, the negotiations were a failure. This was a major blow to a very important sector of United States trade and a far cry from the insignificant trade implications of the Arusha Convention.

Many minor items were added to the growing list of American grievances: (a) border tax adjustments in the European Community; (b) 'burden-sharing' not only in respect of European defence, but also in relation to aid to developing countries and in the sense of accepting a larger share of Japanese exports; (c) the extension of preferential arrangements to remaining EFTA countries and so forth. To make matters worse, the United States was also going through one of its periodic bouts of protectionist sentiment, with various sectional interests asking for, and usually obtaining, emergency protection against a growing flood of imports from Western Europe and Japan. [6] That the cause of this sudden loss of American competitiveness was an over-valued dollar was not perceived. Instead one blamed the GATT trading system, the 'unfair' pricing policies of European and Japanese companies and the non-tariff barriers which prevented American exports from competing in world markets. In short, the United States was disenchanted with the whole system, which seemed only to work in its disfavour.

The European Community, on its side, was unsympathetic to American moans. It drew up a *pro forma* list of grievances with which they countered American complaints — the American Selling Price (ASP) system of customs valuation, the 'Buy American' Act, the 1954 GATT 'waiver' to permit import quotas on agricultural products, emergency import quota restraints, on shoes and textiles, voluntary export restraints on steel — but it was not interested in a negotiation to clear the air. The Community was busy with the negotiations on its enlargement and felt that these problems could wait.

All the same, the list of European grievances was meagre. In fact, as far as the Europeans were concerned, what they could hope to gain from such a negotiation was very much less than what the United States wished to extract from them in the way of concessions. The elements of a balanced bargain were not present. The American tariff was at an all-time low. There were no quantitative restrictions to speak of on products of interest to the Europeans. The United States, the world's most powerful economy, found itself in the paradoxical situation of having lost all its leverage on its trade partners.

**American Response to the European Challenge**

But the United States was also not idle at home. A Presidential commission — the Williams Commission — was instructed to investigate this unsatisfactory commercial policy situation. In July 1971 it produced a three volume (2,000-page) report with technical papers. [7] One of its conclusions was that if America's trade partners continued to show indifference to United States offers to negotiate, she should consider imposing an import surcharge. The reasoning was the same as that which in pre-GATT days led to substantial tariff increases just before a commercial negotiation, in order to establish a negotiating position or, as the French term has it, to erect a *tariff de combat*. But 2,000-page reports are little read and thus the world was taken by surprise when, a few months later, in August 1971, President Nixon suspended the convertibility of the dollar *de jure* (*de facto* it had already been suspended in 1968) and imposed an import surcharge. The new 'get tough' attitude of the Nixon Administration was intentional, not accidental. [8] Its purpose was to improve American leverage which had been so sorely lacking previously. Accordingly while the European Community and Japan smarted under the impact of the 'Nixon measures' and bewailed the effects of the monetary crisis, the United States was calmly building up its trade negotiation position.

Similarly, the Smithsonian Accord of 18 December 1971 expressed United States concern with improving the balance-of-trade advantages. [9] Not only was the dollar devalued — a step long overdue for re-establishing United States balance-of-payments equilibrium. Two concessions in trade policy were extracted from Western Europe and Japan as well, namely (a) the long-term commitment to a major round of GATT negotiations, to start in 1973, and (b) a short-term commitment to negotiate in Brussels on a number of immediate problems — on grains, citrus fruit and tobacco.

Another recommendation of the Williams Commission, to be retained here, was the proposal that the industrialised countries should phase out tariffs as instruments of trade policy by successive 10 per cent cuts over a decade with provisions for 'exceptions' and 'safeguards'. This proposal has been in the air ever since the European Community and EFTA demonstrated that free trade in industrial products between countries at comparable levels of development and efficiency is not only entirely feasible, but also appears to have a very dynamic effect on industrial growth. It reappeared in the report of the OECD (Organisation for Economic Co-operation and Development) high-level group on trade and related problems ('. . . total abolition of duties . . . a reduction of 10 per cent a year on the assumption of total abolition in ten years . . . ')[10] and again was aired at the 1972 plenary session of the GATT's signatory countries by the American representative (and also the Japanese). It was later played down by American spokesmen who had the difficult task of persuading the United States Congress to pass forward-looking trade legislation.

Nevertheless, the proposal is entirely logical, at least for the United States. Zero tariffs, suitably surrounded with flexible safeguards, would provide the perfect answer to European tariff discrimination without sacrificing the right to use emergency measures to protect domestic industry in case of serious difficulties. Equally logically, the European Community has scoffed at the zero-tariff idea as being unrealistic, because zero-tariffs would reduce it to no more than an Association for the Protection of European Peasantry (APEP), with a Scheme for the Harmonisation of Axel Weights (SHAW), a European Social Security Fund (ESSEF) to join the FEOGA and other such bodies. Would this be the end of Europe? Or can Europe maintain its identity without the help of protectionism?

Interestingly enough, the Williams Commission espoused the zero-tariff idea before the devaluation of the dollar, but it only became more-or-less official United States policy towards the end of 1972, when the implications of a floating dollar were more fully understood. As the dollar floated downwards, so the import pressure on United States business was gradually released, thereby cutting the grass from under the feet of the protectionist lobbies. From that it was just a short step to realising that tariffs are no longer needed to keep business happy as long as a realistic exchange rate prevails. The key to ending over five years of frustrating trade relations with the European Community now seemed to be within America's grasp.

A zero-tariff world may be premature at the present time, because of the European Community's patent lack of maturity and inability to do without the common external tariff as a symbol of European unity. But it is definitely on the cards for the future. The mutual benefit would be enormous and the flexible exchange rate system which will probably emerge from the current series of monetary upheavals makes it socially and politically feasible.

The world has moved into an era of quickly changing contemporary events — belonging more to the domain of the press than to that of scholarly analysis.

It was clear from the monetary developments in the first few months of 1973 that the United States and the European Community were still at loggerheads. The European Community and Japan are themselves the victims of successive dollar devaluations, tributaries of a rate of inflation decided for them by the Federal Reserve Board, and vassals of the dollar system. They would like to see the United States act on its money supply to prevent a further depreciation of the dollar. They propose that the United States should raise interest rates in order to entice dollars back home, impose direct controls on capital outflows and support the dollar in the open market. But now the European Community and Japan have lost their power of leverage over the United States. The latter will not allow its interest-rate policy to be dictated by any other consideration than that of the needs of the United States national economy. Direct controls on capital movements are anathema to the liberal-minded American, be he Congressman, President or businessman. As for supporting the value of the dollar in terms of other currencies, nothing could be further from the United States national interest. It would mean borrowing money it did not want, to buy dollars it did not need, to maintain an exchange rate it did not like, for governments which were not being particularly agreeable.

The American counter-proposal has suggested that one should act on the demand for dollars in the world, and that if the countries of Western Europe and Japan wish to maintain a high exchange-rate for the dollar, they have but to increase their demand for dollar goods. In other words, the European Community should open its markets to United States agriculture (that is, improve the conduct of the common agricultural policy) and to United States high-technology goods (that is, put in a more realistic perspective efforts to develop a European technological community), and at the same time should recognise the error of its ways as far as preferential agreements are concerned. If all this were done, why then one might consider supporting the dollar in the foreign exchange market!

Two initial trade negotiating positions confront each other. The United States position is made up of both sticks and carrots. Tariff-free trade in industrial goods is offered in the firm conviction that the European Community and Japan would benefit more from zero-tariffs than the United States. At the same time the possibility of tariff increases is waved as a stick to persuade the reluctant European Community to move. On the home front, safeguards are spread out to reassure Congress that tariff-free trade does not mean no protection.

The position of the European Community appeared to soften when the ability of the Nixon Administration to produce a fairly remarkable piece of trade legislation was no longer in doubt. Tariffs may be reduced but not eliminated right across the board. Non-tariff barriers may be negotiated on a basis of reciprocity. The CAP is no longer totally non-negotiable. And the Community is in favour of a more flexible 'safeguards' clause. On the other hand, the European Community would resist a close 'link' between trade and money since this is where the United States bargaining power really lies. As long as the Europeans fail to put their own monetary house in order they only have themselves to blame if they find it impossible to escape from implications of a floating dollar standard. It is unrealistic to believe that the United States will not use this very powerful lever in order to obtain what they want on the trade front; that is, zero or near zero tariffs, backed by suitable safeguards.[11]

## NOTES AND REFERENCES

1. This chapter is based on a paper given at a conference on 'International Trade Negotiations: Conflict or Co-operation?' sponsored by the Fiera Internazionale di Milano, Milan, 16 April 1973.

2. This explains why the United States negotiated separate joint declarations with the European Community and with Japan as steps towards the launching of a seventh round of multilateral trade negotiations. These joint declarations were lodged with the Secretariat of the General Agreement on Tariffs and Trade (GATT) in February 1973.

3. For a discussion of the establishment of the post-war international trading system, see Gerard Curzon, *Multilateral Commercial Diplomacy* (London: Michael Joseph, 1965).

4. Because of its international obligations under the GATT, the United Kingdom resisted the temptation to develop the Commonwealth preferential trading system, the expectation being that it would be eroded by the process of trade liberalisation.

5. An analysis of the Kennedy Round negotiations can be found in Ernest Preeg, *Traders and Diplomats* (Washington: Brookings Institution, 1970).

6. A brief descriptive analysis of the sense of frustration in the United States over foreign economic policy is set out in Hugh Corbet, 'Australian Commercial Diplomacy in an Era of Negotiation', *Australian Outlook*, Melbourne, April 1972.

7. Presidential Commission on International Trade and Investment Policy, *United States International Economic Policy in an Interdependent World*, Williams Report (Washington: US Government Printing Office, 1971), formally submitted to President Nixon in July 1971 but not published until September.

8. Harald B. Malmgren, 'Managing International Economic Conflicts', Annals of International Studies, Geneva, 1972, p. 189.

9. See Chapter 1 for a fuller discussion of the events before and after the Smithsonian Accord.

10. High-level Group on Trade and Related Problems, *Policy Perspectives for International Trade and Economic Relations*, Rey Report (Paris: OECD Secretariat, 1972), p. 58.

11. The negotiation of a more effective 'safeguard' mechanism is discussed in Chapter 15 below by Jan Tumlir.

## *Part II*

# GENERAL FACTORS AFFECTING NEGOTIATIONS

# CHAPTER 3

## Divergent Philosophical Approaches to Foreign Policy

ROBERT JACKSON

Since the early 1960s there has been a continuous shift in the distribution of power among the nations. At the heart of this development has been the decline in the relative strength of America. Her politico-strategic position has been transformed by the establishment of parity in nuclear armaments by the Soviet Union and by the emergence of China as a potential intercontinental nuclear power. The political confidence and influence of the United States has been drastically diminished by its failures in Indo-China and a further reduction is foreshadowed in its growing dependence upon Middle East sources of energy. At the same time, the European Community and Japan have emerged, in the international economic system, as two new poles of economic power of a size comparable with the United States, and the Soviet Union is also becoming a major factor in the world economy. While the political purposes and institutions of the United States have been cast into doubt by its failures abroad and at home in the 1960s, both in the European Community and in Japan the resurgence of economic strength has has been accompanied by strivings after the definition of new and distinctive forms of political personality, appropriate to the restored economic vitality of their societies.

### Three Lines of Interpretation

In the West at least three significantly different lines of interpretation have been brought to bear upon the emerging pattern of world politics created by those trends in the distribution of power. Each of them draws upon a different tradition of thought about international relations. The first school, that of realism, grows out of the classical European diplomatic tradition — a line which runs from Thucydides through Machiavelli to de Gaulle. This realist version holds that after a brief period (1945-70) of 'bi-polar' competition for hegemony between two super-powers, the world is now returning to a more normal condition of 'multi-polar' competition to sustain a balance between several great powers, each of which is actuated primarily by purposes which it is compelled to define for itself in the light of the prevailing balance. The doctrines of this school are based on the concepts of state interest, balanced power and flexible alliances. Its most fundamental assumptions are that the tendency of political entities is to differentiate themselves and that the relations between the powers are essentially competitive.

The second line of interpretation has a less ancient and distinguished descent than the realist school. It originated in the period of the immense growth of intercourse between societies after the beginning of industrialisation early in the 19th century. Its chief exponents are the liberal capitalist descendants of Adam Smith, especially some of the exponents of West European integration; and it is also a powerful influence upon the socialist descendants of Marx and Engels. This might be called the 'functionalist' school because it holds that the underlying characteristic of the development of the international 'system' — especially since 1945 — has been the growing complexity of functional interrelations between the different societies which make up that 'system'. Since the end of World War II, and more especially since the late 1950s, there has been a dramatic expansion in international commerce and investment — encouraged in part by the liberalisation of trade and capital flows — in technology, in transport and communications and in collective provisions for security; and the functionalist school argues that the inner logic of each of these activities is leading to the progressive integration of historically differentiated societies and to the creation of a complex and subtle web of interdependencies between them. The basic assumption of functionalism is the primacy of the social and the economic over the political aspects of man's life. As political animals men may seek to define distinct identities for themselves within mutually exclusive groups; but as economic and social animals they act in such a way as to erode those distinctions from within and to substitute quite other principles of association.

When it seeks to interpret the contemporary situation in the West the functionalist school is divided. On the one hand, there are those —primarily Anglo-Saxons — who hold that the network of interdependence is tending to the consolidation of the whole range of Western interests into a single coherent system which links together, in an increasingly intimate association, the different elements of Western Europe, North America and the Western Pacific. On the other hand, there are those who hold that the pattern of those interests is becoming increasingly diversified and incoherent: that 'international politics are moving away from the simple pattern of clearly defined, all-purpose alignments and towards a pattern of overlapping but non-coincidental relationships and groupings in different functional areas'.[1] There is also a difference of emphasis between those functionalists who think primarily in terms of regional integration and those who think globally. And the contradictions in the way these two processes of integration are being pursued have become regarded as one of the major sources of strain in the modern world economy.

The third school — the rationalist — overlaps with functionalism, with which it shares the doctrine of the inner logic and transforming power of social and economic development; but it adds a metaphysical dimension to the pragmatic and materialist assumptions of the functionalist school, and unlike functionalism it sees alongside the process of social growth a parallel evolution in the field of men's political relations. Thus at the same time it also shares with realism its conviction of the fundamental importance of politics. But unlike realism, it identifies in political life a tendency not to differentiation but to integration: a progressive unification of economic and social organisation which is closely bound up with the progressive unification of all moral and policial values by the light of reason.

'It will surely come to pass,' says Origen, 'that all who are endowed with reason shall come under one law . . . Our belief is, that the Word shall prevail over the entire rational creation, and change every soul into his own perfection.' [2] The roots of the rationalist philosophy may be traced from Plato through a branch of the Christian tradition down to Kant and Hegel, where it sub-divides into Marxist eschatology on one side, and Western rational liberalism on the other. The central principles of the rationalist school in its Western form are individualism and legalism. Its starting-point is the doctrine that the individual is the essential political unit, and that because all human beings are equally endowed with reason their rational interests are fundamentally harmonious and can thus be brought under universal regulation by a single unified and coherent system of law. Man's life in history is a progress in rationality and the unfolding of the moral will. Therefore the tendency of relations between states is towards the progressive articulation of the common interests of humanity into a single unified and coherent world order. This is the founding principle of the United Nations: mankind is building himself a United States of the World; and consequently the problem of relations between states is essentially the same as that of the relations between citizens within the state.

As Harold Malmgren argues in Chapter 6 below: 'In trying to find a better system for managing economic interdependence while ensuring a large degree of freedom for national governments to deal with their own social and economic problems, one cannot help recalling the centuries-old philosophical debate about how to ensure freedom to the individual citizen in the context of orderly communal relations. The same kind of issues arise in the management of international economic affairs and one is drawn to the conclusion that real freedom for a national government can only be found, in this highly interdependent world, within a framework of international rules, procedures and tacit or explicit understandings.' [3]

## Shifts in Distribution of Power

Of all the governments and institutions participating in the present attempt to reconstruct the international economic system, the United States Administration is probably that with the most coherent strategy and the most highly articulated set of philosophical pre-suppositions. Such proposals as that of Henry Kissinger, first made when he was adviser to President Nixon on foreign policy,[4] for a 'New Atlantic Charter' must stimulate consideration of which of the three contemporary schools of thought which we have identified concerning the nature of the international order most accurately interprets the tendency of contemporary history. For one of the most profoundly important aspects of the drifting apart of the European Community, the United States and Japan which it is America's avowed object to prevent is the re-emergence on either side of the Atlantic and the Pacific of divergent views upon these questions of the philosophical basis of mutual relations.

During the quarter century after the end of World War II the shifts which have taken place in the constellation of power in the West were mediated through a complex structure of formal relationships and institutional arrangements in the fields of trade, finance and security. The institutional foundations of this system were laid in the 1940s; and it evolved through successive stages, from the Atlantic Charter — which enunciated some of the philosophical pre-suppositions of the system — to the Bretton Woods agreements of 1944-45 establishing the International Monetary Fund and the International Bank for Reconstruction and Development, to the negotiation of the General Agreement on Tariffs and Trade in 1947, the European Recovery Programme of the same year, the establishment of the North Atlantic Treaty Organisation in 1949, and to the signature of the Security Pact between the United States and Japan in 1951. At the centre of this system stood the strength of the United States, whose philosophy and institutions seemed to represent the hope of the future, whose exports dominated world markets, whose currency provided the essential reserves of the world monetary system and whose nuclear and conventional forces were the foundation of Western security. Only the United Kingdom, and to a lesser extent Canada, played a significant part in what was otherwise a largely American design.

By the 1960s, however, the emergence of the European Community — hovering between economic power and political impotence — became a new factor of growing importance, together with the resurgence of the Japanese economy. In addition, a range of new middle powers — Australia, Brazil, Mexico — assumed a larger place on the world scene. After the completion of decolonisation in Asia and Africa the voices of the new countries of the 'Third World' rang out increasingly loudly in the councils of the world. Atlantic conceptions became increasingly inappropriate, particularly in view of the shift of the focus of international tension away from Europe to Asia. These changes have been the prelude to the 'era of negotiations' which is now beginning within the non-Communist world. The European Community, Japan, the United States and the other advanced industrial societies, together with the countries of the developing world, have embarked on a complex and interrelated set of negotiations seeking to define new arrangements to govern their trading, monetary and security relations and, also, to regulate their competition for access to natural resources. Out of these discussions a new system of international association will emerge in the non-Communist world; and it is probable that the arrangements which result will be of the same profound consequence for the present and for future generations as those which were developed in the post-war era.

It would be unfair and inappropriate simply to dismiss the American appeal for a philosophical approach to these negotiations merely on the ground that a favourable response might open the way to that organisation of the negotiations which most favours the views of the United States. The most obvious task of the negotiators is to devise new arrangements which both reflect the real contemporary distribution of strength among the parties and which are, at the same time, capable of flexible adjustment to the shifts in relative power which will continue to take place in the future. But the Nixon Administration's initiative is of much more fundamental importance. It challenges other governments and institutions to formulate clearly and explicitly the philosophical conceptions upon which their policies are based, and to seek to determine how far their various conceptions can or should be brought into identity. For beyond and above the problems of institution-building there inevitably lies before all the parties, whether acting severally or individually, the further task of understanding the philosophical principles of which the new arrangements will be the application.

This philosophical task cannot be evaded: for every political arrangement embodies its own logic, whether explicit or implicit.[5] It is therefore inevitable that the system or systems of international association which result from these negotiations will reflect the philosophical preconceptions of those who participate in their creation. Whether or not these preconceptions are articulated and made explicit, and whether or not they unite or divide the parties, in the nature of things their ghostly presence will be palpable around the conference table.

## Rationalist Approach of the United States

American preconceptions in the field of international relations are comprised of an ever-mobile dialectic between the realist and the rationalist schools. Realism is a part of America's European inheritance, and it has made the United States a great exponent of power-politics, whether as an isolationist power enjoying the economic advantages of its former immunity from attack, or as an interventionist power exploiting its overwhelming economic and military superiority. Rationalism on the other hand has given the United States an ideology — a concept of a world order lying beyond and above power-politics. This central concept in the American tradition has its roots in the historical experience of the United States as a revolutionary nation consciously willing itself into existence as the embodiment of self-evident and universal truths and seeking subsequently to interpret those truths and draw out their meaning. Notions drawn from this experience and its interpretation possessed the minds of those American statesmen who were largely responsible for building up the post-war system of international relations; and they helped to give their actions and utterances a powerful and distinctive ideological flavour. [6] Their broad international strategy was consciously based upon this philosophical conception, which linked together and gave an ideal meaning to the institutions of what they called 'the free world'. When their successors look back upon this inheritance in the retrospect of history they are inclined to see in it an enchanting unity and intellectual coherence. For as with every manifestation of mankind's political creativity, the philosophies upon which men base their actions must not be regarded merely as a means of rationalising and justifying the exercise of power. They also lend to power a purpose and dignity without which those who possess it would be oppressed by a sense of meaninglessness and futility. [7] *'J'écoute Roosevelt me décrire ses projets. Comme cela est humain, l'idéalisme y habille la volonté de puissance.'*

Although the Nixon-Kissinger partnership in the United States has demonstrated great virtuosity since 1969 in maintaining the diplomatic initiative from a position of growing weakness in a multipolar world, their philosophical approach to the problems posed by the decline of America's relative power has not diverged fundamentally from the established tradition of American foreign relations. During Richard Nixon's first term, when he was devising his new approaches to the Soviet Union and China, the realist element in that tradition seemed to be uppermost in the President's mind. It was in this period that the notion of a penta-polar world was popularised by the White House, together with the classical realist doctrines of state interest, balanced power and flexible alliances. But at the same time, in all President Nixon's philosophical utterances, these realist analyses continued to be scrupulously located within a framework of concepts derived from the rationalist element in the American tradition.

Thus in President Nixon's successive 'Reports on Foreign Policy' the manoeuvres required to create a new balance of power have always been represented as an advance towards the creation of a new and more enduring form of world order — a 'structure of peace' in which an increasingly coherent and rationalised system of international arrangements would gain a deeper and more permanent legitimacy from the consent and participation of all the great powers. Even when Mr Nixon was acting unilaterally to overturn established legal arrangements — as in the new international economic policy promulgated in August 1971 — the realist rhetoric of 'the national interest' was balanced by the insistence that his actions were merely a prelude to the construction of a more lasting and rational order. As *The Round Table* pointed out in an editorial discussion of 'Mr Nixon's Philosophy of Foreign Policy' in October 1972, [8] the new relationship with Peking was regarded as the first step along a road on which the new relationship with Moscow marks a further stage, and the new relationship with America's allies something like an ultimate destination. With China the task was defined as being 'to establish a civilised discourse on how to replace estrangement with a dialogue serving to benefit both countries'. With the Soviet Union the object was to 'move from the mere assertion to the harmonisation of conflicting national interests'. And with the alliances: 'they must now be flexible enough to permit members to pursue autonomous policies within a common framework of strategic goals'. [9]

At the end of 1971 it seemed for a time that the realist theme might have established a permanent ascendancy in the President's thinking. The new international economic policy announced on August 15 followed hard upon the announcement on July 15 that Mr Nixon had been invited to Peking. But over the months since the temporary resolution of the world economic crisis in December 1971 it has become apparent that the underlying rationalist theme has increasingly reasserted itself, especially in America's attitude to her relations with her allies and friends in the non-Communist world.

Dr Kissinger's proposals for a 'New Atlantic Charter' are perhaps best understood as one of the latest manifestations of this way of thinking. As has been already remarked, the realist philosophy acknowledges that relations between the Americans, the Europeans and the Japanese are conducted on the basis of the pursuit of maximum advantage by three more or less independent centres of power. Realism would therefore indicate that the task of 'joint statesmanship' was to manage this ineluctable competition in such a way as to balance the power of the three centres and to reduce as far as possible the friction occasioned by their rivalry. But in his 'Year of Europe' speech Dr Kissinger did not adopt this view of the problem. Rather, he espoused the rationalist conviction that 'we can no longer afford to pursue national or regional self-interest without a unifying framework'. Instead of requiring that the three centres should define their own goals for themselves and seek to realise them as far as the balance of power allows, he charges them to come together to define a set of over-arching common goals — 'a new balance between self-interest and common interest'.[10]'We must evolve a new Atlantic Charter setting the goals for the future — a blueprint that . . . creates for the Atlantic nations a new relationship in whose progress Japan can share.'

### Obstacles to Politico-Strategic Coherence

In contemplating this philosophical task, however, everyone — not only the Americans — is haunted by the recollected unity and coherence of the post-war system; and there is a widely held view, especially in the European Community, that any kind of philosophical discussion must be avoided, partly because there is something of a conceptual vacuum in the Common Market countries and partly because such an enterprise seems to be irretrievably associated with the particular concepts upon which the post-war order was built. This is one of the several reasons why the American Government's references to the Atlantic Charter have been unfortunate. The philosophical premises of that document were essentially those which distinguished the post-war international system. Oversimplifying, it might be said that it is against the background of the Atlantic Charter, and the apparent simplicity and certitude of its principles and ideals, that the modern political disenchantment in 'the West' is silhouetted.

What has changed? On the level of power it is, of course, the relative decline of the United States which marks the most fundamental change since President Roosevelt and Mr Churchill met on board HMS *Prince of Wales* on the eve of America's entry into World War II. America's dependents of that time, and her soon-to-be-defeated enemies, are now her rivals in every sphere save that of military activity. But changes in the structure of power, even when they are of such magnitude, are not sufficient to explain the apparent divergences of outlook which the American proposal of a 'New Atlantic Charter' is designed to resolve. It is necessary also to look into the fate of that philosophy which the original Charter sought to express.

At the deepest philosophical level it might be argued that Atlanticism has lost its relevance because of some inherent flaw in the rationalist concept of One World upon which it was founded. But short of that point it is possible to identify two major developments which have brought into question the feasibility of defining an over-arching framework of common goals among the nations of the non-Communist world. The first of these concerns the relations between America and her Communist rivals. The second concerns the nature and destiny of the European Community and the Empire of Japan.

The changes which have taken place since 1945 in the relations between the United States, Russia and China cannot be described merely in terms of a quantitative growth in the power of the two Communist states. There has also been a qualitative change which has inevitably had a profound effect upon America's outlook upon the world.

Until the early 1960s the United States stood outside some of the permanent realities of international politics because the facts of its geo-political position on an island continent surrounded by broad oceans exempted America from the disciplines which geography and history impose upon the more vulnerable powers who govern the lives of the rest of mankind. Consequently America was free to conceive her role in the outside world primarily in moral and philosophical terms. And indeed since the realist philosophy tended to support a non-interventionist attitude in international relations, it was necessary for those Presidents who wished to carry their country-men with them in playing an active role abroad to justify their interventions overseas in terms of the universalist ideologies upon which America's history as a nation was itself based. Thus one of the most striking features of the Atlantic Charter is the emphasis given to ideology in interpreting the conflict with Germany. 'The President and the Prime Minister,' it commences, 'have considered the dangers to world civilisation arising from the policies of military domination by conquest upon which the Hitlerite government of Germany has embarked.' Since in terms of classical realism the

United States had no vital interest at stake in the European war, the only justification for intervention lay in interests of a philosophical character, deriving from the alleged existence of a spiritual challenge to America's fundamental values. According to Roosevelt in June 1940 'we of the United States cannot safely permit the United States to become a lone island, a lone island in a world dominated by the philosophy of force'. Over the period since the collapse of 'the philosophy of force' in its Axis version this conception of America's role has been refined and reiterated by successive Presidents in their dealings with the Communist world. By the same token the anti-Communist coalition led by the United States inherited the ideological values of the anti-Axis coalition.

But since 1945 the emergence of Russia and China as intercontinental nuclear powers has placed the United States for the first time in a position where its international policy must be determined primarily by the logic of power rather than by the logic of ideology — whether the ideology of anti-Fascism or that of anti-Communism. At the same time the disintegration of the ideological unity of the Communist world has helped to make it easier for America to abandon the philosophical paraphernalia of the anti-Axis and anti-Communist coalitions. Strategic parity made an ideological foreign policy impossible; multi-polarity made it unnecessary. As discussed above, the most notable achievement of President Nixon's first Administration was the development of a more flexible relationship with Russia and China, based upon the application to American circumstances of the classical doctines of state interest, balanced power, secret diplomacy and the reversal of alliances. America's global role as the leader of a world-wide coalition has now in many respects been repudiated, and indeed the entire constitutional order of this recent imperial-presidential phase in America's history has been cast into the melting-pot of the Watergate scandal. Meanwhile, the ideological element in the attitude of the United States to its Communist rivals has largely disappeared. What room remains for ideology, therefore, in America's relations with her allies?

## Economic Basis for International Cohesion

In 'the West' today can one hope to rediscover the philosophical coherence which underlay the post-war order? The answer seems likely to be in the negative. In addition to all the changes to which the post-war international order has been submitted, and the fundamental change in the character of America's relations with the outside world, there has arisen, as Dr Kissinger has remarked of Western Europe and Japan, 'a new generation — to whom war and its dislocations are not personal experiences — which takes stability for granted. But it is less committed to the unity that made peace possible and to the effort required to maintain it'. What is true of the peoples is also true of the governments: the success of the United States in balancing the power of its adversaries and in fostering economic recovery and civilian values among its allies and friends has reduced the compulsion upon them to submit to the discipline of a unifying framework or to a consensus defining a set of common Atlantic goals.

Yet this reluctance is not to be attributed to mere indolence on the part of the Europeans and the Japanese. Their reservations in the face of Dr Kissinger's Atlantic proposals go deeper. Both Japan and the European Community are complex societies in search of political personality. That is to say they are seeking, in one case, to renew, in the other, to develop a capacity to define their own purposes. And although those purposes as yet remain obscure, there is a growing awareness that societies whose history and geo-political situation are as different as are those of the European Community, the United States and Japan cannot expect to have an identical set of political and strategic goals — however willing the Americans might be to uphold Dr Kissinger's generous insistence that 'it will be quite feasible, indeed desirable, for the several allies to pursue these goals with considerable tactical flexibility'.

Both the Europeans and the Japanese are deeply conscious of the extent to which their destiny has for a quarter of a century been dependent upon the power of the United States. Their gratitude, as might have been expected, is tempered by resentment. Both societies are still very much aware of the extent to which their politico-strategic and economic interests are bound up with the American alliances. But there is a growing disposition to see this intimate relationship as a phase preparatory to a more complete independence.

Realism will teach the Europeans and the Japanese that they must pay a price for the continuance of American support in those areas where it is still needed. Functional integration may bring them closer together in some areas as well as dividing them in others. For governments will be obliged to accept the political implications of the growing economic interdependence that arises from the pro-gressive integration of the world economy as a whole. It may indeed be in economic terms that they stand the best chance of finding a philosophical basis upon which to build their future relations. But in the years that lie ahead there seems to be little likelihood that they will learn to embrace the concept of a deeper and wider Atlantic or trans-oceanic community.

NOTES AND REFERENCES

1. Ian Smart, 'The New Atlantic Charter', *The World Today*, London, June 1973, p. 242.

2. Origen, *Contra Celsum*, Bk. 8, Ch. 72, translated by W.H. Cairns in *Ante-Nicene Christian Library*, Vol. XXIII, 1910.

3. See *infra*, p. 00.

4. Henry Kissinger, 'The Year of Europe', an Address to the Associated Press of America, New York, 23 April 1973. At the time Dr Kissinger was Assistant for National Security, in the White House, but shortly after he became Secretary of State in the Nixon Administration.

5. A 'philosophy' in this sense might be defined as the logic of a political arrangement brought before consciousness and its implications inspected: so that, if necessary, a new arrangement might be adopted embodying different implications arising from a different philosophical framework.

6. Harold Macmillan, the former British Prime Minister, recalled in describing his visit to the United States in March 1959: 'We left Camp David by road at 4 p.m. In the course of the drive Eisenhower "talked at large about the future of the world. He is certainly a strange mixture. With all his crudity and lack of elegance of expression, he has some very remarkable ideas". His chief theme was the need to "institutionalise" the nations of the free world. Somehow or other Britain and the Commonwealth, Europe and the United States ought to be able to develop more precise methods of resisting Communism all over the world. "He developed this theme at some length — monetary, tariff and all other policy could be unified . . . ".' See Harold Macmillan, *Riding the Storm: 1956-59* (London: Macmillan, 1971), p. 649. The internal quotations are extracts from the former Prime Minister's diary.

7. Charles de Gaulle, *Memoires de Guerre: L'Unite*, Vol II (Paris: Plon, 1952), p. 292.

8. *The Round Table*, London, October 1972, pp. 403-10.

9. Richard Nixon, *US Foreign Policy for the 1970s: a Report to the Congress by the President of the United States*. (Washington: US Government Printing Office, 1972), p. 8.

10. Kissinger, *op. cit.*

# CHAPTER 4

## External Relations of the European Community

RALF DAHRENDORF

Jean Monnet's claim that 'necessity is the great federator of Europe' is nowhere more appropriate than in the field of the external relations of the European Community. It is here that the need for common action — the inability of the smaller and medium-sized countries of Western Europe to pursue their goals effectively by themselves — is most acutely felt. It is in the field of external relations also that most countries and their political representatives are most reluctant to 'admit defeat' (to use a phrase employed by one well-known British politician describing with resignation the negotiations on British membership). As a result there is no area of European activity where it is more difficult to be systematic. The following notes thus make no claim to being exhaustive or even comprehensive. They can do no more than help to explain some of the issues, factors, motives and problems involved in the European Community's external relations, as seen by one who was responsible for these relations in the Commission of the Community, from 1970 to early 1973.[1]

### Expectations and Fears

In the last few years, every foreign minister of the European Community, in his wanderings around the world, has had an experience which in itself is not to be under-estimated. In talking to his colleagues abroad, he found them obviously interested in his country, but at some stage the conversation invariably turned away from questions of bilateral relations and towards the responsibilities of the foreign minister as one of the representatives of the European Community. Whether a European minister goes to the United States or China, to Mauritius or Fiji, to Indonesia or Venezuela, to Gabon or Bangladesh, he invariably finds himself in the role of a *European* as well as a German, French, British minister. It is worth recounting some of the things he is likely to hear.

In Latin America — and there is no particular reason for the sequence in which I am going to refer to various parts of the world — our fictitious foreign secretary would still encounter a great deal of criticism of the European Community. This is directed against what Latin Americans feel is an exaggerated, indeed almost exclusive, interest of the Community in Africa. The real basis of the criticism is, however, that there are many in Latin America who look upon the Community as a great opportunity for themselves. They want it to provide them with many of the economic advantages which the United States offers without the political disadvantages that, in the view of most of them, go with the American connection. For that reason, twenty-one Latin American states came together in 1971 to make the Declaration of Buenos Aires, inviting the European Community to engage in a dialogue with a view to defining a system of effective economic and financial co-operation.

Co-operation without dependence is in fact a major theme of the expectations of many countries as they look at the European Community. In the Mediterranean region there is an additional element attached to this interest. In many countries of the region, and notably in the Arab ones, there is deep resentment of the option which has dominated their political scene in the last decade — namely that between the United States and the Soviet Union. The European Community to them seems to offer an effective and acceptable alternative — to be sure, an alternative without Eskadra or the Sixth Fleet. It is worth noting that in this notion of 'Europe', Suez and all that is entirely forgotten. The European Community appears as something qualitatively different from its member-states or even the sum of them.

In South-east Asia, our foreign secretary would encounter a different situation again. The countries of the region are trying to create a neutral zone, not committed to any of the super-powers and, if possible, not even dependent on their guarantees. In order to achieve this end, there must be other guarantees. One such guarantee is sought by several of them in a system of regional economic and political co-operation, the nucleus of which may be found in the Association of South-east Asian Nations (ASEAN). It might be said there would be no ASEAN (and, incidentally, no Andean Group in Latin America) without the European Community; the organisation is generally fashioned along the lines of European experience. It is felt at the same time that ASEAN will not be able to serve its purpose without close co-operation with the Community.

Lest it is felt that too rosy a picture of the ways in which the world sees the European Community is being presented, turn to another group of countries, those of the temperate Commonwealth (and South Africa's situation is not entirely different). Our foreign secretary would certainly be politely received in Australia, New Zealand and Canada. But there he would hear a story which he is not likely to forget. By virtue of the process of enlargement of the European Community these countries, and notably those of the

Antipodes, have had to undergo a painful process of re-orientation: looking for new markets, developing their own industry, thinking of an uncertain European Community rather than their traditionally more certain partner, the United Kingdom. The process is still under way, and Europeans will go on being reminded of their responsibilities in it, arising from the relevant protocols to the treaty of accession, from their obligations under the GATT, and from the sense of solidarity with countries which for many reasons have a right to recall Europeans to their obligations.

Our foreign secretary is likely to have a very different experience indeed as he comes to Moscow. His interlocutors there will not be at all eager to talk about the subject of the Community. Instead, they will probe him as to the possibility of settling most, if not all things, including economic relations, on a bilateral basis. The Community exists, certainly, as a sort of capitalist club for the mutual benefit of members; but of course it has no real political significance . . . Our travelling minister may detect a sense of fear at this point. The notion of free countries co-ordinating freely some of their internal as well as external policies is alien both to the traditions and pre-sumably to the interests of the Soviet Union.

Leaving out China, where this same fact makes for an eager though not very well-defined interest in the European Community, there remains of course the other super-power, the United States. Here, it is even more difficult than in other cases to summarise in a few simple sentences the complex mixture of expectations and fears that governs attitudes to the European Community. The United States has consistently supported European political integration and continues to do so. But three developments tend to complicate this picture. One is, that there is growing doubt in the United States as to the political quality of the European Community. Here certain Soviet and certain American views meet, however unintentionally. Secondly, the United States no longer feels responsible for others in the same way as in the 1950s. It thinks in terms of a partnership in which everybody has the same right to look after his interests as everybody else. And thirdly, economics, and notably international economic relations, have come very much to the forefront of the United States' interest in the world; and in this respect there is a feeling — wrongly, I believe — that the European Community is injurious to the United States. Whole books have been devoted to the implications of this set of expectations and fears. [2]

But in any case a long story has been cut very short. No reference has been made to Austria and Sweden, to the countries of Africa, to the oil-producing countries of the world,[3] to regional powers such as India or Brazil or Nigeria, to the non-temperate Commonwealth countries, sugar-producing or not. Yet the panorama of challenges earlier sketched would have to be extended to all of these in order to be anything like complete. It should be apparent that there are few countries left in the world for which the emergence of an enlarged European Community is not relevant and felt to be relevant. It should also be apparent that in many parts of the world there are strong emotional feelings about the Community, sometimes fear, often hope. And as this experience is described, one wonders how the travelling foreign minister can communicate it to his colleagues, both in his cabinet at home and in the Council of Ministers in Brussels.

**European Facts of Life**

For now the other, less insubstantial side of the picture requires our attention. The treaties of Rome (Euratom and EEC) do not have very much to say about the external relations of the Community (and the treaty of Paris, on the ECSC, says even less, leaving a common commercial policy explicitly outside Community competence). To concentrate on the Treaty of Rome, there is the short but substantial Part Four on the association of overseas countries and territories: there are references to trade in the section on agriculture; and there are the Articles 110 to 116 on a common commercial policy. Along with Article 238 providing for 'association' agreements concluded by the Community, Article 113 is the most important single basis for the external relations of the European Community, so that a few remarks about this article seem in place.

First of all, Article 113 stipulates that after the end of the transitional period the Community shall have a common commercial policy, including the treaty-making power that goes with it. This is the logical result of the fact that after that period was accomplished the Community would have become a full-fledged customs union. The end of the transitional period was in fact reached on 1 January 1970, and from that day onwards (a few months later, to be exact, but technically from that day) commercial agreements could no longer be concluded by individual member-states, but had to be negotiated, signed and ratified by the Community according to its own procedures. One exception was made at the time concerning the state-trading countries of Eastern Europe. Here member-states reserved their right to conclude agreements bilaterally for three years. Even so, the Paris summit meeting of October 1972 confirmed that on 1 January 1973 the common commercial policy would go into effect without exception or restriction.

On the formal side of things this is obviously important, but it is only a part of the issue. In terms of substance, Article 113 betrays clearly the traces of the time at which it was drafted, and it is in that context that the seamy side of the Community's external relations becomes evident. For in this article commercial policy is defined as including 'in particular' matters of tariffs, of liberalisation, of protective measures against dumping, and the like. The catalogue is meant to be illustrative. But it is illustrative also of a time when administrative measures in the tariff and quota field were the core of any commercial policy. The Kennedy Round agreement has changed this radically. Today tariffs play but a secondary part in commercial relations. Liberalisation is of diminishing significance even in the two areas in which it continues to have some relevance. with Japan and the state-trading countries. Anti-dumping measures are in any case as much a matter of multilateral consideration as for bilateral agreements. What, then, remains of a common commercial policy for the Community?

The seriousness of the question is not to be under-estimated. For the European Community, external relations are in large part based on the fact that the Community is a customs union. They are external *commercial* relations. In the Treaty of Rome these commercial relations have been defined rather narrowly. Is the lowering of tariffs which are already low, the liberalisation of imports which are already liberal, and the bilateral confirmation of multilateral safeguard procedures really all the Community has to offer? Up till the present moment, there has been no unambiguous answer to this question, and what answers there have been are contradictory in tendency.

A modern commercial policy is necessarily concerned not only with regulating the flow of an already existing trade, but with creating trade and promoting economic inter-change in general. It is, in other words, a policy of economic co-operation, involving credit conditions, marketing aids, industrial co-operation including the setting-up of joint ventures, the exchange of technological information and 'know-how', and so on. This area of co-operation, however, was not included by the member-states in their notion of a common commercial policy. On the contrary — notably though not only with East European countries — member-states have concluded co-operation agreements of long duration which are not regarded as being relevant to the Community prerogatives stipulated in Article 113.

On the other hand, recent commercial agreements concluded by the Community, beginning with the one with Yugoslavia, all include an article setting up a 'mixed' or 'joint commission', the functions of which are not confined to the supervision of the working of the agreement as such. These joint commissions, consisting of the government of the partner state and representatives of the Community institutions, have the right to examine all problems of mutual interest, and they have done so — as have the councils of association in connection with the association agreements — in the general area of co-operation. It is clear, however, that joint commissions cannot make decisions which extend the boundaries of community activity.

One or two other developments might be cited. Mention has not been made of agriculture and the relevance of trade in agricultural products for the external relations of the Community. There are reasons for this reticence. The common agricultural policy is not calculated to make life easy for those responsible for the Community's external relations. But there are cases where the Community, above and beyond tariff decisions, has been able to satisfy some of its partners by agricultural concessions. Beyond agriculture, there is at present a lively debate about the extension of old, or creation of new, instruments of financial assistance, notably for the countries of the Mediterranean region. The experience of the European Development Fund on the one hand, and the European Investment Bank on the other, might be helpful in this respect. In the Mediterranean region also, and probably in the first place in agreements with the three Maghreb countries and with Malta, the Community might also consider setting up a more comprehensive system of economic co-operation as part of its commercial policy. Decisions to this effect have been taken in principle, although their implementation remains to be achieved.

It would obviously be possible to continue at some length this description of the substance of the external relations of the Community. Enough has been said to make an obvious and at the same time clearly unfortunate point. There is an almost absurd disproportion between the expectations of the European Community's partners in the world, and the instruments which the Community has at its disposal in order to respond to these expectations. The Community has been described as a dinosaur, a gigantic creature with a tiny brain. This is not a very complimentary description, suggesting as it does that whenever the monster moves it affects the lives of many without even realising what it is doing. Nor is the description entirely correct. But if there is any major task ahead in the external relations of the European Community, it is that of bringing the instruments of action more into line with goals and expectations, if only in order to prevent the latter being reduced to the modest scope of the former.

## International Tests of the Community

It might be argued that precisely because the European Community is a community of nine countries working out common solutions, it is not particularly well suited to conduct effective relations with individual countries elsewhere. The very awkwardness of the term 'bilateral' in describing, say, relations between the Community and Egypt, indicates a problem that might well deserve more consideration than has been given to it so far. There are almost bound to be incongruent expectations whenever the Community, represented by its institutions, is confronted with the government of one country, and strained comparisons — such as saying that the United States Administration has to get something accepted by Congress just as Brussels officials do by the Council of Ministers — only add to the confusion. It may be no accident, therefore, that in the past the Community has been at its best in multilateral, or what might be called multi-bilateral contexts, notably in the Kennedy Round negotiations and in relations with the African associates. It might be argued, therefore, that tasks and events of this nature provide the touchstone of the Community's ability to develop effective external relations which are in keeping with its character and importance.

There are, first of all, a number of tasks of a multi-bilateral nature to be carried out in the next few years. There has been the problem of renegotiating the Yaoundé agreement, taking into account the probable desire of a number of anglophobe countries in Africa to join the association. In a less formalised fashion, the attempt to evolve a global approach to the countries of the Mediterranean region is also multi-bilateral; it is important to keep it that way and even to set up instruments which by their applicability to the entire region pave the way for an even more strictly multilateral approach. Much of the development policy of the Community will consist in negotiating international agreements; this may well be an appropriate solution for the problems of some Commonwealth countries in various parts of the world. The attempt to develop an effective and appropriate apparatus of instruments of economic co-operation on a world-wide scale might well begin by establishing more formal links with comparable communities, such as the Andean Group and ASEAN. They are likely to understand both the constraints and the potential of a Community much more easily than any individual country.

The two great tests of the Community's approach to international relations in the near future are, however, of a more strictly multilateral nature. One of them is the reform of the system of international economic relations, as it is being redesigned, partly in the framework of the International Monetary Fund, partly in that of the General Agreement on Tariffs and Trade (GATT). The process is going to be without precedent in its complications. Even the liberal has to admit that liberalisation is not enough to describe the task of an intercontinental trade round, nor is monetary reform confined to maintaining convertibility. The numerous connections between trade and monetary problems, a changing definition of the role of the United States and of the dollar in the world, the increasing importance of that elusive set of obstacles to trade called 'non-tariff barriers', the growing significance of multinational companies and international investment, the obvious insufficiency of existing safe-guard arrangements and, of course, the emergence of the European Community as an important and to some extent dominant power in international economic relations: this is a formidable array of problems to be solved in a limited period of time.[4] (The dinosaur's brain may have to grow very fast if the beast is to make its appropriate contributions.)

In the GATT, the Community has a fixed and accepted set of rules for developing and representing its view — which must, of course, be a unified and coherent view. This is part of a common commercial policy. In the IMF this is not yet the case, but here too a high degree of co-ordination has been achieved in a pragmatic manner; progress in the direction of a European monetary union makes this co-ordination imperative. But in both cases, co-ordination *sur place* is not enough. The political will expressed by the Community in December 1971, and again in February 1972, to engage in world-wide talks in order to create 'a new equilibrium on the international level which makes possible a rise in the standard of living by extending international economic relations and continuing to liberalise world trade' has to be rendered more specific. There is a need to define more precisely the open world economy which is being sought and for which the European Community will have a major responsibility. This will clearly be one of the major tasks on the agenda of the institutions of the enlarged Community.

The other responsibility which the Community has is that in proving that as a community of states it is not the forerunner of a new world of blocs, it is possible to form a community as Europe is doing, and yet remain open for co-operation with others. Perhaps two other points should be added to this statement. It is possible, indeed desirable, to form a community without forcing everybody else to act in a similarly concerted manner. And it is possible, indeed desirable, to co-operate with others without arresting the internal development of the Community.

## Problem of Divided Responsibility

One final remark remains to be made, less in order to complete these notes which are by design incomplete, than to fill the most obvious gap that has been left open so far. I began by describing some of the expectations which challenge Europe in the world. These expectations are often complex, involving not only economic, but also political and even military considerations. Perhaps the example of the United States is the most topical case in point. The United States no longer regards as three distinct things its wish to see Europe strengthened politically, its interest in its own balance of payments, and its interest in the North Atlantic Treaty Organisation (NATO). Indeed, much of American foreign policy in the early 1970s may be understood as an attempt to evolve, in part by trial and error, a coherent approach to all three aspects of policy.

Nobody will be surprised if what is difficult for the United States turns out to be even more difficult for the European Community. But to be surprised, or not, is hardly a sufficient response in this important area. Part of the disproportion between expectations and realities which overshadows the external relations of the European Community is due to the fact that in its very design the Community is a partial institution, one that conducts whatever external relation it has either in ignorance of the wider implications of its actions or, in any case, in impotence *vis-a-vis* these effects. If the United States hints at the risk of a withdrawal of the Sixth Fleet as a result of the European Community's preferential agreements with countries in the Mediterranean region, there is nobody in the Community who can respond adequately; and this is only a striking instance of many less dramatic, although often no less important examples of the effects of fragmentation on the external relations of the Community and its member-states. A fragmented foreign policy weakens those who try to conduct it. Considering the fact that all member-states have by now discovered the need to join forces in certain important areas of action, the consquences to be drawn from this insight are almost obvious.

I do not want to engage in an institutional controversy at the end of these notes. Perhaps it may be said, however, that the response found so far to the problem of fragmentation in external relations is no more than minimal in relation to the needs. After the summit conference at the Hague in 1969, preparations were made for setting up a procedure of 'political co-operation'. This has led to regular meetings between the political directors of the foreign offices of member-states and to meetings of the foreign ministers as well. At the Paris summit it was suggested that such meetings should be held even more frequently than before. Here important matters such as relations with the Middle East are being discussed and to some extent settled. It should be clear that in several respects what has been started here can be no more than a nucleus of a far more effective co-ordination of foreign policy in the European Community.

Necessity is indeed a great federator. But history has known individuals and countries who failed to recognise their needs. Here, too, the enlargement of the Community is not so much the end of a road as the beginning of something long overdue. The European Community's external relations, like other aspects of this great co-operative effort, hold out hope as well as difficulties in the future. Much, in other words, remains to be done.

## NOTES AND REFERENCES

1. An earlier version of this chapter was published as 'Notes on the External Relations of the European Communities', *The Round Table*, London, January 1973.

2. See, for example, Theodore Geiger, *The Fortunes of the West: the Future of the Atlantic Nations* (Bloomington and London: Indiana University Press, 1973).

3. The problems involved in relations with oil-producing countries are discussed in Chapter 7 below by Frank McFadzean.

4. The issues listed here are dealt with in the chapters of this volume by Harald Malmgren (6), Harry G. Johnson (9), Peter Lloyd (11), David Robertson (8) and Jan Tumlir (15).

# CHAPTER 5

## *Internal Adjustment Problems of Japan*

NOBUYOSHI NAMIKI

The industrial structure of a country changes according to such factors as its adaptability to changes in the world economy, to changes in the pattern of domestic demand, to technological progress, to changes in resource conditions and so on. In the process industrial adjustment takes place. Industrial adjustment means that, in facing its changing industrial environment and finding it difficult to continue in the same line of business, an enterprise decides to transfer to another sector of industry or to remain in the same sector but specialise more and change its production methods in order to lower costs and improve quality. By behaving in this way the firm might stay in existence and develop its future. [1]

Japan has experienced the highest economic growth among leading industrial countries. This shows that the capacity to adapt to economic changes is high in Japan; and consequently the scope for industrial adjustment, in the process of 'creative destruction', is also high. Over the past decade Japan's capacity to adjust internally has stood her in good stead as she has become more involved in the world economy through the liberalisation of controls on trade and investment. In a country very different culturally and historically from other developed economies, these adjustments have involved deep and widespread social implications, the nature of which may not be fully appreciated abroad. Further adjustments have to be contemplated as Japan enters another round of multilateral trade negotiations aimed at reform and liberalisation.

Industrial adjustment takes different forms according to a firm's industry, its size and the time available. Observations about an industry and its scale of operations are usually tied together. But in the following pages I will for the sake of convenience discuss the problems separately. Then an outline will be given of Japanese Government policies in this field. To illustrate the characteristics of industrial adjustment in the Japanese economy some important concrete cases will be explained, namely the textile and mining industries, together with the policy problems they pose.

Furthermore, as international economic integration proceeds, especially with industrialisation in developing countries, it is vitally important for the sound development of international economic relations to settle smoothly the problems of international industrial adjustment. Finally, therefore, some policy proposals on industrial adjustment will be presented. In this paper, then, the following four topics will be pursued: (a) problems of industrial adjustment by sectors, (b) problems of industrial adjustment by scale of firm, (c) problems on how to handle adjustment problems in some industries, and (d) problems of international industrial adjustment.

## Problems of Industrial Adjustment by Sectors

First of all, to obtain a general idea of the problems, attention should be paid to the statistics relating to the changes in the long-run pattern of production, employment and trade (Tables 1-6). These macro data, showing the high rate of growth and the wide structural fluctuation, indicate the large possibilities for adjustment problems to make themselves felt in the Japanese economy. These macro-data show only in rough outline the magnitude of adjustment problems. They do not show up any important social, economic, managerial, cultural or political factors affecting change

The growth of Japanese industry is due, in large part, to its high sensitivity to changes in the rest of the world. Japan, troubled at one time by a shortage of foreign exchange, tried to foresee trends in international demand, and to develop industries which could meet that changing demand. Thus the structure of domestic production supporting exports has been well maintained through various forms of industrial adjustment. Exports have accordingly grown at a rate higher than the world average. For the period 1960-67, world trade in the goods listed in Chapter 5 of the Standard International Tariff Classification (SITC) increased by 10.4 per cent, but Japan's exports rose 25.1 per cent; in SITC Chapter 7, world trade increased 10.7 per cent, but Japan's exports rose 24.1 per cent; and in SITC Chapters 6 and 8, world trade increased 8.2 per cent, but Japan's exports rose 13.8 per cent.

Japan's imports are alleged to be institutionally controlled to a very great extent. Whether or not this is in fact the case, the image should change within a few years. Seen from a bilateral point of view, Japan's restrictions have been no worse than those of her partners.[2] After all there have been very considerable discriminatory restrictions imposed against Japan in the form of 'voluntary' export restraints. And Japan does not exercise any discriminatory restrictions as a member of a trading block. Be that as it may, the relaxation of what controls have existed, or do now exist, will call for further industrial adjustment measures.

Adjustment in the form of industrial conversion takes place whenever the labour, capital, technology, land or products of an enterprise change to meet a new situation. The data only show,

TABLE 1 International Comparison in the Rate of Growth of Real Gross National Product (GNP) and Industrial Production

*Percentage at annual rate*

| Countries | Prewar Periods | | Postwar Period | GNP in 1970 (100 millions of dollar) |
|---|---|---|---|---|
| | 1880-1910 | 1910-1940 | 1960-1970 | |
| **Growth Rate of Real GNP** | | | | |
| Japan | 3.8 | 4.4 | 11.1 | 1,962 |
| United States | 3.9 | 4.3 | 4.1 | 9,741 |
| United Kingdom | 1.9 | 1.9 | 2.8 | 1,210 |
| France | 1.1 | 0.9 | 5.8a | 1,415b |
| West Germany | — | — | 4.8 | 1,855 |

| Countries | 1880-1910 | 1910-1930 | 1960-1970 | Industrial production (100 millions of dollar) |
|---|---|---|---|---|
| **Growth Rate of Industrial Production** | | | | |
| Japan | 20.9 | 8.0 | 14.4 | 1,920 |
| United States | 4.3 | 2.4 | 4.9 | 6,400 |
| United Kingdom | 1.6 | 0.8 | 2.9 | 960 |
| France | — | — | 6.1 | |
| West Germany | 4.4 | 0 | 6.0 | 1,430 |

Source: Japan Economic Planning Agency, Tokyo

a1960-69    b1969

TABLE 2  Change in Work Force

*(In thousands)*

| Year | Total Population | Work Force | | | | Percentage Composition | | | |
|---|---|---|---|---|---|---|---|---|---|
| | | Primary Industry | Secondary Industry | Tertiary Industry | Total | Primary Industry | Secondary Industry | Tertiary Industry | Total |
| 1880 | 36,649 | 16,076 | 1,092 | 3,535 | 19,572 | 80.9 | 6.5 | 12.6 | 100.0 |
| 1900 | 43,847 | 17,331 | 3,427 | 4,550 | 25,308 | 68.5 | 13.5 | 18.0 | 100.0 |
| 1920 | 55,391 | 14,441 | 5,576 | 6,949 | 26,966 | 53.5 | 20.7 | 25.8 | 100.0 |
| 1940 | 72,500 | 14,192 | 8,419 | 9,620 | 32,231 | 44.0 | 26.1 | 29.9 | 100.0 |
| 1947 | 78,101 | 17,812 | 7,427 | 8,090 | 33,329 | 53.5 | 22.2 | 24.3 | 100.0 |
| 1950 | 83,200 | 17,208 | 7,812 | 10,605 | 35,626 | 48.4 | 21.9 | 29.7 | 100.0 |
| 1960 | 93,900 | 14,346 | 12,731 | 16,604 | 43,691 | 22.6 | 29.2 | 38.2 | 100.0 |
| 1970 | 103,356 | 10,066 | 17,651 | 24,309 | 52,042 | 19.3 | 33.9 | 46.7 | 100.0 |
| Principal Countries | | | | | | | | | |
| United States (1969) | 203,213 | 3,606 | 24,225 | 50,071 | 77,902 | 4.6 | 31.1 | 64.3 | 100.0 |
| United Kingdom (1965) | 55,283 | 423 | 10,835 | 13,625 | 24,883 | 1.7 | 43.5 | 54.8 | 100.0 |
| France (1965) | 49,920 | 3,121 | 7,796 | 8,824 | 19,741 | 15.8 | 39.5 | 44.7 | 100.0 |
| West Germany (1969) | 58,707 | 2,533 | 12,936 | 11,353 | 28,822 | 9.4 | 48.2 | 42.3 | 100.0 |

Source:  Japan Economic Planning Agency, Tokyo

**TABLE 3   Changes in The Distribution of National Income by Industry**

*(Percentages)*

| Year | Primary Industry | Secondary Industry | Tertiary Industry | Total |
|---|---|---|---|---|
| 1880 | 41.9 | 17.9 | 40.2 | 100.0 |
| 1900 | 33.8 | 24.4 | 41.8 | 100.0 |
| 1920 | 28.7 | 26.9 | 44.4 | 100.0 |
| 1940 | 24.2 | 35.8 | 40.0 | 100.0 |
| 1947 | 35.4 | 28.6 | 36.0 | 100.0 |
| 1950 | 26.0 | 31.8 | 42.2 | 100.0 |
| 1960 | 15.6 | 37.5 | 46.9 | 100.0 |
| 1970 | 8.9 | 39.2 | 51.9 | 100.0 |
| **Principal Countries** | | | | |
| United States (1969) | 3.2 | 35.8 | 61.0 | 100.0 |
| United Kingdom (1969) | 3.1 | 43.5 | 53.4 | 100.0 |
| France (1969) | 6.1 | 46.3 | 47.8 | 100.0 |
| West Germany (1969) | 3.6 | 54.4 | 42.0 | 100.0 |

Source: Japan Economic Planning Agency, Tokyo

TABLE 4  Changes in the Composition of Industrial Production
(*Percentages*)

| | Light Industry | | | | Heavy Industry | | | | Grand Total |
|---|---|---|---|---|---|---|---|---|---|
| Year | Foodstuff | Textiles | Wood Products | Total | Machinery | Metals | Chemicals | Total | |
| 1900 | 18.4 | 50.6 | 2.7 | 80.4 | 5.4 | 4.2 | 10.2 | 19.6 | 100.0 |
| 1920 | 13.4 | 44.4 | 3.4 | 72.8 | 9.7 | 5.6 | 11.9 | 27.2 | 100.0 |
| 1930 | 16.1 | 38.0 | 2.8 | 64.6 | 10.6 | 9.6 | 15.3 | 35.4 | 100.0 |
| 1940 | 9.1 | 18.4 | 3.8 | 30.0 | 31.2 | 21.8 | 17.1 | 70.0 | 100.0 |
| 1947 | 9.8 | 11.7 | 9.4 | 43.5 | 25.6 | 14.4 | 14.6 | 56.5 | 100.0 |
| 1950 | 13.5 | 23.2 | 7.6 | 55.8 | 13.9 | 16.0 | 12.9 | 44.2 | 100.0 |
| 1960 | 12.4 | 12.4 | 4.5 | 43.6 | 25.8 | 15.8 | 9.4 | 56.4 | 100.0 |
| 1970 | 10.3 | 7.7 | 4.2 | 37.8 | 32.3 | 19.3 | 8.1 | 62.2 | 100.0 |

Source:  Japan Economic Planning Agency, Tokyo

**TABLE 5** Changes in the Composition of Industrial Production

*(Percentages)*

| Countries | Year | Light Industry | | | | | Heavy Industry | | | | Grand Total |
| --- | --- | --- | --- | --- | --- | --- | --- | --- | --- | --- | --- |
| | | Foodstuff | Textiles | Wood Products | Total | | Machinery | Metals | Chemicals | Total | |
| United States | 1939 (1) | 15.7 | 14.6 | 4.9 | 55.6 | | 25.2 | 8.9 | 10.3 | 44.4 | 100.0 |
| | 1953 (1) | 13.5 | 7.7 | 4.0 | 45.6 | | 29.0 | 14.9 | 8.7 | 54.4 | 100.0 |
| | 1967 (2) | 10.9 | 6.9 | 3.5 | 41.2 | | 33.1 | 14.4 | 9.0 | 58.6 | 100.0 |
| United Kingdom | 1935 (1) | 15.6 | 19.0 | 3.3 | 56.4 | | 28.2 | 7.3 | 8.1 | 43.6 | 100.0 |
| | 1954 (3) | 10.4 | 14.7 | 3.0 | 42.9 | | 34.2 | 14.3 | 8.6 | 57.1 | 100.0 |
| | 1963 (3) | 11.7 | 10.9 | 2.8 | 41.2 | | 35.7 | 13.4 | 9.7 | 59.8 | 100.0 |
| West Germany | 1936 (4) | 19.3 | 14.7 | 4.2 | 49.5 | | 20.9 | 22.0 | 7.7 | 50.6 | 100.0 |
| | 1955 (4) | 15.3 | 12.0 | 3.8 | 45.4 | | 25.6 | 19.1 | 7.9 | 54.6 | 100.0 |
| | 1967 (4) | 15.7 | 7.7 | 3.2 | 39.9 | | 28.6 | 16.1 | 10.4 | 60.1 | 100.0 |

Source: Japan Economic Planning Agency, Tokyo

TABLE 6  Changes in the Composition of Exports by Commodity
(*Percentages*)

| Commodity | 1850 | 1900 | 1920 | 1930 | 1955 | 1960 | 1965 | 1970 |
|---|---|---|---|---|---|---|---|---|
| Food and tobacco | 38.1 | 11.3 | 7.3 | 9.0 | 6.8 | 6.3 | 4.1 | 3.4 |
| (Tea) | (26.2) | (4.0) | (0.9) | (0.6) | (0.5) | (0.1) | (0.0) | (0.0) |
| Crude materials and fuels | 6.9 | 13.1 | 5.6 | 5.1 | 3.2 | 2.2 | 1.5 | 1.0 |
| Textiles: | 40.1 | 51.3 | 63.2 | 63.9 | 37.4 | 30.3 | 18.8 | 12.6 |
| Raw-silk | (30.8) | (22.3) | (20.0) | (29.8) | (2.5) | (1.0) | (0.1) | (0.0) |
| Cotton yarn and thread | (—) | (10.3) | (8.0) | (1.0) | (1.2) | (1.0) | (0.2) | (0.0) |
| Cotton fabrics | (0.1) | (2.9) | (17.5) | (19.0) | (11.4) | (8.7) | (2.6) | (1.0) |
| Rayon and spun rayon fabrics | (—) | (—) | (—) | (2.4) | (7.1) | (4.3) | (1.9) | (0.5) |
| Synthetic fabrics | (—) | (—) | (—) | (—) | (—) | (0.8) | (2.2) | (3.3) |
| Clothing | (0.1) | (3.0) | (4.0) | (4.1) | (5.3) | (5.5) | (3.4) | (2.4) |
| Non-metallic mineral manufacture: | 1.9 | 1.7 | 3.4 | 3.3 | 6.4 | 4.2 | 3.1 | 1.9 |
| Chinaware | (1.7) | (1.2) | (1.6) | (1.9) | (2.1) | (1.7) | (1.0) | (0.7) |
| Cement | (—) | (0.1) | (0.5) | (0.7) | (1.1) | (0.6) | (0.3) | (0.2) |
| Paper manufacture thereof | 0.4 | 0.9 | 1.9 | 2.3 | 0.9 | 1.3 | 0.9 | 0.9 |
| Others: | 4.4 | 9.4 | 7.3 | 7.0 | 7.5 | 11.5 | 9.2 | 7.2 |
| Toys | — | (0.2) | (1.1) | (0.8) | (2.1) | (2.2) | (1.2) | (0.7) |
| Plywood | — | (—) | (—) | (0.04) | (0.2) | (1.5) | (0.8) | (0.4) |
| | 46.8 | 63.3 | 75.8 | 76.5 | 52.2 | 47.3 | 32.0 | 22.6 |

Light Industry {

| | | C1 | C2 | C3 | C4 | C5 | C6 | C7 | C8 |
|---|---|---|---|---|---|---|---|---|---|
| | Machinery and equipment: | 0 | 0.3 | 3.1 | 3.1 | 13.8 | 25.6 | 35.4 | 45.6 |
| Heavy Industry | Vessels | (—) | (0.0) | (0.8) | (0.3) | (3.9) | (7.2) | (8.9) | (7.3) |
| | Motor vehicles | (—) | (—) | (—) | (—) | (0.3) | (1.9) | (2.8) | (7.0) |
| | T.V. receivers | (—) | (—) | (—) | (—) | (—) | (0.07) | (1.0) | (2.0) |
| | Textile machines | (—) | (0.0) | (0.2) | (0.3) | (1.3) | (1.2) | (1.0) | (1.0) |
| | Watches and clocks | (—) | (0.1) | (0.07) | (0.1) | (0.09) | (0.09) | (0.3) | (0.2) |
| | Metal products: | 4.0 | 7.1 | 3.5 | 3.8 | 19.3 | 14.1 | 20.5 | 19.9 |
| | Iron and steel products | (—) | (—) | (0.7) | (0.6) | (12.9) | (9.6) | (15.4) | (14.9) |
| | Chemicals: | 4.2 | 4.9 | 4.7 | 2.5 | 4.7 | 4.5 | 6.5 | 6.5 |
| | Fertilizers | (—) | (—) | (0.1) | (0.1) | (2.1) | (1.5) | (1.9) | (0.8) |
| Total | | 8.2 | 12.3 | 11.3 | 9.4 | 37.8 | 44.2 | 62.4 | 73.0 |
| | | 100.0 | 100.0 | 100.0 | 100.0 | 100.0 | 100.0 | 100.0 | 100.0 |
| Grand Total | | 27.9 | 200.2 | 1,915.9 | 1,434.6 | 720,966 | 1,454,320 | 3,025,293 | 6,898,729 |

Source: Japan Economic Planning Agency, Tokyo

however, when an enterprise changes its products. **Data** on industrial adjustment in Japan are included in the *Integrated Basic Survey of Medium and Small Enterprises* and in the *Industrial Statistics*. Since the former attempts to clarify the special features of medium and small enterprises, it covers features of most enterprises which have to undergo industrial adjustment, which means the data is useful when studying the state of industrial adjustment. But the survey only applies to a limited period.

On the other hand, the *Census of Manufactures* tabulates continuously, but the items dealing with industrial adjustment were only added recently. Consequently *Industrial Statistics* also only covers a limited period. Fortunately, the items in the *Census of Manufactures* almost coincide with those in the *Integrated Basic Survey of Medium and Small Enterprises*, which is to say one can study a fairly long period by combining the two. In this way statistics on work or plant conversion for the periods 1960-62, 1964-66 and 1967-69 have been estimated. Of course no totals for industrial conversion are shown in the ordinary publication of *Census of Manufacture*. Inquiry sheets have therefore been reworked and the results are utilised in this paper.

These data are rarely found in any country and are quite valuable. For they can be used to trace the change of activity of businesses in manufacturing industry. But entries to, and exits from, manufacturing industry are not traceable. This is a weakness of the data. Since there exists no statistical survey in the Ministry of International Trade and Industry (MITI), of non-manufacturing industries, use has had to be made of fragmentary questionnaires in that area. The problems of industrial adjustment are not confined to manufacturing industry; they also extend to agriculture and tertiary industry. Using this fragmentary information I will outline the conversion problems of non-manufacturing industries in order to make clear some of the characteristics peculiar to the adjustment of Japanese manufacturing.

*Conversion in Agriculture*

The adjustment problems in Japan's agriculture and in America's are somewhat different. The biggest difference lies in the fact that when the younger members of a Japanese farm family leave home in search of urban work the other members stay behind on the land, whereas in American farm families if the father leaves all the members are likely to follow him. In the United States the conversion from rural to urban employment is made at one time and not over an extended period as in Japan. According to D. Gale Johnson, of the University of Chicago, 80 per cent of those in America leaving their farms are leaving with all their family.[3] The following reasons might be given for this difference:

(a) Reforms after World War II made landowners of all Japanese farmers. It is perhaps partly because of an increase in the value of farm land that the whole family usually does not want to leave agriculture.

(b) An aspect of agricultural policy is that the prices of farm products are heavily supported.[4] In addition, as a result of Japan's economic growth, the extra income from non-farming work has increased. Thus farmers' incomes (from farm and off-farm work) tend to exceed those of non-farmers.

Although there are many opportunities for part-time employment for farmers willing to commute, young people and those unable to find employment near their farms often leave home altogether to work in urban districts. Such work may be seasonal labour as construction workers, when the farm does not require intensive labour, or it may be work in manufacturing industry. How Japanese agriculture in ten to twenty years will be affected by the current movement of young people to the cities will very much depend on future policies concerning agriculture. But the slow rate of conversion in agriculture, an adjustment accompanying a change of generation, will in turn effect directly or indirectly the adjustment process in other industries.[5]

*Adjustment in Manufacturing Industry*

The dates of conversion in sectors of Japanese manufacturing industry shown in Table 7 indicate a rising trend. It is seen to be rising every two years: for 1960-62 the rate of conversion was 9.6 per cent; for 1964-66, it was 12.7 per cent; for 1967-69, it was 15.1 per cent. The way in which these rates are obtained can be seen in the following example. From 1967 to 1969 there were 49,024 enterprises in the manufacturing industry which converted their production and, during the same period, 325,625 manufacturing enterprises continued in the same business. The work conversion rate is thus 15.1 per cent.

Conversion rates in the manufacturing field differ according to the type of industry. Among the industries which have high work-conversion rates (above 12 per cent) are transport, electrical, industrial and precision machinery. Among those which have less high rates (12 to 6.2 per cent) are non-ferrous metals, iron and steel, rubber, chemicals and leather. Some which have rather low rates (6.2 to 3 per cent) are clothing, oil, coal, furniture, paper, pulp and

TABLE 7   Rates of Conversion in Manufacturing Industry by Sector *(Percentages)*

|  | 1960-62 | 1964-66 | 1967-69 |
|  | Rate of Conversion | Rate of Conversion | Rate of Conversion |
| --- | --- | --- | --- |
| Manufacturing industry total | 9.6 | 12.7 | 15.6 |
| Foods | 2.8 | 3.4 | 5.9 |
| Textiles | 5.0 | 8.7 | 7.3 |
| Clothes | 6.6 | 11.3 | 16.1 |
| Lumber and products | 4.2 | 9.9 | 9.7 |
| Furniture | 5.3 | 9.5 | 16.8 |
| Paper and pulp | 6.0 | 12.2 | 17.1 |
| Printing and publishing | 4.0 | 7.3 | 9.2 |
| Chemicals | 2.4 | 11.9 | 15.1 |
| Petroleum and coal | 4.0 | 5.0 | 21.0 |
| Rubber | 4.5 | 14.0 | 19.9 |
| Leather | 3.4 | 11.5 | 18.9 |
| Ceramics | 4.0 | 7.4 | 9.0 |
| Iron and steel | 13.3 | 21.2 | 19.3 |
| Non-ferrous metals | 13.4 | 20.6 | 22.1 |
| Metals | 10.7 | 25.4 | 25.8 |
| Industrial machinery | 21.3 | 34.3 | 25.3 |
| Electric machinery | 21.8 | 32.2 | 27.6 |
| Transportation machinery | 11.7 | 27.4 | 38.6 |
| Precision machinery | 12.9 | 21.4 | 26.8 |
| Other manufactures | 5.9 | 13.9 | 21.7 |

Source:    Data for 1960-62, *Integrated Basic Survey of Medium and Small Enterprises*, Tokyo, and data for 1967-69, *Census of Manufacturers*, Tokyo.

timbers. And some of those with very low rates (3 per cent and below) are provisions, textiles, publishing, printing and ceramics. There is some relation between the conversion rate of a certain industry and its growth rate. Among those industries with high conversion rates, the growth rate is high in all except iron and steel and rubber, while those which have low conversion rates, with the exception of furniture and ceramics, have a low growth rate. Generally speaking, conversion is active in growing industries; and sluggish in stagnant industries.

It is interesting to trace the fields into which 23,386 establishments — that is, offices, factories and so on: not always the enterprises themselves — converted their business from 1968 through 1969. In the provisions, rubber, leather and ceramics industries, destinations are irregular. But the following industries tended to convert according to a regular pattern: textiles converted to clothing; timber to furniture or other manufacturing industries, such as pulp and paper; pulp and paper to publishing, printing and other manufacturing industries; iron and steel to metal and machinery; non-ferrous metal to metal and to industrial, electrical and transport machinery; industrial machinery to metal and to transport and electrical machinery; electric machinery to metal and industrial machinery; transport machinery to metal and industrial machinery; and precision machinery to metal and to electrical and industrial machinery. These conversions might be classified into two general categories.

(a) In cases such as textile into clothing or timber into furniture, industries moved vertically into fields requiring more processing or intensified information.

(b) In the conversion of machinery-making enterprises, the aim might be to further the development of a division of the enterprise.

There are a few cases which look like a reverse of the above: clothing into textiles for instance. But they are exceptions to what seems to be a justifiable rule.

When conversion is aimed at the development of a division of a business, it is not contradictory to find that the conversion rate is high in the high-growth activities and low in the low-growth areas. If conversion took place from a manufacturing to a non-manufacturing activity, it would probably be from a low-growth sector rather than from a high-growth one, but there are no statistics to prove as much.

Numbers were given to twenty kinds of industries classified according to their rate of growth. A matrix was drawn showing exits and entries between different kinds of industries as shown in Figure 1. It is a percentage distribution chart with a total exit number of 100. Every section with a dot shows 10 per cent and blank sections less than 10 per cent. Efforts of an enterprise in a low-growth industry to expand into a processing industry would be valued highly as would be the efforts of an enterprise in a high-growth industry to become a conglomerate. It must be realised, however, that conversion has its limits and that the new business of an enterprise usually maintains a close relationship to its previous business.

The survey on actual conditions of medium and small enterprises which have converted compiled by the Medium and Small Enterprises Agency in December 1971 produced the following results:

(a) Equipment: firms using old equipment 54.0 per cent; those using part of old equipment, 34.9 per cent, those using totally new equipment 11.1 per cent

(b) Technology: firms using old technology 40.8 per cent;

those using part of old technology 44.9 per cent; those using totally new technology 14.3 per cent

(c) Customers: almost no change, 25.7 per cent; partly changed, 54.1 per cent; totally changed 20.2 per cent.

This survey was supposed to have been carried out on the enterprises which had strong tendency to convert. In respect of equipment, technology and customers there was thought to be a strong inclination towards total renovation. But in spite of this bias the results show that firms have been hanging on the shadows of their previous business activities.

How have 'converted' firms been faring? Using data from the *Medium and Small Enterprises Movement Analysis*, published by the Medium and Small Enterprises Agency, a comparison can be made between the rate of growth of value added per ten employees of enterprises which stayed in the same business and the same

FIGURE 1 Matrix of Exits by the Degree of Growth

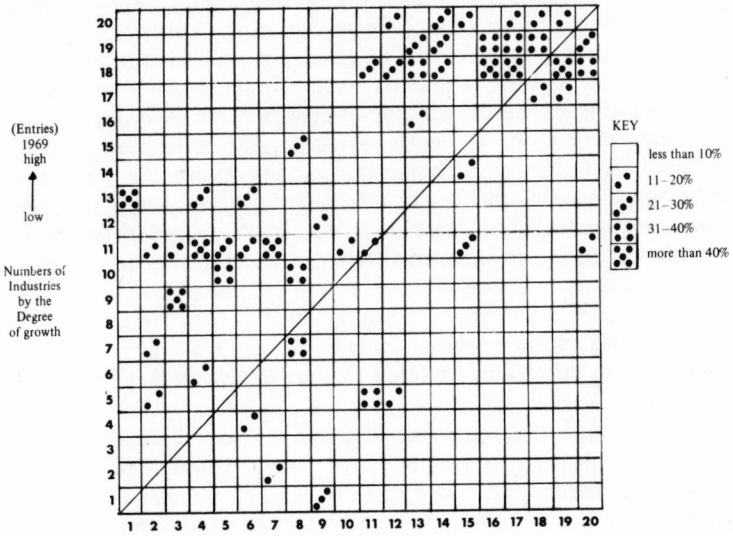

(Exits) 1968 (low→high) Number of Industries by the Degree of growth

Notes:
1. The numbers of industries by the degree of growth are the same in both 1968 and 1969. The larger the number is, the higher the growth rate of the industry is.
2. The distribution of the industry to which conversion has taken place is indicated by percentage composition of the key.

Source: *Integrated Basic Survey of Medium and Small Enterprises*, Tokyo, 1971.

measurement of enterprises which converted during the period 1967-69. In three manufacturing industries (paper-pulp, oil-coal, iron-steel) out of twenty, rates of the former enterprises exceed the latter, but in the remaining seventeen industries converted enterprises were doing better than those following the same business. Generally speaking, then, their conversion has been successful.

Conversion to a highly developed industry is said to have shown a growth rate on average 23 per cent higher than conversion to a low-growth industry. An irregular growth rate was found, however, in highly developed industries in which there is much competition (statistically standard deviation is much higher).

## Conversion in the Service Industry

In the service industry changes in the pattern of demand, in the flow of distribution and in competition are the chief causes of adjustment. There is no authentic statistical survey on these cases. But some special surveys and case studies compiled by the Medium and Small Enterprises Promotion Association and the Kyoto Prefectural Office give an idea of conversion in the industry.

An increasingly large variety of articles are handled in wholesale businesses. Moreover, wholesale establishments often convert to retail handling of the same kinds of articles. The following conversions have been seen: wholesale textile goods into restaurant, hotel and clothing businesses; wholesale personal effects into restaurant and transport; wholesale textile articles into manufacture of paper-processed articles, and agricultural and livestock products; wholesale marine products into provision manufactures; and wholesale construction materials into timber and wood manufactures. Conversions from service industries to manufacturing industries, like cases of conversions within manufacturing industries, show a tendency for enterprises to enter fields related to that in which they had dealt previously.

Generally speaking, a retail business is easy to open and, in consequence, it is apt to run into strong competition. When articles handled by retailers are low-growth or 'sunset' items, conversion is necessary. In this situation, one quite often sees the conversion take place with a change in generation, as in agriculture, but if the proprietor is not aged he will try to convert his business to any other retail business or restaurant. Examples of conversions in various service industries are: restaurants into hotels, game centres or bowling-alley halls; freight-car transportation into car maintenance; barbers into retail furniture or utensil stores; cinemas into retail provisions, restaurants, game centres or bowling-alley halls.

These cases make the Japanese feel gigantic social changes taking place around them. In the background of these conversions are transient changes in social customs which mark the coming of a new age.

Conversions to the service industries, and conversions within the service industries, are hard to clarify for lack of data. This is the case not only in Japan, but also in the rest of the world. In any analysis of domestic adjustment to international integration due consideration should be given to such fundamental currents as the influence of the distribution 'revolution', the evolution of the leisure industry and the impact of mass communication. The sector in the vanguard of economic development, but a straggler when it comes to social adjustment, is the so-called service industry and it poses challenging problems for policy makers.

## Problems of Industrial Adjustment by Scale of Firm

### Conversion of Medium-size Firms

According to the survey of the Medium and Small Enterprises Agency shown in Table 8, the number of employees is decreasing in enterprises with ten to fifty employees; and the number of employees is increasing in enterprises with 200 to 1,000 employees. These data on changes in the size of enterprises were based on enterprises which have not converted production. They can, however, be used to forecast the chance of success in conversions by scale of the firm.

According to a survey made by the Medium and Small Enterprises Promotion Association in 1967, conversions by comparatively large firms have a higher chance of success. The critical scale for decreases or increases in size vary according to the type of industry. For instance in the provision industry 50 to 100 employees is considered the critical scale. Enterprises having fewer than fifty employees are apt to decrease the number of their employees; and those with more than 100 employees are apt to increase the number of employees. In the clothing industry, as another example, thirty to fifty employees is the critical scale.

The importance of size in considering industrial adjustment can be seen in the case of branch factories established by the clothing manufacturers of the city of Gyoda in Saitama Prefecture. Gyoda was once the centre for the production of a special type of Japanese socks. In answer to a change in demand, the firms converted to the manufacture of children's clothes, school uniforms and work clothes. This conversion was highly successful. What attracts attention here is the fact that several enterprises of Gyoda have, or are now constructing, branch factories in the Tohoku region, an area where spare labour for sewing can still be found. K Company is

TABLE 8  Conversion by Scale of Firm Manufacturing Industry, 1964 to 1966

(Percentages)

| 1964 Employees per firm | Total firms | 1966 Employees per firm | | | | | | | | | | | Converted to other firms | Not covered by the survey |
|---|---|---|---|---|---|---|---|---|---|---|---|---|---|---|
| | | 1-3 | 4-9 | 10-19 | 20-29 | 30-49 | 50-99 | 100-199 | 200-299 | 300-499 | 500-999 | 1000 + | | |
| 1-3 | 520,137 | 29.2 | 25.9 | 10.4 | 3.6 | 2.8 | 2.0 | 0.9 | 0.2 | 0.2 | 0.1 | 0.1 | 12.7 | 1.8 |
| 4-9 | 212,340 | 63.8 | 9.1 | 0.3 | — | — | — | — | — | — | — | — | 11.1 | 1.3 |
| 10-19 | 186,186 | 8.7 | 58.4 | 9.1 | 0.3 | 0.2 | 0.3 | — | — | — | — | — | 13.4 | 2.0 |
| 20-29 | 55,062 | 0.5 | 11.2 | 57.0 | 6.7 | 0.9 | 0.8 | 0.1 | — | — | — | — | 14.9 | 1.9 |
| 30-49 | 25,896 | 0.2 | 1.4 | 18.6 | 44.2 | 11.2 | 10.1 | 0.3 | — | — | — | — | 15.2 | 2.0 |
| 50-99 | 18,399 | 0.1 | 0.4 | 2.2 | 13.2 | 50.8 | 58.1 | 6.7 | 0.1 | — | — | — | 14.7 | 2.5 |
| 100-199 | 12,630 | — | 0.1 | 0.4 | 1.5 | 10.8 | 12.3 | 57.6 | 5.8 | 0.7 | — | — | 14.2 | 2.4 |
| 200-299 | 5,390 | — | 0.1 | 0.2 | 0.3 | 1.2 | 1.5 | 20.3 | 42.6 | 14.9 | 0.1 | — | 14.1 | 3.2 |
| 300-499 | 1,688 | — | 0.1 | 0.1 | 0.1 | 0.3 | 0.4 | 3.7 | 14.6 | 56.7 | 0.9 | 0.1 | 12.4 | 3.5 |
| 500-999 | 1,150 | — | — | — | 0.2 | 0.3 | — | 0.7 | 2.2 | 15.4 | 7.0 | — | 8.6 | 5.1 |
| | 760 | — | — | — | — | — | — | — | — | 15.4 | 60.8 | 5.9 | 7.5 | 5.5 |
| 1,000 + | 641 | — | — | — | — | — | — | — | — | 0.6 | 7.2 | 77.8 | 7.4 | 4.5 |

Source: *Integrated Basic Survey of Medium and Small Enterprises*, Tokyo, December 1966

constructing a branch factory for 100 workers in Akita Prefecture. L Company has a factory with 100 workers in Miyagi Prefecture and K Company has a factory with 80 workers in Iwate Prefecture. Success would not have been possible for these companies with a smaller number of employees in each branch factory. In short, technology, capital, market exploitation and so on are necessary for conversion. And the chance of success is higher in larger enterprises.

## Conversion of Small Firms

According to the recalculated data of the *Census of Manufacture*, in every manufacturing industry, without exception, linear ratios exist between the size of an enterprise, the rate of capital accommodation per worker and the size of value added per worker. Thus, when the firm is small, neither technology nor capital are intensive; value added per worker is low and, in consequence, wages are also low. Low productivity (value added per worker) is the result of the difference of the bargaining power between small and big firms, and of low physical productivity.

In the process of economic growth, rising wage levels place small enterprises in a difficult position. There is pressure on them to convert and many conversions do in fact take place. Through the entry of formerly employed workers who became independent, and also through the declines of large enterprises, the number of small firms in existence is likely to remain stable. On the other hand, the number of plants in manufacturing industries will on average, keep growing (Table 9).

When small enterprises convert, what forms do they take? To show the direction in which an industry made up of small enterprises converted, look at the case of artificial flowers. The makers of artificial flowers were dealt a heavy blow by the entry into the Japanese market of competing products made in Hong Kong. The number of members of the industry's association was 181 in 1968, but during the previous ten years 117 had left. The breakdown of those leaving was: fifty-two closed their business; thirty-eight changed the nature of their work. With the rest there is no information. Firms converted into retail premises, hotels, real estate, recreation service and apartment houses. The destinations were all, in a broad sense, service industries. Most enterprises converted during the period 1961-63 when the industry was strongly affected by the import of Hong Kong flowers.

The textile industry offers another example for it was severely affected by the Japan-America Textile Agreement and many textile enterprises all on the small side, were obliged to change their production. The new field of activity for those engaged in the firms

TABLE 9  Annual Rate of Growth in Establishment of Manufacturing Industries
(*Percentages*)

|  | 1959-61 | 1961-65 | 1965-69 | 1957-69 |
|---|---|---|---|---|
| Manufacturing Total | 1.48 | 3.21 | 3.76 | 2.82 |
| Medium and Small Scale (1-299) | 1.43 | 3.21 | 3.76 | 2.80 |
| 1-9 | 0.08 | 4.16 | 4.07 | 2.76 |
| 10-19 | 3.32 | 0.44 | 4.50 | 2.74 |
| 20-99 | 6.59 | 0.92 | 0.86 | 2.75 |
| 100-299 | 10.67 | 3.72 | 3.80 | 6.01 |
| Large Scale (more than 300) | 10.82 | 3.39 | 3.93 | 6.00 |

Source:  *Census of Manufacture*, Ministry of International Trade and Industry, Tokyo

were as follows: 22 per cent became white-collar workers in other companies; 16 per cent went into businesses related to the textile industry (secondary processing and retail); 14 per cent went to agriculture; 8 per cent went into service industries; 5 per cent joined other manufacturing businesses; 3 per cent retired from business altogether; and 25 per cent appeared undecided. A quarter of converted manufacturers of textile goods changed to another business within the manufacturing industry. The remaining three-quarters converted into other areas. The fact that 14 per cent of the employees of the textile firms turned to farm work shows that the industry is highly localised and that textile manufacturers and farmers had a certain close tie before the conversion.

When small manufacturers try to change their business they tend to go into the service industry or industries other than manufacturing. For instance, in the case of machine processing sub-contractors, conversion involves a change to secondary sub-contraction work, then tertiary sub-contraction work and finally factory work (or other work in the manufacturing or service industries).

*Conversion of Large Firms*

Large enterprises have become increasingly multifarious as they often develop into conglomerates in their quest for survival. Activities to which they turn are usually in non-manufacturing industries: leisure, real estate, housing, city building *etcetera*. On some occasions in Japan a bank may establish a new company in order to let a large manufacturing enterprise enter a new field.

The conversion of a large enterprise is a very serious problem. This paper, in dealing with industrial adjustment in the development of international economic relations, is not concerned with problems of this kind and so I will not go further into the subject.

**Outline of the Government Position**

Japan follows two broad policies for the furtherance of industrial adjustment. First of all, the decisions of entrepreneurs and other businessmen are influenced by long-, medium- and short-range forecasts. Such forecasts are often made by governments and large enterprises in a modern industrial country. They can then be co-ordinated implicitly, as in case of the United States and the Federal Republic of Germany or explicitly and institutionally, as in case of Japan and France. The co-ordination formula adopted in the French case is the *l'economie concertee*.

The Japanese and French systems of co-ordination, implemented according to this formula, resemble each other to a fairly large extent in the way public and private forecasts are co-ordinated and

TABLE 10  Movement of Labour (Exits)

*(Conversion rate by size of work force)*

| Industry | 4-9 | 10-19 | 20-29 | 30-49 | WORK FORCE 50-99 | 100-199 | 200-299 | 300-499 | 500-999 | 1000+ | Total |
|---|---|---|---|---|---|---|---|---|---|---|---|
| 18 Foods | 0.6 | 0.5 | 0.7 | 0.6 | 0.4 | 0.5 | 0.3 | 0.4 | 0.3 | 5.9 | 0.6 |
| 20 Textiles | 2.1 | 2.7 | 2.0 | 1.6 | 2.1 | 1.5 | 0.4 | 0.4 | 0.5 | 1.3 | 2.0 |
| 21 Clothes | 5.8 | 5.7 | 4.8 | 3.8 | 4.7 | 3.1 | 4.3 | 4.0 | 0.0 | 0.0 | 5.5 |
| 22 Lumber and products | 3.5 | 2.5 | 1.7 | 3.0 | 2.9 | 2.2 | 2.2 | 0.0 | 0.0 | 0.0 | 3.0 |
| 23 Furniture | 4.9 | 7.2 | 6.0 | 6.1 | 6.6 | 5.0 | 0.0 | 5.1 | 0.0 | 0.0 | 5.5 |
| 24 Pulp, paper and paper products | 6.4 | 6.9 | 5.7 | 3.6 | 3.4 | 3.4 | 0.0 | 2.0 | 0.0 | 0.0 | 5.9 |
| 25 Printing, publishing | 2.6 | 2.4 | 2.0 | 1.9 | 1.8 | 3.4 | 1.0 | 0.0 | 0.0 | 0.0 | 2.5 |
| 26 Chemicals | 9.0 | 7.7 | 5.1 | 5.4 | 3.0 | 3.2 | 2.7 | 0.0 | 1.7 | 1.2 | 6.2 |
| 27 Petroleum and coal products | 9.5 | 4.7 | 1.5 | 7.5 | 1.7 | 0.0 | 0.0 | 9.1 | 0.0 | 0.0 | 5.5 |
| 28 Rubbers | 9.4 | 9.5 | 7.3 | 6.5 | 7.2 | 4.7 | 13.9 | 7.3 | 2.6 | 3.4 | 8.7 |
| 29 Leather | 7.3 | 5.6 | 8.6 | 6.5 | 5.2 | 5.6 | 11.1 | 0.0 | 0.0 | 0.0 | 0.9 |
| 30 Ceramics, stone and day products | 2.1 | 2.8 | 2.6 | 2.6 | 1.7 | 1.9 | 1.4 | 0.0 | 0.0 | 3.7 | 2.3 |
| 31 Iron & steel | 15.8 | 10.5 | 6.4 | 5.3 | 5.3 | 6.1 | 1.8 | 0.0 | 1.4 | 0.0 | 9.4 |
| 32 Non-ferrous metals and products | 13.6 | 11.3 | 7.5 | 6.5 | 5.5 | 5.4 | 2.0 | 0.0 | 4.3 | 0.0 | 10.4 |
| 33 Metals | 11.2 | 11.7 | 8.9 | 9.1 | 9.6 | 9.0 | 5.4 | 3.6 | 6.9 | 8.3 | 10.9 |
| 34 Industrial machinery | 15.1 | 14.7 | 10.9 | 8.5 | 8.6 | 6.2 | 3.0 | 2.9 | 3.7 | 3.2 | 13.2 |
| 35 Electric machinery | 18.5 | 14.2 | 11.3 | 7.5 | 7.0 | 3.4 | 3.3 | 1.2 | 1.1 | 3.6 | 13.0 |
| 36 Transportation machinery | 24.5 | 24.8 | 16.7 | 13.5 | 13.2 | 10.4 | 4.3 | 4.5 | 2.7 | 2.2 | 20.8 |
| 37 Precision machinery | 13.5 | 12.3 | 9.3 | 9.6 | 9.2 | 7.6 | 4.8 | 4.3 | 4.8 | 3.7 | 12.0 |
| 39 Others | 8.4 | 9.2 | 10.3 | 8.0 | 7.0 | 8.1 | 4.1 | 2.7 | 2.5 | 15.4 | 8.6 |
| Manufacturing industry | 6.3 | 7.0 | 5.7 | 5.2 | 5.2 | 4.3 | 2.6 | 1.7 | 2.0 | 2.3 | 6.2 |

## TABLE 11  Movement of Labour (Entries)

*(Conversion rate by size of work force)*

| Industry | WORK FORCE | | | | | | | | | | Total |
|---|---|---|---|---|---|---|---|---|---|---|---|
| | 4-9 | 10-19 | 20-29 | 30-49 | 50-99 | 100-199 | 200-299 | 300-499 | 500-999 | 1000+ | |
| 18 Foods | 0.5 | 0.6 | 0.6 | 0.7 | 0.7 | 0.3 | 0.0 | 0.9 | 0.0 | 0.0 | 0.5 |
| 20 Textiles | 1.8 | 2.3 | 1.7 | 1.8 | 1.9 | 1.6 | 1.5 | 1.3 | 1.0 | 1.3 | 1.9 |
| 21 Clothes | 6.9 | 5.6 | 4.7 | 4.6 | 4.3 | 3.7 | 2.9 | 0.0 | 0.0 | 0.0 | 6.1 |
| 22 Lumber and products | 3.2 | 2.3 | 1.7 | 2.0 | 2.4 | 4.4 | 1.1 | 0.0 | 0.0 | 0.0 | 2.8 |
| 23 Furniture | 4.5 | 5.4 | 6.0 | 6.9 | 7.0 | 2.2 | 4.3 | 0.0 | 0.0 | 0.0 | 4.9 |
| 24 Pulp, paper and paper products | 4.8 | 6.2 | 5.1 | 3.2 | 3.5 | 3.1 | 3.7 | 4.1 | 0.0 | 0.0 | 4.9 |
| 25 Printing, publishing | 3.4 | 2.9 | 2.5 | 1.5 | 1.8 | 1.9 | 0.0 | 1.8 | 0.0 | 0.0 | 3.0 |
| 26 Chemicals | 9.0 | 6.3 | 4.1 | 2.3 | 3.3 | 1.3 | 1.1 | 2.6 | 0.8 | 2.4 | 5.4 |
| 27 Petroleum and coal products | 7.5 | 5.2 | 4.6 | 9.0 | 1.7 | 0.0 | 0.0 | 0.0 | 0.0 | 0.0 | 5.3 |
| 28 Rubbers | 8.1 | 8.7 | 5.5 | 4.5 | 7.3 | 9.3 | 2.8 | 0.0 | 2.6 | 0.0 | 7.4 |
| 29 Leather | 5.3 | 6.7 | 6.6 | 2.2 | 3.7 | 8.3 | 5.6 | 0.0 | 0.0 | 0.0 | 5.5 |
| 30 Ceramics, stone and clay products | 2.1 | 2.3 | 2.5 | 1.4 | 1.7 | 2.9 | 0.7 | 1.1 | 4.7 | 0.0 | 2.1 |
| 31 Iron and steel | 14.6 | 14.9 | 6.2 | 6.1 | 5.4 | 5.8 | 0.9 | 2.1 | 4.3 | 0.0 | 10.4 |
| 32 Non-ferrous metals and products | 12.6 | 15.4 | 9.1 | 7.6 | 8.3 | 4.6 | 4.0 | 0.0 | 4.3 | 3.0 | 11.4 |
| 33 Metals | 15.2 | 16.1 | 13.3 | 11.6 | 13.2 | 10.4 | 6.8 | 0.9 | 6.9 | 25.0 | 14.8 |
| 34 Industrial machinery | 14.2 | 11.5 | 9.6 | 8.7 | 8.3 | 6.8 | 5.0 | 2.4 | 2.2 | 8.4 | 11.9 |
| 35 Electric machinery | 17.5 | 15.3 | 10.3 | 9.5 | 8.0 | 6.1 | 2.7 | 2.0 | 1.7 | 1.0 | 13.2 |
| 36 Transportation machinery | 17.2 | 17.6 | 12.7 | 12.7 | 9.4 | 6.7 | 3.5 | 3.0 | 4.5 | 1.4 | 15.0 |
| 37 Precision machinery | 12.0 | 12.8 | 7.9 | 10.6 | 9.2 | 5.8 | 3.2 | 6.4 | 0.0 | 0.0 | 11.2 |
| 39 Others | 8.3 | 9.8 | 9.7 | 10.0 | 8.4 | 7.0 | 6.8 | 4.1 | 2.5 | 0.0 | 8.7 |
| Manufacturing industry | 6.2 | 7.1 | 5.7 | 5.5 | 5.5 | 4.4 | 2.7 | 1.9 | 2.1 | 2.2 | 6.2 |

in the content of deliberations based on these forecasts. The fundamental difference is that the chairmanship of the French council for such deliberations is assumed by a government representative and its reporters are also government officials. A similar Japanese council, though, is chaired by a representative of the private sector and its reporters are also from private circles. In a sense the Japanese private sector charts its own economic course. In this sense the concept of 'Japan Incorporated' is illusory. As is pointed out in a report by the Department of Commerce in the United States, government can only play a leadership role in a limited field. Deliberations in Japan, relating to the co-ordination of public and private opinions and predictions, are carried out more democratically than in France and there is a greater chance that the private sector will be affected by the process.

The second broad line of policy is more direct. This includes financing by government organisations and tax prerogatives. Among the organisations involved are the Japan Development Bank, the Small Enterprise Finance Corporation and the People's Corporation. The second of these also provides low-interest loans to small enterprises capable of meeting specified requirements. The tax prerogatives include accelerated depreciation (according to the Small Enterprise Modernisation Promotion Law, the Law on Provisional Measures for Small Business against Preferential Tariffs, and the Law on Provisional Measures for Small Business relating to the Enforcement of International Economic Adjustment Measures) and a system to provide reserves of funds for the structural modernisation of the small business sector (according to the Small Business Modernisation Subsidisation Law).

These policy measures are virtually directed, as far as industrial adjustment is concerned, at small enterprises. With respect to large enterprises the Japanese Government mainly relies on the guidelines delineated in the forecasting process — indicative planning. Although the rapidly growing Japanese economy could afford the costs of industrial conversion, the large-business sector can overcome difficulties rather easily, but the small business sector cannot always do so.

The ensuing section will furnish prominent examples of the support provided by the Japanese Government for industrial adjustment and, through the examples, the characteristic traits of its handling of the industrial adjustment problem should become clear.

### Policies for Adjustment Problems

In Japan industrial conversion is interpreted as a structural problem in the sector concerned. In the United States it is interpreted as the direct problem of each enterprise and its workers.

Already the general problem of industrial conversion has been discussed in this paper. But the earlier observations were mainly on a macro-economic level. They did not go into the Japanese peculiarities of industrial adjustment. In this section two cases will be adduced to demonstrate more concretely how the industrial adjustment problem is handled in Japan and what policies are taken to solve the problem. The cases relate to the textile sector and the mining sector (coal and sulphur mining). They will not only serve as the primary example of industrial adjustment in Japan. They are also the rare cases where international comparisons are possible.

## Industrial Adjustment in the Mining Sector

The main industrial adjustment problems in the mining sector are the development and dissemination of new energies (the energy revolution), the competition of some products (like sulphur) with by-products as a result of anti-pollution measures, the drain of energy resources and the pollution caused by some products (like copper). Attention will focus here on sulphur mining which has been most heavily influenced by changes in the external situation.

## Adjustment in Sulphur Mining

Production of recovered sulphur in Japan was started in 1955 with 5,000 tons (metric tons). Along with the full-scale enforcement of anti-pollution measures and resort to the method of de-sulphurisation with heavy oil, the output of recovered sulphur made a steep climb to 379,000 tons in 1971. This was more than 90 per cent of Japan's total sulphur output (419,000 tons). (Japan's recovered sulphur output rose from 46,000 tons in 1965 to 88,000 tons in 1968 and increased more than fourfold from 1968 to 1971.)

On the other hand, Japan's output of mine sulphur reached 258,000 tons or a new high in 1957, but due to a business depression was down to 214,000 tons or a new low in 1965. In step with business recovery, the output turned for the better, reaching 260,000 tons in 1967. Affected by the sharp rise in the production of recovered sulphur, the output of mine sulphur dropped steeply to only 43,000 tons in 1971.

To cope with this situation, the Mining Council, a body which advises the Minister of International Trade and Industry, submitted a *Report on Policy Measures for Sulphur* in July 1968. In July 1969, the Commerce and Industry Committee of the House of Representatives adopted a resolution calling for the 'establishment of a policy for sulphur'. In response to these steps, the Japanese Government took such measures as (a) the formulation of a sulphur demand-and-supply programme, (b) the promotion of sulphur exports with the emphasis placed on recovered sulphur, and (c) the subsidisation of sulphur mines to permit the rationalisation of their operations. (Government expenditures made for this last purpose from 1968 to 1970 totalled 38.7m year.) In spite of these measures, and affected by declining sulphur exports and spiralling labour costs, one sulphur mine after another closed down. The number of employees continued to decrease from 6,000 in 1965 to 2,700 in 1970 and the decrease is till going on.

The emphasis of government policy for the sulphur mines has been on the maintenance of reserves for retirement allowances. When the Matsuo Sulphur Mine, the biggest in Japan, was closed down, the oil refineries, at the Government's request, contributed 150m yen for allowances for retiring miners. With the closing-down of such mines as Horobetsu, Ogushi, Ishizu and Kohonoe the Government asked the oil refineries to contribute 22,000 tons of recovered sulphur (worth 154m yen) and devoted the sum thus raised for retirement allowances. When the Matsuo Mine converted its sulphur mining operations into pyrite mining, the non-ferrous metal producers contributed 60m yen in support of the conversion.

In this way the conversion (or closing-down) of sulphur mines was realised with the co-operation of affiliated industries rather than by disbursements from the Treasury. It attests, it might be said, to the competency of the industrial policy-making authorities that the difficulties of the sulphur mining companies were overcome not by the appropriation of taxes — that is, by a contribution from the general public — but by contributions from closely related interests.

In addition, it is likely that the sulphur problem will develop into a more complex one as the products of waste gas emitted by non-ferrous metal producers, pyrite and recovered sulphur compete to become a resource for the production of sulphuric acid. It is also anticipated that there will arise competition between the gypsum produced as a by-product of a sulphuric acid and mine gypsum. These problems are now under deliberation by the Japanese Government.

## Adjustment in Coal Mining

Japan's coal output reached 55,410,000 tons or a new high in fiscal 1961, then went down because of the energy revolution. The figure for fiscal 1972 is estimated at 27,500,000 tons. The regular workers employed by the coal mines totalled 366,000 in fiscal 1952 (the output for the fiscal year was 43,750,000 tons) which was a new high, but the figure dropped to 34,000 in fiscal 1972, or less than 10 per cent of the peak figure.

Coal mining in Japan passed from the so-called 'priority production' period right after the end of World War II to the period of
increased and efficient production, and in 1962 entered a period of
decreased but efficient production. The fact that while the employment of the coal mines dropped after 1952, the output continued to
rise till 1961 is evidence that the period was one of 'increased and
efficient production'. In that period output rose by 11,670,000 tons,
but employment dropped by 154,000 as the *per capita* (monthly)
output rose from 9.9 to 21.7 tons. The weight carried by coal in the
distribution of energies dropped from 47 to 31 per cent. During the
period of 'decreased but efficient production', the conversion or the
closing-down of coal mines has been going at full swing. The coal
output for 1967 was 47,060,000 tons, and employment was 92,000.
Both output and employment continued to drop steeply to 27,500
tons and 34,000 workers in 1971. In terms of *per capita* coal output,
Japan ranks above France and the United Kingdom, but below West
Germany.

Japan's coal output for 1975 is estimated at 20m tons. It is
anticipated that the figure for 1980 will be short of 10m tons because
of the difficulty of recruiting a sufficient labour force and other
difficulties. The labour force available at that time will be no more
than 10,000. Coal miners below thirty-five years of age accounted, as
of March 1972, for 2.5 per cent (8,500 miners) of Japan's total coal
mining work force, as against 52.6 per cent (140,000 miners) in
December 1958.

Making adjustments in the area of coal mines is also a problem
for West European countries. The United Kingdom, which has
maintained its coal output at a comparatively high level, estimates
its output for 1975 at 118m tons as against 154.3m tons in 1970.
West Germany estimates her coal consumption for 1975 at 80m tons
as against the 88.7m tons in 1970 (97.5m tons consumed and 8.8m
tons imported). Considering the increasing trend of coal imports,
West Germany's output for 1975 might be around 60m tons. France
estimates her coal output for 1975, at 25m tons as against 39.9m
tons in 1970. France's estimated production in 1975 is thus closest to
that estimated for Japan. The production of coal mines in Western
Europe and Japan will be unavoidably reduced as other sources of
energy gain in importance — in spite of the oil 'gap'.

It would be useful next to compare the Japanese and European
performances in the adjustment of their coal mines. It is appropriate
to compare them in terms of the per-ton cost of conversion and
closing-down, the contribution to regional reforms and development, and the efficiency of conversion.

In comparing the costs incurred in conversion and closing-down a difficulty arises in the relevant expenditure accounts vary from country to country. To make a comparison of the actual government expenditures for coal mines, the per-ton expenditures in France and Japan are respectively 2,460 yen (for 1970) and 2,200 yen (for 1972). The Japanese figure for 1970 was 1,820 yen. Since there was a per-ton 250 yen loss on the Japanese coal mines in the same year, one can conclude that the Japanese 1970 figure may actually have been slightly less than the French figure. The per-ton price of West German coal is higher by about 1,500 yen than the Japanese price because of the Federal Republic's tariff quota and fuel consumption tax. There was an expenditure of 600 yen per ton in 1971 and a loss of 1,450 yen per ton on Ruhr Coal (a joint stock company). It can therefore be said that the social cost on the maintenance of Japanese coal mines is slightly less than the German cost.

As regards the regional performance, Japanese coal mines in general are not well located to make a contribution to regional reforms and the development of a high rate of economic growth. With the development project for the coal-producing region, implemented from 1962 to 1971 at a cost of 89,600m yen, it might be said that regional problems were kept from getting worse.

As for the efficiency of adjustment, the conversion and closing-down of Japanese coal mines might have promoted the high rate of economic growth, but there is no evidence for this of course.

Some coal-mining companies started to convert as early as 1965, began to branch out into new industrial lines, and lived off their coal mining activities from 1969 to 1970 bearing in mind the timing and other factors involved in going into new lines. The new lines were mostly in the tertiary industry, notably real estate development (the construction of housing units), tourism and the refining of non-ferrous metals (as joint enterprises with affiliated companies). There are other areas in which coal-mining companies could make use of their specialised technology.

A case in point is the Taiheiyo Coal Mining Company which is not affiliated to any *Zeibatsu* group. Since 1960 or so the company was seen creating subsidiaries producing raw concrete, petroleum products and air-conditioning equipment. In 1967 the company established Taiheiyo Kohatsu Kaisha as a subsidiary for real estate development. The new subsidiary made smooth development. Then the company made its coal mining department independent and merged Taiheiyo Kohatsu with another subsidiary. At the same time the old company was re-named Taiheiyo Kohatsu Kaisha by assuming the name of its subsidiary in real estate development. In one year after the restart, the company's real estate development department returned 4,300m yen with a profit of 300m yen. Coal sales returned

13,900m yen with no profit. It was a plus factor that agreement had been reached between the management and the union over the conversion. Conversion is often delayed when labour and management are pitted against each other.

It can be concluded that the conversion of Japanese coal mining companies is going smoothly thanks to their own efforts, an appropriate government adjustment policy and a high-rate of economic growth.

## Adjustment Problems of the Textile Sector

The Japanese Government has implemented four major policies for structural improvement of the Japanese textile sector. The first policy was contained in the Law on Provisional Measures on the Equipment of the Textile Industry of 1956 (old law). The second was implemented by the Law on Provisional Measures on the Equipment of the Textile Industry (revised law) of 1964. The third was based on the Law on Provisional Measures on the Structural Improvement of Specially Designated Textile Industries of 1967. And the fourth was the Provisional Special Policy for the Textile Industry of 1971, which was implemented according to the inter-governmental textile agreement concluded between Japan and the United States. Since 1970 an additional policy, based on the Law on the Promotion of Small-enterprise Modernisation, has been implemented for the small-business sector.

The 1956 and 1964 measures were basically aimed at disposing of surplus plant and equipment. For this purpose a registration system for plant was adopted so that only registered plant could be used. Surplus equipment had to be stored, sealed or scrapped. The storing, sealing and scrapping costs were, in principle, covered by related enterprises with no aid from the Government. The latter policy differed from the former in two ways: a scrap-and-build system was adopted to encourage the voluntary scrapping of surplus equipment, and surplus equipment for chemical and synthetic textiles was disposed of through the co-operation of 'concerted economy' between government and industry.

The 1967 policy was developed to allow the textile sector to recover from the effects of the structural improvement of the industry's competitors in advanced countries, from the impact of the long-term agreement with the United States, from the rapid strides being taken by developing countries in this field, from the slowing down in demand and from the labour shortage. Its aims were (a) the disposal of surplus equipment, (b) the modernisation of plant and (c) the enlargement of the scale of production to enable firms to compete with larger enterprises (involving the grouping of small enterprises).

The following are the rates of structural improvement in various parts of the textile sector and were measured in 1971 against the annual structural improvement programmes framed for the industries from 1969 to 1973. In the spinning industry 68 per cent of plant was modernised and 100 per cent of surplus plant was disposed. Nine groups were formed in the industry. The weaving industry achieved 69.6 per cent success in plant modernisation, 23 per cent in surplus plant disposal, and 67.9 per cent success in the grouping of weaving enterprises. The knitting industry achieved 17.4 per cent success in the grouping of enterprises and 20.7 per cent in plant modernisation. The dyeing industry achieved 17.5 per cent success in the grouping of enterprises; 56 per cent in plant modernisation.

By and large, the success rates for plant modernisation are high, whereas the rates for disposal of surplus equipment and the grouping of enterprises are low. The surplus plant of the spinning industry, however, was disposed of as scheduled by the programmes because the industry consists mostly of large enterprises. It is difficult to step up the disposal of surplus plant in an industry made up of small enterprises. For example, some small enterprises in the weaving industry are concurrently engaged in farming. They can make do with small profits and are unwilling to dispose of their plant and equipment.

The Law on Provisional Measures on the Structural Improvement of Specially Designated Textile Industries specified that the Government would provide low-interest loans for plant modernisation. As an encouragement, enterprises in the weaving industry which had suspended more operations than scheduled were made eligible for a subsidy equal to half the excess cost incurred on the part of the suspension over the planned level. The subsidy was small and the greater part of the cost, not covered by the subsidy, was borne by enterprises in proportion to the number of looms held by them. According to the laws of 1964 and 1967, government subsidies were granted in exceptional cases, and the cost incurred on structrual modernisation was mainly covered by firms. The Government of Japan was willing to give advice rather than money.

Things changed when textiles became a problem between Japan and the United States. Even before the conclusion of the Japan-United States Textile Agreement, it was decided by the Japanese Government to subsidise 90 per cent of the cost of the scrapping, in order to lessen the damage incurred by the decline in exports to the United States. After the conclusion of the agreement this percentage was advanced to 100. Why did the Government give such subsidies? It did so because the textile issue was settled by an inter-governmental agreement. Such a subsidy was granted also on the grounds that the final beneficiaries are the exporters of developing countries — because they can increase their exports at the expense of Japanese enterprises. These government subsidies thus amounted to 26,564m yen by September 1972.

In view of the fact that the 1967 law is to lose effect in 1974, the Japanese Government has been studying a plan for the textile sector. The plan is (a) to develop the sewing industry so that it could branch off into the manufacture of garments, (b) to integrate the spinning (materials), weaving (finished textiles) and secondary textile product parts of the industry and (c) to up-grade, diversify and fashion secondary products according to modern tastes. It is anticipated that new adjustment problems will crop up as the textile industry progresses in this new direction. What will become of the government subsidy? The Japanese textile producers have learned much from the import restrictions imposed on them and there is the possibility that they will seek restrictions of imports on their own behalf. The only alternative to import restrictions, as pointed out in the Culvert Report, [6] is adjustment assistance.

And after the Japan-United States textile issue it seems that the idea of adjustment assistance is gradually becoming accepted in Japan. In this way the harmonisation of producer interests and taxpayer interests will become important.

## International Industrial Adjustment

In discussing the problems of industrial adjustment in Japan the case of the textile industry has just been explained. But to discuss the problem one has to face the question of international industrial adjustment as a part of international economic policy — the other part being international monetary adjustment. The maintenance of harmony between the monetary system and the industrial organisation of a country is the minimum requirement for ensuring economic development. Likewise the maintenance of smooth relations between the international monetary system and international industrial organisation is the minimum requirement for ensuring the healthy development of the world economy.

It is desirable that the present international monetary system should be reformed by the adoption of an SDR standard (that is one based on special drawing rights) and fixed-but-adjustable exchange rates. Businessmen as well as economists are beginning to see the necessity for this reform and it is likely that it will be realised. On the other hand, for the smooth operation of the international industrial (trading) system, safeguards against the disruption of international industrial activities and the establishment of an Industrial Conversion Fund need to be introduced in every advanced country.

The international adjustment of national industries must be carried out with a full understanding of the changes taking place in the conditions of competition between the advanced and developing countries. Various factors must be considered such as differences in factor proportions, the transfer of technology and capital, the literacy of the peoples involved and so on.

In an industry where developing countries enjoy roughly the same conditions as advanced countries with respect to raw materials and technology, such as the cotton industry, there is a limit to which industrialised countries can bridge the wage gap with high productivity. Imported cotton goods accounted for 2.1 per cent of America's domestic consumption in 1955, but this percentage increased to 6 per cent in 1960. This brought about the Long-term Agreement on Cotton Textiles. When the United States was making an issue over competition with low-cost countries in cotton textiles, the European Community was making an issue over competition with low-cost countries in textile goods, chinaware, sewing machines and metal toys. The Gremze Report in West Germany,[7] issued in 1960, suggested that low-cost countries might be countered by adopting a mixed tariff system — imposing specific duties on low-price commodities. But the plan was not realised.

The problem of 'low-price commodities', which accompanies the industrialisation of developing countries, raises a new issue for the GATT. At its fifteenth annual meeting in the autumn of 1959, Douglas Dillon, as Under-Secretary of State in the United States Administration, proposed that effective counter-measures against low-price commodities should be considered. In response to this proposal a definition of 'market disruption' was agreed. It was decided that the following conditions combine to constitute market disruption:

(a) When there is a sharp and substantive increase, or the possibility thereof, in the import of a specific product from a specific source;

(b) When a product is offered on the market of an importing country at a price considerably lower than a comparable domestic product;

(c) When the price differential between the imported and domestic product is not attributable to government interference with price formation, or price decisions, nor to a dumping practice; and

(d) When serious injury, or the danger thereof, is caused to producers in an importing country.

Defining market disruption thus, the GATT decided to establish a Committee on Market Disruption. This Committee was supposed to implement plans for action which were not detrimental to the rights and obligations of GATT signatories, by securing a multilateral approach without causing injury to third countries and incurring trade restrictions. It was plain, however, that the move would result in discriminatory restrictions against developing countries and against Japan. It was the cotton industry in developed countries that was then feeling most strongly the need for such action. Accordingly the Long-term Agreement on Cotton Textiles materialised in 1962. The Committee on Market Disruption ended without actually carrying out any actions.

Thus 'safeguards' have tended to fulfill the role for advanced countries of counteracting the industrialisation of developing countries as well as acting as a safety valve against trade liberalisation. Since this tendency is harmful to the sound development of the world economy, the Japanese Government considers that safeguard actions, and accompanying measures, should be reviewed internationally.

Safeguards should be accorded the key position in international economic policy. By this it is not meant that safeguard measures should resolve all problems, but if they are developed to play an important role, governments might adopt forward-looking attitudes towards tariff reductions, the abolition of quantitative restrictions and other non-tariff distortions. In other words, when trade liberalisation makes real headway, a new safeguard mechanism should display its real worth. A new safeguard mechanism, providing for emergency protection, must achieve the following policy goals:

(a) Industrial rationalisation and conversion in advanced countries;

(b) The promotion of economic growth in developing countries by pushing their industrialisation; and, by these means,

(c) Effective distribution of resources in the world economy as a whole.

Of these policy goals, no advanced country would be negative toward the promotion of industrial rationalisation and conversion in advanced countries, but it can hardly be said that progress is being made in reality. Is this due to limited government funds or to strong protectionist tendencies in the business community generally?

As for the industrialisation of developing countries, the United Nations Conference on Trade and Development (UNCTAD) pushed to the fore the 'preferential treatment' approach influenced by Raoul Prebisch's fondness for Latin-type political splendour. But any cool observation of generalised preferences in practice makes it clear that a more effective approach would be for advanced countries to promote industrial conversion and to refrain from import restrictions. One effective method might be for UNCTAD to press advanced countries to set aside a certain portion of their GNP, perhaps 0.1 per cent, to finance industrial conversion. Developing countries should not oppose this because 1 per cent of the GNP is meant to be used for aid to themselves. Neither would advanced countries be able to oppose it because the funds would be used on their own industrial conversion. The existence of such funds would in itself build up a mood for promoting adaptation to changing economic conditions.

Lastly, on the effective distribution of resources in the world economy, the problem is that agricultural difficulties can hardly be streamlined by counter-measures. Effective distribution of resources in secondary industries has been pushed considerably, and this should exert beneficiary effects on tertiary and primary industries.

The framework of a reformed safeguard mechanism for achieving these policy goals should cover ten major points.

1. *Condition for Invocation*: The condition for invoking emergency protection should be market disruption. What is important, as a practical problem, is whether it is possible to judge objectively the four factors that were mentioned earlier to constitute market disruption. Regarding a sharp and substantive increase in imports, for instance, an increase in imports may well be relative when compared with an importing country's domestic consumption, even if it is not an absolute increase over the previous year, according to the interpretation given to the relevant Article 19 of the GATT. This leaves considerable latitude for judgment. The second factor (the price differential) and the third factor (the non-existence of the government interference and of dumping) can be determined relatively objectively. But there is a limit to the objective determination of 'serious injury or the danger thereof'. It is possible to use various related indices such as the rate of imports against domestic consumption, the shift in the level of employment in the industry conerned, the direction of domestic production, price fluctuations and decrease in earnings. But it is impossible to formulate objective general criteria applicable to all industries. All the same, I will take market disruption as the condition for invocation. The question of subjectivity, in making a judgement, should be left to be covered by other factors.

2. *Procedure of Invocation*: As for the forms of invocation, various formulae can be considered, such as (a) unilateral invocation in an emergency, but with consultations afterwards, (b) invocation after prior notice and consultation, and (c) invocation only with prior notice, but without consultations (or when consultations have fallen through). Such situations are provided for in Article 19 of the GATT (which provides for emergency protection). As a rule, though, invocation should be with prior notice and consultations. In short, the governments should conduct constant and careful studies on the industries in their own countries and competitive countries elsewhere, lest they should be taken by surprise when there is an increase in imports (which is then interpreted as a 'sharp increase').

3. *Instruments of Emergency Protection*: The instrument for implementing 'safeguard' protection should be an increase in tariff duty or the imposition of a quantitative restriction. This concurs with the provisions of Article 19. In cases where countries invoked Article 19, a little less than 40 per cent imposed quotas and a little more than 60 per cent raised tariffs (or withdrew concessions).

4. *Security of Access*: A safeguard-invoking country must guarantee access to its market for the country against which it has taken action. What is in question here is how to determine the period over which emergency protection should be applied and how to determine the rate at which it should be removed. A period of one year to six months before the date when the problem is alleged to have appeared should be reviewed to determine the quantity of imports that should be guaranteed access during the period of emergency protection. With regard to the rate at which imports should be allowed to increase under emergency protection, the rate of increase in the three years up to the period when 'market disruption' is taken to have begun should be the absolute minimum, but when this latter rate is a minus figure the minimum should be a levelling-off. When the instrument of emergency protection is a tariff, access should be guaranteed by a tariff quota, which should then be increased at an agreed rate — as would be the case where the instrument was a straight quantitative restriction.

5. *Retaliatory Measures*: One of the difficulties with safeguard measures is the handling of retaliatory measures by the exporting countries affected by the imposition of emergency protection. The Treaty of Rome (Article 226), the Stockholm Convention (Article 20) and the Benelux Economic Alliance Treaty (Article 14) do not provide as a matter of course against retaliatory measures. The

retaliatory measures provided for by the Long Term Agreement on Cotton Textiles are indirect. Article 7 of this Agreement provides that a country affected by import restrictions can request the other party to conduct consultations. In case consultations have broken down, the question can be referred to the Cotton Goods Committee. The opinion of this committee is to be taken into consideration by a group of signatory countries when the problem is referred to this group through the procedures stipulated in Article 23 of the GATT. Inasmuch as Article 23 provides for remedy in the case of nullification or violation of GATT-granted interests, it will be possible to take retaliatory measures at this stage, depending on the situation.

On the other hand, bilateral safeguard provisions invariably provide for retaliatory measures. For instance, the safeguard provisions between Japan and France, and between Japan and the Benelux countries, permit an importing country to impose quantitative import restrictions under certain conditions and provide that an exporting country can impose quantitative import restrictions, as a counter-measure, within a limit not exceeding the effect of the measures taken by the importing country. The safeguard between Japan and Britain does not specify the measures to be taken by an importing country, unlike the cases of Japan-France and Japan-Benelux. It does not specify either the counter-measures to be taken by an exporting country.

Such are the provisions for counter-measures under existing safeguard arrangements. What should counter-measures be like under a new safeguard system? To prevent the abuse of safeguards, counter-measures should be recognised. Counter-measures, though, are difficult to recognise even in the case of industrial adjustment compelled by developing countries' growth. Consequently, as an intermediate plan between these two, an importing country could offer compensation unilaterally, without recognising an exporting country's counter-measures. Such compensation should be subject to scrutiny and recommendation by a safeguards committee.

6. *Term of Emergency Protection*: Varied terms for the use of emergency protection measures should be set up for individual industries and such safeguard periods determined by whether or not rationalisation and conversion of the industry concerned is difficult. As concrete standards, the labour/capital equipment ratio, the most appropriate technical scale, the degree of popularisation of technology and the novelty of the industry concerned should be consulted. In determining the protectionist period concentrated preparatory work by a panel of first-rate economists and administrators becomes necessary. As the term of emergency protection is the

period of continuous application — for instance, one year for cotton spinning, 1.5 years for chemical fibre spinning, two years for chemical fertilizer and three to four years for iron and steel — determination, though necessary, is difficult.

7. *Extension*: When an emergency protection measure is used, extension after the expiration of the term mentioned above should not be permitted. The protective measure for the same industry cannot be re-applied at least before the same length of time as the protectionist period for that industry (or 1.5 times thereof) has lapsed following its expiration. Any violation of this should be subject to a penalty to be determined separately.

8. *Preparation of Adjustment Measures*: A country that has invoked, a safeguards committee should examine the rationalisation and a conversion plan, for the industry concerned and release them within three months after invocation of 'escape-clause' action. Funds for rationalisation and conversion plans should be disbursed out of an industrial conversion fund and these plans should be revised periodically.

9. *Safeguards Committee*: When emergency protection is being invoked, a safeguard committee should examine the rationalisation and conversion plans mentioned above and make recommendations where necessary. The committee should meet periodically, analyse the development of various conditions surrounding the safeguard invoked and make recommendations as and when necessary.

10. *Non-discriminatory Application*: Discriminatory application should not be permitted in order to prevent misuse. [8]

This then, is the outline for new emergency protection measures. As can be seen, the safeguard measures themselves have built-in provisions not only for protection but also for promoting industrial conversion. In other words, they are aimed at promoting the adjustment of protected industries in developing countries into new export industries; at allowing advanced countries a minimum time required to convert or rationalise their affected industries; and at pushing forward the rational and progressive development of the industrial structure of the world economy.

This, coupled with the above-mentioned industrial conversion fund (based on an UNCTAD resolution), should control the spread of protectionist tendencies in the world in the future and enable forward-looking ideas to gain strength in five to ten years to come. Under present political conditions, it appears that import restrictions are more favourably accepted than industrial adjustment, but import restrictions must be avoided by all means.

The United States Congress did not approve the Nixon Administration's 1970 Trade Bill which called for a more flexible interpretation of the Trade Expansion Act's provision for adjustment aid. It appears, though, that the United States Tariff Commission is still behind the 1970 bill. In 1969 the Commission determined four cases of alleged damages, although no determinations of this kind had been made until that year. The number of cases rose to nine in 1970. The determinations mostly related to workers' eligibility for damages, but it seems that adjustment assistance in the United States is just getting under way. The Congressional appropriations for industrial adjustment increased from $26m in fiscal year 1971 to $110m in fiscal year 1972.

On the other hand, Chapter 5 of the Report of the OECD High-Level Group on Trade and Related Problems maintains that, in view of the significance of the safeguards clause in the recommendations relating to the adjustment problem, common rules and procedures should be established. [9] The report and the proposals made in this paper are basically in line. It is hoped that the proposals will be used as reference material for putting the report into effect.

### NOTES AND REFERENCES

1. An earlier version of this paper was given at the Fifth Pacific Trade and Development Conference sponsored by the Japan Economic Research Centre, Tokyo, 9-13 January 1973.

2. For an account of Japanese non-tariff barriers, see Kiyoshi Kojima, 'Non-tariff Barriers to Imports into Japan', in Harry G. Johnson and Stanley D. Metzger (eds.), *International Negotiations on Non-tariff Barriers* (London: Allen & Unwin, for the Trade Policy Research Centre and the Brookings Institution, 1974).

3. D. Gale Johnson, *World Agriculture in Disarray* (London: Macmillan, for the Trade Policy Research Centre, 1973).

4. Japanese agricultural-support policies are discussed in Michael Tracy, *Japanese Agriculture at the Crossroads*, Agricultural Trade Paper No. 2 (London: Trade Policy Research Centre, 1972).

5. For a fuller account of agricultural adjustment in Japan, see Kenzo Hemmi, 'Structural Adjustment of Japanese Agriculture', in Kiyoshi Kojima (ed.), *Pacific Trade and Development*, Vol. 6 (Tokyo: Japan Economic Research Centre, 1973).

6. This report was prepared by the Foreign Economic Policy Subcommittee of the Senate Committee on Foreign Relations, United States Congress.

7. *Tariffs as Trade Policy Measures against Low-cost Countries*, Gremze Report (Bonn: Ministry of Economic Affairs, 1960).

8. For a full discussion of the ramifications of emergency protection, see Chapter 15 below by Jan Tumlir.

9. High-level Group on Trade and Related Problems, *Policy Perspectives for International Trade and Economic Relations*, Rey Report (Paris: OECD Secretariat, 1972).

# CHAPTER 6

## Need for a New System for World Trade and Payments

### HARALD MALMGREN

When President Nixon sent his Trade Reform Act of 1973 to the Congress of the United States in April 1973 he emphasised that sweeping changes in international relations since the close of World War II had not been matched by sufficient change in the international trade and monetary systems. On the one hand, the world has become far more interdependent economically; on the other, national and international rules, practices and institutions have not been adopted. The rigidity of the international system and national practices has been exerting an increasing stress on economic resource and financial flows and political frictions have been generated among, as well as within, nations as a consequence of distortions of trade and investment. Economic friction in turn threatens to pull nations apart at a time when efforts should be directed towards consolidating relationships and negotiating solutions to mutual political and economic difficulties. This is true both for relåtions among the major trading powers and for relations between these countries and the developing nations of the world.[1]

President Nixon therefore repeated in his trade message to Congress, which accompanied the bill, what he had said in his address to the Governors of the International Monetary Fund (IMF) in September 1972, that 'our common goal should be to set in place an economic structure that will help and not hinder the world's historic movement toward peace'.

It is in this broad politico-economic context that the United States Administration has been trying to outline what needs to be done. What Americans are talking about is an economic system which provides flexibility to adapt to new circumstances with sufficient adjustments to permit long-range business commitments. The economic adjustments made necessary by the energy crisis that followed the Arab-Israeli conflict of 1973 are strong reasons to develop such a system.

### Two Major Objectives of New Order

In other words there are at least two major objectives that should be sought. First, there is a need to restore order and a high degree of collective discipline in world economic relations. Second, there is a need to provide sufficient flexibility in the international mechanisms of adjustment so that domestic economies may be managed effectively, and yet be allowed to adapt on a continuing basis to the evolution of the global economy.

In seeking these objectives account has to be taken of the very high degree of economic interdependence which exists among nations today. Actions or policies in one country often do have a direct effect on economic circumstances within other countries. Often these effects are transmitted quickly, and sometimes disruptively, to particular industrial sectors, regions of the country or types of workers. Even the form of policy instruments chosen by one government can effect the interests of others.

In trying to find a better system for managing economic interdependence, while insuring a large degree of freedom for national governments to deal with their own social and economic problems, one cannot help recalling the centuries-old philosophical debate about how to insure freedom to the individual citizen in a context of orderly communal relations. The same kinds of issues arise in the management of international economic affairs and one is drawn to the conclusion that real freedom for a national government can only be found, in this highly interdependent world, within a framework of international rules, procedures and tacit or explicit understandings.

The system, however, cannot easily be dealt with on a piecemeal basis. If there is reform, for example, of the monetary system without any change in present trading rules and practices, the purposes of monetary adjustment will tend to be thwarted by trade measures used to insulate major economic sectors from pressures for economic adjustment. Put another way, with a well-functioning monetary system, there could well be increased incentive for governments to intervene to protect sensitive regions or sectors, adding to the present array of trade barriers and distortions around the world. Conversely, reform of the trading system itself would leave governments free to offset the effects by financial, exchange-rate and other devices, without regard to the agreed objectives of a reformed trading system. Moreover, while certain monetary experts may forget, it should be remembered that the monetary system does not exist for its own sake; it is there to serve trade and to serve investors.

Taking these considerations into account, it becomes clear that progress in the reform of both systems is essential. This does not mean there must be day-to-day parallelism. It does mean though that the logic of creating a better system compels governments to move on both fronts through whatever channels seem most widely acceptable and useful. This much is agreed among the experts of many governments.

But the problem has to be complicated a little further. Suppose that a better monetary system and a better set of trading rules are created. Would it then be possible to sit back and be satisfied that the system is adequately balanced and sufficiently subject to collective discipline? The answer must be 'no'.

## 'Third Area' of Concern in New Order

There is a 'third area' that must also be addressed. This is the question of investment flows and the influences upon them. Government policies which affect the location and nature of investment could otherwise be utilised to offset the intended effects of the trade and monetary mechanisms which are created. It is not solely a matter of tax incentives and subsidies to locate in this or that part of a country or the world. It is also a matter of incentives to technology, incentives which affect methods of production and, too, incentives to promote home production over imports. Industrial and regional policies are relevant to these considerations.

The question of multinational enterprises can be put in this context, because they are simply one institutional manifestation of international investment flows and business relations. To the extent that these institutions appear to cause problems for particular governments, the problems ought to be seen as difficulties primarily arising out of differences among national policies. Of course there are differences in the home-country and home-office influences as well. But there is a tendency to emphasise problems relating to certain companies from one country, the United States, and a surprising degree of blindness to the fact that today nearly half the larger multinational enterprises in the world are European, Canadian or Japanese in origin. If there is a problem for governments it is an international one. If something were to be done, it should be done within a collective approach. And such an approach should be in the wider context of all policies and policy differences which influence the form, volume and direction of international investment.

The 'third area' being discussed here is more complex than the traditional monetary and trade issues, because it involves parts of national policies of which in the past discussion has never been considered possible internationally. Yet national policies to promote certain industrial sectors, or certain high-technology advances, can and will affect the interests of other nations.

Wherever governments intervene in this way, their intentions are to alter the long-term outlook for their economies. Basic national policy objectives are usually involved. Thus governments are faced with the problem of reconciling on an international basis these long-term adjustment objectives, and the methods of managing them, among the various countries of the world.

When some of the key non-tariff barrier questions are dealt with in the coming international trade negotiations, it will become apparent that issues of internal policy and legislation are affected. One has only to mention consumer and safety standards and government procurement policies to make the point clear. But other measures, such as the control of export-subsidy practices, quickly shade into what appears to be internal policy. Suppose government assistance is used to induce construction of a new plant in a certain high unemployment region for the sole or main purpose of selling its output in export markets. Is this just a question of internal assistance or is it also a question of an export subsidy, *de facto*? Some of these 'grey area' issues will be covered partially by the trade negotiations through the writing of new trade rules. But it would also seem logical to carry over consideration of some of these issues, to put them in the broader context of the 'third area' referred to earlier.

Thus to be coherent in any approach to improving the world economic system, governments must conceive of a wide-ranging review of all the elements of the international system of trade and payments. This must include (a) particular attention to monetary reform; (b) liberalisation and reform of the trading system; and (c) negotiation of some new rules or consultative procedures to help improve the management of international relations in the 'third area'.

In this comprehensive context the question of international economic adjustment to changing circumstances needs to be re-examined. Economic adjustment takes place as a set of forces working simultaneously on several different levels and within different time-frames. Exchange-rate adjustment or adjustments in interest rates and capital movements have a duration of their own. Adjustments in specific industrial sectors, or in agriculture, are made in a different time-frame in relation to a number of micro-economic circumstances, and in relation to other forces which are at work in social policies and in national politics.

To boil all of this down to its basic essentials, ways need to be found for insuring *orderly* adjustment at all levels, in order to create a 'stability of expectations' which is conducive both to prolonged and expanding world economic activity and to economic expansion and readjustment to changing social requirements within countries. It is this kind of stability in the world economic system that is important. It is not a question of how often exchange rates change. Rather it is a question of whether the adjustments which inevitably must take place do so in an orderly way, without crises, and in a manner sufficiently predictable or controllable that business plans can be laid and investments made on a long-term basis.

## Basic Principles of Equitable and Symmetrical Adjustment

To create such a 'stability of expectations' thought has to be given to better mechanisms for adjustment at what economists call the micro-economic level, as well as on the macro-economic, or monetary level. Some basic principles of equitable adjustment should be developed. For example, if governments are forced by internal circumstances to intervene to provide assistance to industries for transitional periods in times of difficulty to facilitate economic adjustment, then the costs of such programmes and adjustments required by them should in the first instance be borne by the nation introducing them. Workers in the same industry in another country should not have to bear much of this burden — nor should my farmers pay for your farmers subsidy programmes. That is a principle of fairness that few can quarrel with, but it is frequently breached in international economic relations.

Where a government considers that some transitional devices are needed to protect a programme of adjustment for a domestic industry, and these devices do in fact affect other countries, then the measures should be taken within an internationally agreed framework. There ought to be some rules and procedures to govern these exceptional cases and ensure that they are truly transitional and in accord with long-term objectives of flexible and fair world adjustment to evolving economic circumstances.

It is within this framework that consideration should be given to the recommendations of various experts — including especially the report of the high-level group of eminent experts chaired by Jean Rey [2] — that there should be developed a new multilateral safeguard mechanism to control or manage the national actions taken by governments to safeguard particular industries from import pressure. Where such import-restricting actions are taken, they should be subject to international surveillance, and there should be some means of ensuring that restrictive actions are temporary and are used to provide transitional relief during a period of structural readjustment of the industry concerned. If orderly change is to be sought there should be as much emphasis on the 'change' element of this expression as on the 'orderly' element.

Thus there is a logical interdependence between the various levels and techniques of international economic adjustment, and this constitutes a strong reason for ensuring consistency between the trading and monetary systems.

Looking ahead, it seems that whatever the outcome of the forthcoming economic negotiations, it is evident that the new system which is devised should be able to resolve problems *before they become crises*. What should be negotiated is a system which not only allows but encourages orderly transition whenever an economic adjustment becomes necessary.

Consistent with this approach to reform of the world economic order, is the need for a monetary framework which provides a variety of adjustment options to governments, but which also creates incentives and penalties which induce the taking of action when it is needed. On the American side, certain monetary reform ideas have been floated (if a pun be allowed), including the notion of 'reserve indicators'. Contrary to popular impressions, the reserve indicators proposed by the United States do not establish a specific obligation on a nation to change its exchange rate. Instead the idea is that there should be a general obligation to take action when the indicators suggest. The form of the action could be any one of a number of alternative adjustment measures that could effectively remove a payments surplus or deficit. A country experiencing a large increase in its reserves, for instance, could discharge its obligations by increasing the demand for imports, either through suspension of import restrictions or an increase of domestic income. It is also assumed that countries would normally take appropriate adjustment actions long before changes in reserves established an adjustment obligation.

The object is to secure a symmetry of incentives and obligations among both surplus and deficit countries. This search for symmetry is not a new problem. The debates between Harry Dexter White and John Maynard Keynes in the early 1940s, in planning the post-war economic order, often stuck on precisely the same question: How to create a suitable penalty on surplus countries to encourage them to take action? One of the proposals discussed at that time was to wipe the slate clean of a certain proportion of a surplus position if the surplus country did not take action and the surplus continued for a specified period. The problem with this quickly became apparent. The debtor countries would have, under this procedure, a strong incentive to run persistent deficits if they knew part of their debts would be voided after some specified period.

In spite of the difficulties some devices are needed to put escalating pressure on surplus countries. It is not enough to focus attention on the debtor-country positions. For example, 'convertibility' has become a central issue in the reform debate, because it is assumed to put pressure on deficit countries to moderate policies which allow deficits to develop on a large scale. But convertibility does not provide any incentive or penalty on the surplus side. Until that assymmetry is altered, convertibility is an unrealistic proposition, especially given the starting point of the existence of substantial dollar balances held around the world.

There has to be a *numeraire*, or a common unit of account of reserves, which would constitute the basis for clearing deficit or surplus positions. This *numeraire*, if it is to be used as a reserve unit, would have to be relatively attractive, as compared with holding national currencies. It should in other words be worth holding, as compared with interest-earning assets, and it should involve an element of protection against devaluations or revaluations of specific national currencies. This commonly accepted reserve unit cannot, however, solve all problems; on the contrary, the more reliable and attractive it becomes, the less countries will be willing to hold currencies. Its back could easily be broken by the weight it might have to bear. Thus discussion is still brought back to the fundamental question of how to force balance-of-payments adjustment and how to insure that the adjustments which take place are orderly.

Probably this can only be achieved through negotiation of some new undertakings which would be subject to multilateral surveillance and required consultation procedures among nations. And this in a sense is why the United States has sought to establish the concept of an objective measurement of performance as a basis for international consultation. To sum up, we need rules which are equitable and fairly symmetrical in their applicability, a means of measuring performance of nations in adherence to the rules, and incentives to encourage nations to channel their actions in directions consistent with the international undertakings.

**Need for New Institutional Framework**

On the trade side, one objective of negotiations will be liberalisation of trade in the traditional sense of reducing barriers to trade. Another objective, however, should be the pursuit of a new international framework for channelling economic decisions of national governments as they apply to specific sectors or industries, moderating conflicts where they occur and stabilising, and making more equitable, the basic conditions of competition for trade and investment activities. The second objective of reforming the rules and procedures of the trading system is an essential element of any coherent and universal framework for the conduct of economic relations among nations.

Such a reform need not require rewriting from top to bottom the General Agreement on Tariffs and Trade (GATT), the instrument which has governed international trade over the last quarter of a century. If, for example, agreements are negotiated to eliminate or harmonise practices in the non-tariff barrier area, such agreements will take the form of new commitments. Some government practices and procedures will be ruled out, while others will be formally allowed. The commitments will vary from one problem area to another. There may even be variation among the number of countries committing themselves in each problem area. The sum totality of the new set of commitments, taken together with the expected reduction in tariffs and in the present degree of discrimination where it exists, will constitute *de facto* reform of the international trading system.

There will probably have to be more, as for example in the rules governing trade measures used for balance-of-payments adjustment. This question had been raised by the United States in the Committee of Twenty, established by the IMF to prepare proposals for the reform of the international monetary system, although traditionally the question has been thought to be a GATT matter (covered specifically by the GATT's Article 12). Such broader questions can, in the course of negotiations, be taken up in light of developments in monetary reform and in trade reform more generally.

It must also be candidly recognised that the GATT rules and procedures are neither comprehensive, nor consistent, nor adhered to in all cases. Agriculture is in an ambiguous situation. Free trade areas are less and less controlled by the GATT rules because the rules are more and more liberally interpreted by key governments.

Again, as in the monetary area, there is a need for better consultative and surveillance procedures and to develop some means for adjudication or measurement of performance which is meaningful. This will not be easy. Governments value highly their sovereign rights to intervene to protect the interests of specific sectors of their countries' economies. From a political point of view, the sensitivities on this score are clearly greater in trade questions than in the monetary area.

The problem is further compounded by the political alignments and special-interest coalitions which tend to form among the various countries. More and more the developing countries take a common stance. The countries associated with the European Community are obviously heavily influenced by Community thinking and they are increasingly unlikely to challenge formal positions adopted by the Brussels Eurocracy. The possibilities for timely and definite decisions within the GATT framework have therefore diminished. To remedy this, new life has to be given to GATT procedures, and especially to GATT panels which might rule on certain types of issues. If panels were used more often, and if they actually decided issues, and if their findings were binding in terms of definition of rights and obligations, significant progress would have been made over the present situation. But there are too many 'ifs' here.

Other countries not formally in either the GATT or the IMF may wish over the next few years to become more fully integrated into the systems. This includes certain developing countries. Also it may be safely assumed that the non-market economies of Eastern Europe, the Soviet Union and China will in due course have reason to become more directly involved within a systematic framework. What the relations of these latter economies to the Western system should be is not an easy question to answer. Nonetheless, before long there will be a need for some new rules and procedures which provide a framework for conduct of commercial activity between centrally-planned and market-oriented countries. Given the potential size of trade between them and the strength of some of their economies, the past *ad hoc* arrangements built around bilateral agreements will not be sufficient. Indeed, present arrangements extended much further will lead to aggressive inter-governmental competition outside the normal patterns and forms of commercial affairs. Reform of the world economic order cannot really be consistent and complete without recognition of this fact of life.

Taking all of these problems together, one may seriously ask whether the solution does not lie in creation of a new, comprehensive institution which covers all international economic issues. To achieve creation of such an entirely new institution would be very difficult. To negotiate its rules from scratch would be nearly impossible, given the number of countries and the diversity of their interests. To expect it to deal in one common context with general issues of monetary co-operation, including co-operation in financial market management, and specific issues of trade in such matters as oranges and orange juice would be wishful thinking.

It may, on the other hand, be possible to come up with a general inter-governmental declaration of economic principles which could provide a broad, high-level political framework within which the respective institutions, and the experts within them, would work. Something by way of an overall political framework was first publicly suggested by President Pompidou in December 1972 (in a *New York Times* interview). It was suggested by Henry Kissinger, when he was President Nixon's assistant for national security, in his Year of Europe speech, but the subsequent effort fell short.

It may also be necessary to maintain a variety of institutions: some of which are built around rights and obligations and the enforcement of them, and some of which are built around co-operation in day-to-day management of the international interaction of national economic policies. This variety is what exists at present and it may turn out to be the best means of managing the world economic system, provided reforms are made, as was decided in Rome in January 1974 by the Committee of Twenty with respect to future IMF operations. There is the additional advantage of multiplicity that different kinds of problems involve different kinds of countries. The developed countries, for instance, have particular problems with each other which are, at least for the present, often matters of lower priority to developing countries, and the Organisation for Economic Co-operation and Development (OECD) can cope with these.

In pursuing a better world economic order, care shall have to be taken to avoid a resurgence of mercantilist thinking, and especially to avoid bilateral mercantilism in policies between the larger trading nations. Bilateral balancing cannot be achieved in trade without damage to world trade. It would leave no opportunity for one country's bilateral surplus with another country to be used to finance its bilateral deficit with a third country. This goes against everything the world has learned about economies. It would be like devising policies on the basis that the world is flat. But speaking of flat worlds, we should also guard against the theory that regional bloc formation is the answer to many of the problems which lie before us. From an economic point of view, Japan has done better than the rest of the world both internationally and at home, without being a member of any regional economic grouping. Conversely, competitive groupings or power blocs could well freeze the workings of present institutions and rules, while leaving an array of 'orphaned' nations unable or unwilling to join one or another bloc. It may even be found before long that a situation has been created where developing nations are forced to choose the spheres of influence to which they tie themselves and those they align against, in a hard choice which can only prejudice their economic opportunities and narrow the maneouverability of their national political freedom.

The objective for the major trading powers must be far more sophisticated than objectives of negotiations have been in the past. In the long-term, the establishment of a more flexible, equitable and worldwide economic system which encourages prompt adjustments between diverging economies is what must be sought. In this broad perspective of what the objectives ought to be, the question of who gets and gives what fades into a secondary position in assessing the value of negotiations. We can be confident that negotiations to liberalise and reform the world economic system can be beneficial to all countries, and to all of the world economy, provided we all make an effort, and rise above the pressures of narrow interests, whether they be within nations, or whether they spring from regional preoccupations.

## Commitment of Major Powers to Reform

During the discussion leading up to and at Washington's Smithsonian Institution, in December 1971, there was agreement to start the process of monetary reform in 1972, and to start wide-ranging trade negotiations in 1973. In early 1972, the United States and the European Community, on the one hand, and the United States and Japan, on the other hand, signed undertakings which committed these economic giants to initiate global trade negotiations in 1973 on the basis of 'mutual advantage, mutual commitment, and overall reciprocity'. These undertakings have subsequently been supported by many other countries. They were the basis on which world trade talks were begun in September 1973.

This may be worth repeating here because there is some hesitancy in some countries, and especially in business quarters, about whether the time is right, and whether the national objectives can be fitted together peaceably, particularly in view of the formidable problems posed by rising energy costs. If the world economy is to move forward efficiently, equitably and with a reasonable degree of stability, such doubts have to be controlled. The political commitments to move forward have in any case been by the major countries involved. The momentum is there for thorough-going reforms. Hesitation can only make worse the problems of international economic management that have to be faced in the mid-1970s.

Governments have been reviewing their attitudes in the light of the major shifts in world supply-and-demand relationships in certain commodities — not only in oil. Agricultural-importing countries have been asking how they can be assured of supplies if they provide greater access to agricultural-exporting countries. Oil-exporting countries in the Third World have been finding that because of world shortages they cannot import certain products required for industrial and agricultural development. Industrial countries have been feeling the strains of having to impose some export controls and provide some stimulation to imports in the face of domestic inflation and, at the same time, seek larger export markets in order to pay for larger import bills for oil and raw materials. It is because of these issues, and of the uncertainties in them, that the need for talks on world trade has been growing.

Rather than reopen the question of timing and the feasibility of a grand effort, endeavours should now be concentrated on involving as many countries as possible. In the United States the Trade Reform Act of 1973 sets up authorities to negotiate with all countries. Specific proposals have even been made for dealing with the Soviet Union and other state-trading or non-market nations. Further special benefits for developing countries have also been proposed through implementation of a generalised scheme of tariff preferences. These provisions are aimed at opening more widely American relations with the whole world, and not just its relations with the largest trading powers. To do what is needed, and especially to create an enduring result, will require a great effort of common will and what Henry Kissinger has called 'joint statesmanship'.

The free-enterprise world is now embarked on an era of negotiation, to create a better world economic order. The present system is the point of departure and it has much in it which should be retained. Nonetheless, past preoccupations with narrowly defined reciprocity and with maintaining rigidly the walls which protect great sectors of economies from change, can no longer be considered unchallengeable. The obligations of suppliers, alongside the obligations of importers, will have to be taken much more seriously than hitherto. Everything requires a new look — and without a comprehensive approach, the weaknesses and rigidities of the present situation can be expected to encourage more and more crises. There is little to commend the management of world affairs by muddling through from crisis to crisis, and from conflict to conflict among civilised countries. The opportunity is at hand to develop a new order, and to escape from this pattern which has plagued broader international relationships in recent years. But only an act of 'joint statesmanship' can accomplish what really needs to be done.

### NOTES AND REFERENCES

1. This chapter was first published as 'Reforming the World Trade and Monetary System: Need for a New Institutional Framework', *The Round Table*, London, July 1973.

2. High-level Group on Trade and Related Problems, *Policy Perspectives for International Trade and Economic Relations*, Rey Report (Paris: OECD Secretariat, 1972).

*Part III*

OUTSIDE ISSUES OF SIGNIFICANCE

# CHAPTER 7

# Economic Implications of the Energy Crisis

FRANK S. McFADZEAN

The essence of the energy crisis is that if consumers continue to use energy at the present rate, by the mid-1980s the demand for energy in the world as a whole will have doubled; and the industrial countries, which cannot now produce at home all the energy they need, will by then have become even more dependent on oil from outside — particularly on oil from the Middle East and Africa. For it is in those areas that are to be found the only readily expandable sources of energy on the scale required.

## WORLD COMMERCIAL ENERGY DEMAND 1945-1972 [1]
### (excl. USSR, China & E. Europe)

m.b/d o.e.

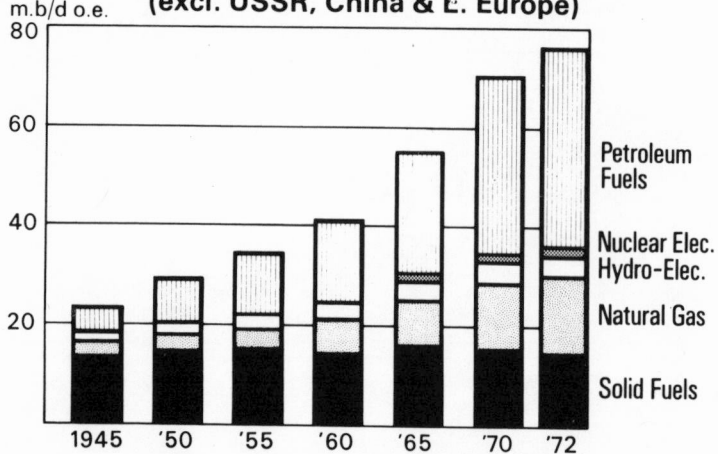

In many respects this is a familiar situation — at least for the Europeans and Japanese. But one key factor had changed well before 1973. It was clear that the countries of Western Europe, the United States and Japan would not be able to go on drawing from the Middle East as much oil as they needed. For it was evident that the oil-producers were able and apparently prepared to restrict the rate at which oil production could grow. There was thus a prospective problem of supply. Oil-importing countries were confronted then with a growing cost for oil which, after the Middle East war of 1973,

## WORLD COMMERCIAL ENERGY DEMAND 1972-1985 [1]
### (excl. USSR, China & E. Europe)

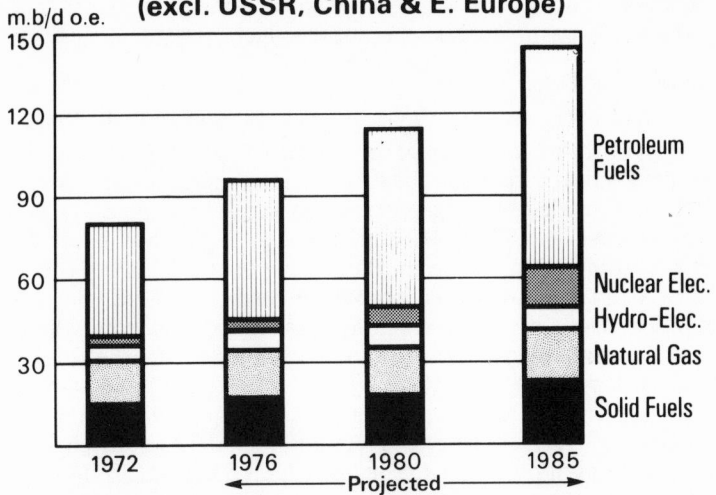

## WORLD ENERGY GROWTH RATES 1945-1985 [1]
### (excl. USSR, China & E. Europe)

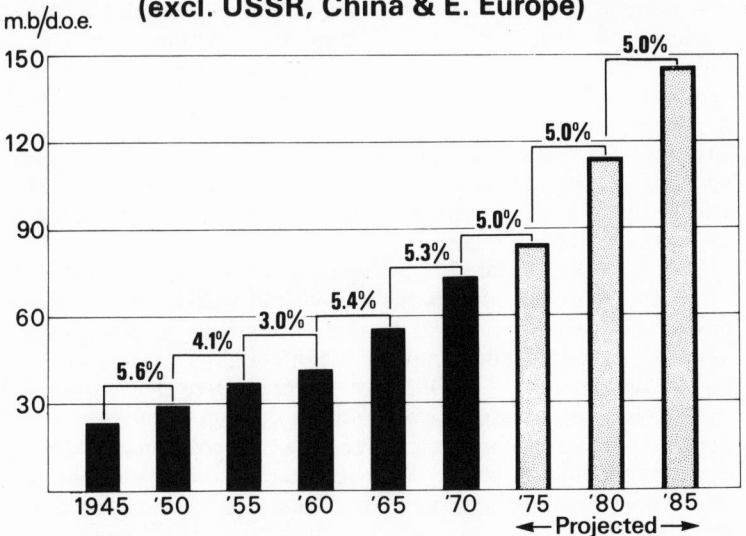

increased sharply with the quadrupling of crude oil prices at the start of 1974, having profound implications for national economies, balances of payments and the world monetary system.

**Supply and Price**

In spite of the fact that demand was rising substantially there was a buyer's market in crude oil in the 1950s and 1960s. Most oil-producing countries in the eastern hemisphere looked to Western Europe as their only large-volume market. The United States was then almost self-sufficient; and although Japan was becoming a larger customer for oil, the market there was still relatively small. In those years the established producing companies were joined by a number of smaller companies, the so-called independents, who were seeking new low-cost oil for shipping to American markets. In their search they were successful, first in the Middle East and then in Africa. But after the supply had begun to develop, the outlet was suddenly closed. United States legislation in 1959 effectively barred access to foreign oil and the independents were left to fight for a share of the markets in Western Europe. This gave Western Europe abundant supplies of oil at low prices, which in turn had the effect of encouraging the substitution of oil for coal, thereby helping to raise oil's share of total energy to its present dominant position.

These developments led to the formation of OPEC — the Organisation of Petroleum Exporting Countries. At a time of surplus production, 'posted' prices were reduced by the companies; and some governments of producing countries became concerned about a fall in royalty payments and revenues from taxation. One of OPEC's first acts was to try to secure the re-establishment of posted prices at the levels of 1958. This was an attempt to ensure that, even if the companies might feel obliged to offer discounts to their customers, the impact would not make itself felt on the revenues accruing to the producing countries. In its early years, OPEC's efforts did manage to achieve some increases in revenues, although they were not spectacular.

But as the 1960s wore on the demand for oil began to catch up with supply. By the end of the decade the market in Japan had grown considerably and the United States was becoming a net importer of oil. Crude supplies became tighter. Prices became higher. By 1970 and 1971, OPEC governments were able to conclude the Teheran and related agreements with the oil companies, which agreed to substantial increases in the levels of government 'take' in the oil-producing countries. These agreements were followed in 1972 by a supplementary agreement in Geneva to provide for future increases in payment to host governments as a consequence of changes in currency rates against the dollar. The days of cheap oil were over and prices were being pushed to a new plateau by the financial demands of the producer countries.

With the growing dependence on oil it was plain the price of Middle East oil could rise at least to the level of alternatives produced elsewhere. The technical costs of alternative sources of conventional oil are certain to be higher than those of current fields, because new discoveries are, in general, smaller in size and are often located in remote or difficult places. The costs of new forms of energy — or of developing alternatives, such as coal, tar-sands and oil shale — are also appreciably higher. Even at the higher cost it is doubtful whether by the mid-1980s there could be sufficient energy from alternative sources to provide genuinely effective constraints on the price of oil.

## Supply and Demand

If oil's share in the total world supply of energy remains at around 70 per cent in the mid-1980s, the doubling of energy needs will call for the production of oil and natural gas equivalent to around 100 million barrels a day — or, to put it another way, 5,000 million tons a year. The great expansion of demand will be in Western Europe, Japan and the United States. Japan is the country in which oil demand is growing most rapidly. Western Europe is the largest buyer of crude oil; it consumes nearly one-third of all the oil used outside the Soviet Union, Eastern Europe and China. The United States consumes more oil than the whole of Western Europe. Together these regions require twice as much as the rest of the world. By the mid-1980s their combined demand will have risen from 34 million to around 75 million barrels a day.

With very few exceptions — notably the Soviet Union — no country's oil needs and oil supplies balance. The more highly developed an economy, the more energy it consumes; and, if a country's economy is growing rapidly, so is its consumption of oil. The critical fact for the industrial countries is that most of their growing oil requirements will have to be *imported* — in spite of the very substantial effort so far made to develop indigenous production.

Western Europe, in the mid-1970s, produces only 15 per cent of its combined needs of oil and natural gas and the realisation of the high hopes for energy developments in the North Sea will not materially change its dependence on outside sources. Japan produces virtually no oil. In the advanced industrial countries of the West only the United States has substantial oil and gas production of its own: but it has been emerging as a big importer. As its needs for imports increase the United States will therefore compete

# GROWTH OF OIL IMPORTS (mb/d) [1]

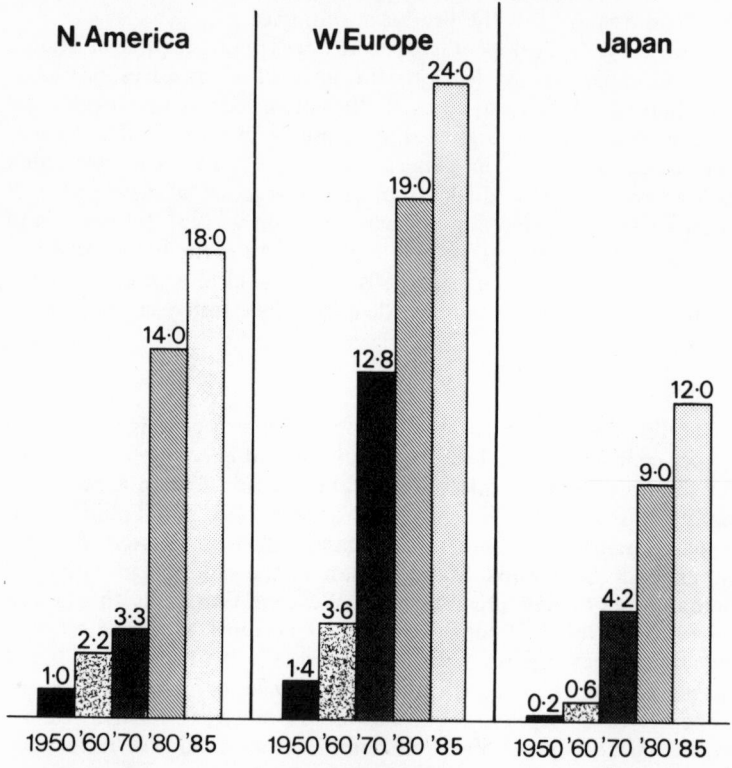

on the international market with Western Europe and Japan for the available oil.

On the supply side little alleviation from energy derived from alternative sources is expected before the mid-1980s. Many new sources are now being developed, of which nuclear power is probably the best-known example. The belief that nuclear power would become readily available in the 1970s was one of the key assumptions in forming energy policy in the United States during the 1960s, when large numbers of nuclear generating units were ordered. But neither the technology nor the economics of such plants have advanced to the expected levels. Natural gas — made unrealistically cheap by American Government controls — was drawn upon during the 1960s to meet two-thirds of the incremental demand for energy; but the drain was so heavy and the incentive to search for new gas so slight that gas supplies in the United States 'peaked out' in 1971. Moreover, because the advent of nuclear power was thought to be imminent, there was less incentive to develop the abundant sources of coal in America. Until the coming of nuclear power in abundance, three quarters of the energy needs of the United States will therefore still have to be met by oil and gas — of which an increasing proportion will have to be imported. In Japan and in Western Europe the prospects for early nuclear power are no better.

## OIL REQUIRED FROM MIDDLE EAST [1]

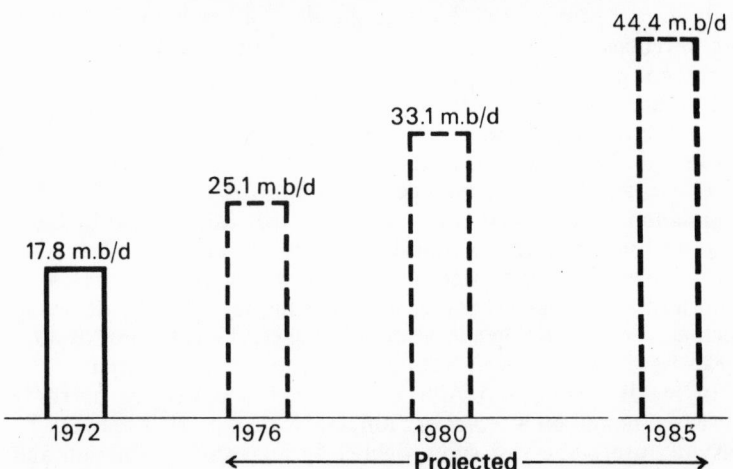

Since the countries of the Middle East supply two-thirds of international oil and hold correspondingly large proven reserves, it is to this zone that the industrial countries will inevitably look to fulfil their import needs over the next decade. For the foreseeable future there is simply no alternative source. Middle East production has been expanding substantially and — in purely physical terms — could indeed be expanded further. Technically, Iran and Abu Dhabi could raise their production by half, and Iraq could double and Saudi Arabia treble their production. This would more or less meet the new demand. It would also mean that Western Europe, the United States and Japan would have become dependent on the Middle East and Africa for 90 per cent of their petroleum imports.

The 1974 increase in oil prices thus provided a strong incentive for oil-importing countries to economise on their use of oil and to accelerate the development of alternative non-oil sources of energy. Fears for the world economy subsequently caused the oil exporters to wonder if they had not increased prices too much.

**Incentive to Produce**

As we have seen, the question has been asked whether those countries will continue to be willing to produce oil simply because the industrial countries need it: whether, in fact, there will be sufficient incentive for them to do so. The incentives are all-important. The countries that are among the world's largest producers are each placed in a different situation, which implies that they might each pursue different oil production policies. Some countries of the Middle East and North Africa have comparatively small oil reserves and large accumulated earnings from oil. Others with larger reserves must face the problem of being able to absorb big revenues. Others, again, have adequate reserves as well as economies thirsty for development funds.

Iran and Iraq are countries with comparatively large populations and a framework within which their economies can grow. They can make full use of the funds brought in by oil. There is therefore an incentive for them to produce more. In Kuwait and Libya the population is small and reserves are limited. Accordingly in these countries it is natural to consider whether to increase production now or to wait, in the expectation of a steady national income over a long-term future; and if prices are rising the incentive for deferring increases in production can be even stronger. Thus before the 1973 Arab-Israeli war, Kuwait put limits on the growth of output.

In Saudi Arabia and Abu Dhabi the economies are narrowly based, although oil reserves are ample. In such cases it may not be easy to absorb the vast sums yielded by increased production and higher government 'take'; and countries concerned might prefer not to draw to the fullest extent on their resources of oil. Saudi Arabia's annual income from oil by the mid-1980s could be high enough to give it an income-per-person from oil revenues twice that of the present income per capita of the United Kingdom; but although she has an area ten times as large as the United Kingdom her total population is smaller than that of London. Not surprisingly, the Saudi Minister for Oil Affairs has recently questioned whether Saudi Arabia would be able to spend its surplus income inside the country. If it could not, it would have to reconsider, comparing the value of investing the surplus revenues abroad — whether in bank deposits, bonds, industrial equities, or direct investment in industries — with the appreciation in value of oil left in the ground instead.

The restriction by Middle East countries of the production of oil — coupled with the increasing needs of the industrial countries and those of the rest of the world — could bring about a *supply* shortage. The shut-in production capacity in the United States provided a welcome reserve during the adjustment of supply sources and routes after the Suez crises. But there is no such cushion left today. Most spare production potential outside the Middle East has been committed to meet the growth in demand and is no longer available as a reserve. This means that a supply gap could open — reinforcing the effects of the rising *demand* for oil imports by the industrial countries.

**Paying for the Oil**     Even before 1974 the revenues accruing to OPEC governments had already risen to unprecedented levels. Their earnings from royalties and income-tax payments in 1972 amounted to 12 billion dollars. It was clear that the industrial countries would have to face up to the problem of the drain on earnings of foreign exchange; indeed, this drain had already begun. The International Monetary Fund had announced that in 1972 the combined trade deficit of the industrial countries with the oil-exporting countries had risen to 9 billion dollars. The level was more than 40 per cent higher than it was two years before. In those two years Japan's deficit with the oil-producers rose by one-third. In the cases of France and the Netherlands it doubled; and in that of the United States it quadrupled. With the substantial increase in oil prices since then a far higher proportion of foreign exchange earnings in Western Europe will have to be spent on oil imports.

Countries are thus seeking to lessen their dependence on imported oil by improving the base of home sources of energy. As already intimated, attention is being paid to developing nuclear energy at a faster pace, maximising the production of coal and encouraging the production of indigenous sources of oil and natural gas. At the same time, active measures are being considered to prevent waste and to increase the efficient use of existing sources of energy by means of economies in transport, by improving insulation and discouraging the expanded use of electricity and by adopting a thoroughly realistic approach to the whole question of conservation of the environment — particularly in regard to measures which result in using up more energy. But these measures only make an impact over the long term.

**Oil Reserves and Investment Needs**

Meanwhile, problems of another kind are raised by the fact that the deficits of the industrial countries provide surpluses for the oil-producing countries. If they choose to invest most of their incremental revenues in the sound development of their national economies in their long-term interest the import of goods from the industrial countries will rise substantially. But large revenue surpluses are likely to remain, even with expanded economic development. The producing countries might choose to reinvest their oil revenues in the consuming countries. This would help alleviate the problem of foreign payments, but it would also bring about a substantial transfer of capital ownership. If the governments of industrial countries want the benefit of an inflow on capital account to offset their trading deficits they will have to agree to a substantial interest being acquired in their major industries by some of the oil-producing countries.

The existence and growth of large surplus funds in the hands of the oil-producing countries also has serious implications for the international monetary system. Acute problems would arise if these surpluses were to be moved about in the short-term money markets of the United States or Europe. There has been ample evidence of the disrupting effect of flows of hot money on the world's financial system over the early 1970s. To add substantially to this pool would lead to greater instability in times of monetary uncertainty, even though floating exchange rates might help to mitigate its influence.

But so long as the oil-producing countries are prepared to go on holding their accumulating surpluses in the currencies of the consumer countries outside the short-term money markets, no immediate monetary problem is presented either by the increase in their receipts that has already taken place, or by their longer-term accumulation of reserve funds. Their experience with both sterling and the dollar, however, has demonstrated to the oil-producing countries the difficulties inherent in using as a reserve the currency of the debtor countries; and fears about the weakness of the dollar or sterling could be put at a risk much of the hard-won progress made over the last twenty-five years in strengthening the framework of multilateral trade and the free convertibility of currencies. Under foreign exchange controls bilateralism would thrive.

The question of oil supply consequently involves future financial relationships between governments. One of the most important questions to decide is whether the present international monetary arrangements will prove adequate in accommodating change. The search for a solution to international monetary problems seems at present to focus on economic and financial relationships between North America, Western Europe and Japan. If governments in consultation succeed in devising a system of measures to solve these problems or mitigate their effects, will it be one that can also contain the new problems I have outlined — the consequences of the increase in financial power that will be building up in the Middle

East in the decade ahead? The declared long-term objective of consultations which have so far been preoccupied with short-term financial crises is a new multilateral financial system. A decision will have to be reached by governments on what part the oil-producing countries will play in it.

Thus the industrial countries are faced by a series of energy problems: first, the problem of the supply of oil — that is, the physical problem of being able to get what they need and, second, problems affecting their national economies — of being able to afford the oil they need and being able to pay for it out of earnings abroad from selling their goods and services. This gives rise to the third problem — how to accommodate in the existing financial system the consequences of paying for it. The changed composition of the international balance of payments emphasises the need for something to be done. Everyone stands to lose if there is a reduction in the incentives to the governments of oil-exporting countries to allow oil to be produced at the rate it is needed in the industrial regions.

It must not be forgotten that the role of the governments of oil-producing countries is no longer confined to granting concessions and licences. Recent negotiations between oil companies and member governments of OPEC covered many matters beyond the question of the future levels of producer government revenue from royalty payments and taxation. They transformed relationships between the companies and their hosts. Foremost among the changes is a provision for governments to acquire immediately a 25 per cent ownership in the operations of the companies producing within their borders. Further provisions are made for the government share to increase by 1982 to a level of 51 per cent. Participation in the production operations of the companies has been achieved by negotiation of the new general agreement to any of the OPEC countries which now account for 90 per cent of the world's exported oil.

### Time for Initiative

Some felt in the early 1970s that it was premature to worry about the energy problems of the late 1970s. The evidence did not support this feeling. The oil-producing countries had already achieved big increases in revenue. Further annual increases were involved in the obligations contracted under the Teheran and related agreements, which provide that host government levels of 'take' should go on rising steadily until 1975. The potential volume of goods that oil-producing countries would be buying from the industrial countries was increasing correspondingly. It was already clear that when all this demand had been satisfied, a large and growing surplus of money would remain. Some producing countries — Saudi Arabia, for example — were already concerned about opportunities for investment in the industrial countries. In Kuwait a Minister had broached the possibility of an Arab reserve currency in which payments for oil would be made, with the aim of avoiding a mark-down on the nominal value of reserve funds if there should be any devaluation of sterling or the dollar. Already two big producers — Libya and Venezuela — insisted on being paid in their own currency by the oil companies; and it was laid down that the currency must be purchased by the companies through the central bank of each country, at rates determined at the time by the government receiving the payment.

In this difficult situation, what can be done? To keep up the flow of oil and to encourage the producing countries to go on developing their resources, there are two areas which might profitably be examined for action by the governments of industrial countries. The first concerns the broadening of their economic relations with the oil-producing countries, leading to an increase in the flow of the technical, management and financial skills which are vital for economic development. The second involves the discovery of ways and means of bringing the monetary strength of the OPEC countries to play a constructive part in the world monetary system. A start could surely be made by associating the main countries concerned more strongly with existing intergovernmental machinery for dealing with international monetary and trade problems. At present the oil-producing countries play only a minor role.

## NOTE

1. The projections in the charts indicate the prognosis prior to 16 October 1973. While the actual figures will be lower it has not been possible at the time of writing to suggest by how much.

# CHAPTER 8

## Operations of Multinational Enterprises in Perspective

### DAVID ROBERTSON

Concern is being expressed in many quarters about the activities of multinational enterprises. The situation is put under the public spotlight by such events as the scandal in Chile concerning the International Telephone and Telegraph Corporation or the confrontation in Britain between the Monopolies Commission and the Roche pharmaceutical firm. But any politician in Western Europe, or in a developing country, can become newsworthy if he calls for regulations or restrictions on the operations of these international giants on the world stage, even though such statements usually reflect little more than naked chauvinism, show very little regard for the economic self-interest of host countries and, it might go without saying, indicate a lack of acquaintance with the studies that have been carried out on the complex issues involved. Multinational enterprises are coming increasingly under attack in the home countries of parent firms for 'exporting jobs' or aggravating balance-of-payments difficulties through investments abroad.

Contradictory complaints in the countries of parent companies, on the one hand, and in those of subsidiaries, on the other, are symptomatic of a failure at the level of public discussion to appreciate the implications of the rapid integration and growing interdependence of the world economy as a result of the liberalisation of international trade and capital movements in the 1950s and 1960s, and of the technological advances that have been made in transport and communications, not to mention other factors. The phenomenon of multinational enterprises represents the organisation of business operations beyond national borders. In short, multinational enterprises are agents for the international transfer of capital, technology and managerial expertise. There is much to understand about their consequences and ramifications for the national economies in which they operate and for the management of the international economic system. Some analytical studies have been conducted on, for instance, the effects of inward and outward investment on investing and host economies and, too, on the balance-of-payments effects.[1] But there are still many aspects of the multinational-enterprise issue that have not been investigated or are only now being explored.

To introduce regulations without understanding the phenomenon that they are intended to control could be harmful and counter-productive. Proposals to regulate or supervise the operations of multinational enterprises therefore need to be carefully considered. It is with some apprehension that one views discussions on the subject that are getting under way in the European Community, in the Organisation for Economic Co-operation and Development (OECD), in several United Nations agencies, as well as in national governments.

An important source of concern for governments is the sheer size of some international businesses and the economic power they appear to possess. International direct investment flows, almost all of which are undertaken by multinational enterprises, have grown twice as fast as international trade since the late 1950s. The total stock of foreign direct investment at the end of 1972 was around $180,000m. Output from foreign-controlled subsidiaries now substantially exceeds the value of world merchandise trade, which was $372,000m in 1972. American-based enterprises account for more than half of total foreign direct investment and 110 of the 200 largest multinational enterprises. American-based groups of companies, therefore, have played a large part in the rapid development of multinational enterprises. A recent report  estimated that overseas production by American-controlled manufacturing companies alone was $65,000m in 1970. Around 80 per cent of this output was sold in the country of manufacture. Even so, it is estimated that American-based multi-national enterprises accounted for 23 per cent of world trade; and trade controlled by these enterprises was growing faster than total international trade in the 1960s.

It is not just size though that gives rise to government difficulties with multinational enterprises. The real source of conflict is that a multinational enterprise operates over a wider domain than does the nation-state. Decisions can be taken, therefore, that enable multi-national enterprises to evade the jurisdictions of one country, by shifting operations or assets to the ambit of another state. It is in this sense that conflicts arise between the perceived interests of a national economy and the perceived interests of multinational enterprises, which are directed at minimising, or avoiding, the effects of double or divergent regulations between national jurisdictions.

Most conflicts consequently arise from differences in regulations in separate jurisdictions. Since these divergences can provide profit-able opportunities for multinational enterprises to exploit, increased regulations will not eliminate the source of conflicts with, and for that matter between, national authorities unless an effort is made to remove the differences. This requires inter-governmental co-operation. It has accordingly been suggested that some kind of code of practice should be drawn-up, with which multinational enterprises and national authorities should be induced to comply, what has been referred to as 'a GATT for investment'.[3]

Before discussing the sense of, and examining the prospects for, an international agreement on the activities of multinational enterprises, it is necessary to identify the major sources of friction between governments and international business. Because much uncertainty surrounds the economic consequences of some multinational-enterprise decisions, the following discussion covers only the main points in connection with specific problems.

### Extra-territoriality Issues

Extra-territorialities, an ugly and almost unpronouncable word, has been devised as a generic term covering a number of practices by which national governments seek to extend the implementation of their own laws or policies into the jurisdictions of other governments through pressures exerted on the management of multinational enterprises. There are two main problems that have received most attention: anti-trust legislation and restrictions based on 'denial policies' (such as 'trade with the enemy' legislation). But the term covers other attempts to extend policies.

These problems were emphasised as major infringements of national sovereignty by a report prepared for the Canadian-American Committee in 1969.[4] That Committee stated 'that extra-territoriality is the area in which the most serious Canadian-American conflicts of interest have arisen and are most likely to arise and in which solutions most need to be found'. It went on to 'urge that the United States Government review comprehensively its practices relating to the extra-territorial applications of its laws and regulations to the foreign activities of American companies'. Many of the problems seem to have diminished with the passing of time. The Gray Report in 1972[5] on foreign investment in Canada gave them little attention.

In the field of anti-trust legislation, directed against monopoly situations, there are many opportunities for clashes between sovereign powers. Anti-trust legislation is usually confined to domestic industries because of problems of enforcement in overseas jurisdictions. Hence, the major conflicts have involved foreign subsidiaries operating in the jurisdiction to which the legislation applies, when the government from the country of the parent has disputed legal judgments. Historical disputes include the 1951 case in the United States involving Du Pont and Imperial Chemical

Industries (ICI) and the fining by the European Community's Commission in 1969 of ten European chemical firms, including ICI, which was technically outside the jurisdiction of the Commission at the time, for allegedly fixing prices of analine dyestuffs. But there have been attempts by the United States authorities to extend anti-trust enforcement beyond the national jurisdictions by pressing parent companies to adopt certain policies in their overseas subsidiaries. The Canadian authorities have been particularly concerned at the intrusion of American anti-trust policy into the operation of American-owned subsidiaries on their soil.

Over recent years, as reflected in the Gray Report, these policy differences have become less significant. Many difficulties have been worked out through compromises following consultations between governments. Often these have been bilateral, as between Canada and the United States. Consultations have also taken place multilaterally in bodies, such as the OECD, which have also helped to reconcile differences. In addition, there has been a gradual emergence of common attitudes towards anti-trust and competition policy in the advanced industrial countries, helped by the gradual development of a competition policy in the European Community.

When a multinational enterprise is the instrument for imposing the foreign policy of one country on another a direct conflict is almost bound to ensue. Because of the dominance of multinational enterprises controlled from the United States, that country's Trade with Enemy Act is a frequently cited source of this problem. Under this legislation not only an American corporation but its foreign subsidiaries are restricted from exporting to specified Communist countries — China, North Korea, North Vietnam, Cuba — even though the subsidiary's host government may have a more relaxed commercial policy towards these countries. Disputes have arisen over the installation of engines produced by an American-controlled subsidiary in trucks being exported from France to China. [6] There have been several instances with respect to Canadian exports to China and Cuba. Similar problems also arise over products considered to be of strategic value (for example, nuclear power devices, arms and ammunition) where licences would be required to export from the United States and where a subsidiary in Canada, say, might be used as a staging post for re-export further afield. Here exports from the United States to Canada for 'domestic consumption' are acceptable, but restraints are imposed for re-exports. This case obviously has less direct effect on the Canadian economy than the former one which applied to goods of 100 per cent Canadian origin.[7]

The Canadian authorities have been considerably exercised over the years about the intrusion of American foreign policies and various agreements and consultative procedures have evolved to help resolve difficulties. With the easing of relations between East and West, with the United States eagerly seeking commercial links with Russia and China, and with their satellites, the frictions over denial policies seem likely to be a dead-letter in a few years. They have in fact dropped out of the main debate. With the Western industrial countries falling over themselves to grant cheap trade credits, and to supply surplus agricultural produce at prices that consumers and businessmen in their own countries would appreciate (not to mention developing countries), problems of trading with the enemy are being swept away — at least for the present.

While extra-territorialities seem to be of diminishing interest, 'another kind of problem which may be even more important in the future', as the Gray Report states, 'is that governments are likely to begin struggling over the multinational enterprise to have it locate activity in their jurisdiction'. [8] This reverses the earlier problem because here the policies of host countries are influencing the decisions of multinational enterprises against the economic interests of their home country. This issue will be examined under the heading of domestic policy incentives.

A somewhat more remote, but potentially controversial, problem could develop out of the attitude towards multinational enterprises that was adopted in 1973 by the Labour Party in the United Kingdom. [9] If a future Labour Government was to nationalise any British-based multinational enterprises, such as Imperial Chemical Industries or British Leyland, what consequences would it have for the overseas operations of these companies? How would the Australian Government, for example, react towards an ICI subsidiary operating on its soil under the control of a parent enterprise which might be deemed an agent of the British Government? There are emotional reactions in Britain against decisions affecting British conditions being made in Detroit or New York. How much more emotional could be reactions in Australia against decisions affecting Australian conditions being made in Whitehall! This could provide a new twist to the problems of extra-territorial interference. Retaliatory action by host governments could severely curtail the overseas operations of any multinational enterprise that is nationalised.

## Balance-of-Payments Controls

The political interpretations of balance-of-payments disequilibria are often quite enigmatical: surplus countries insist that deficits should be corrected, yet for their part they are unwilling to entertain a reduction in their surpluses. It should come as no surprise, therefore, that conflicts of interest arise in connection with policies directed at correcting an external imbalance which act upon the operations of multinational enterprises. The effects of overseas investment on the balance of payments are uncertain and there is wide disagreement about the efficiency of policies aimed at regulating these flows. Capital controls are, all the same, frequently employed by countries with balance-of-payments difficulties.

Broadly there are three types of balance-of-payments policies which affect the operations of multinational enterprises and which have resulted in clashes of interests between governments. They all illustrate the development of economic interdependence between nations. But because multinational enterprises are at the centre of some of the controversies arising out of some of these policies the issues take on a new dimension.

Trade policy measures, to promote exports or to restrict imports, plainly affect the trade of other countries. When multinational enterprises follow policies of international production planning and administered markets they can lead to re-allocations within the enterprise which affect the economies of several countries. [10] In extreme cases these decisions may lead to plant closures or the diversion of investment towards, or away, from the country imposing the new measures. So far international disputes over new trade policy measures have been handled, within the framework of the General Agreement on Tariffs and Trade (GATT) and elsewhere, in the context of traditional trade patterns. Yet multinational enterprises with centralised control are obviously able to take account of such changes, and make new dispositions accordingly, possibly with ramifications in several countries.

A second type of policy measure that has been employed for balance-of-payments purposes concerns remittances of profits, interest and similar payments. Controls on these have been applied by both host and investing countries. Developing countries, but also others, anxious to preserve foreign exchange earnings, have introduced restrictions or even prohibitions on remittances of various kinds from subsidiaries to foreign parent companies. On the other hand, developed countries with substantial overseas investment have on occasion requested domestic firms to increase their remittances from overseas operations. The United States and Britain have both taken steps to encourage such remittances for balance-of-payments reasons. Thus there can be a direct conflict between these separate national policies. It represents a confrontation between governments. But multinational enterprises get caught in the middle and may become the target of both sides.

There is a third set of measures which concerns the regulation of capital flows overseas. This has been attempted directly through capital controls of various kinds, and indirectly through taxes on overseas earnings to reduce after-tax returns on overseas investment, the purpose being to make such ventures relatively less attractive compared with domestic investment. Strong reactions followed the introduction by the United States in 1965 of 'voluntary guidelines' to restrain capital exports and to encourage profit repatriation. Other countries viewed the move as an unacceptable interference in the affairs of subsidiaries operating in their countries, since it influenced decisions on the location of investments by American-based businesses. Australia reacted by restricting access to the local capital markets for American subsidiaries. And the Canadian Government issued guiding principles for 'good corporate behaviour'.

The main objection to all types of balance-of-payments controls is that they require multinational enterprises to take decisions in the light of changes in national policies which affect the disposition of resources between parent companies and their subsidiaries as well as between different subsidiaries. In the process the interest of some countries will be furthered at the expense of others. Multinational enterprises are the intermediaries by which some of these balance-of-payments measures take effect; and their managements are likely to face the first criticisms from an offended government. In a number of cases where real damage could be shown to have resulted, consultations between governments have, in fact, resolved some difficulties.[11] And in cases where wider objections were raised, such as against the mandatory capital controls which the United States introduced in 1968, specific machinery was established to consider areas where multinational enterprises were faced with conflicting regulations.[12] Even so, it is clear that friction has been caused by balance-of-payments controls; and it is not difficult to foresee similar problems arising when governments are faced with severe external imbalances. A major problem is that if satisfactory compromises cannot be reached where problems do arise, the second country may take retaliatory actions (for example in respect of the repatriation of profits), which could aggravate the situation and make the positions of multinational enterprises very awkward.

## Capital Flows and International Monetary Policy

One of the urgent questions in the debate over international monetary reform concerns the role of multinational enterprises in the foreign currency and short-term capital markets. It has become widely accepted that domestic monetary policy is a rather blunt instrument. For multinational enterprises and international financial institutions can transfer funds between markets very easily. Credit restrictions and increases in interest rates are guaranteed to attract foreign capital inflows. On the other hand, by easing credit restrictions and reducing interest rates, national authorities are likely to encourage a capital outflow, as corporate treasurers seek higher short-term interest rates. Financial flows of this kind are aggravated further by uncertainties over exchange rates. In an attempt to insulate domestic money markets from such movements of short-term capital many new types of restriction have been introduced by central banks with varying degrees of success.

The interdependence of national monetary policies is undeniable. It is generally acknowledged that the reform of the international monetary system must involve extensive inter-governmental co-operation over domestic monetary policies. Short-term funds at the disposal of multinational enterprises are thought to represent a major de-stabilising factor in world money markets. (The report of the United States Tariff Commission [13] estimated that short-term assets of American-controlled multinational enterprises were worth $268,000m in September 1972, a figure which has been much disputed because the method by which it was compiled allowed for double counting.) It should be self-evident though that multi-national enterprises recognise their own interest in maintaining a stable world monetary system. For if they switched, for speculative reasons, just a fraction of their short-term assets in response to prospective movement in exchange rates or interest rates they would swamp the money markets. Hence, although changes in national monetary policies can cause economic repercussions in other countries through the mediation of multinational enterprises, and the businesses themselves may weaken the effectiveness of national monetary policies, the conflicts involved are under permanent discussion in the various international organisations responsible for the reform of the world monetary system.

The fact that these issues are being discussed as part of a much larger problem, and that the conflicts between national policies are therefore recognised, puts the financial implications of multi-national-enterprise operations in a different category from the others that have been discussed.

**Taxation Issues**

Taxation probably poses the most complicated of the inter-governmental problems that are associated with multinational enter-prises. Much manpower and skill are employed in the field by governments and companies and some of the issues are receiving attention in the European Community in the context of fiscal and monetary harmonisation.

Differences in tax regulations between countries are plainly vital considerations when corporate planners in multinational enterprises are framing business and financial strategies. Both the structure of rates of taxation on corporate income and the definition of taxable income are important factors. Financial officers have to try to minimise the total tax liability on a given corporate income by balancing the distribution of earnings according to both criteria. But when income is transferred from one tax jurisdiction to another — for example, if dividends are remitted from a subsidiary to the parent company in another country — questions of double taxation must also be taken into account. A complex structure of bilateral agreements has evolved between governments to protect citizens from paying tax twice over on income earned abroad. These agreements do not usually give total relief from host-country taxation, but they at least limit such taxation and provide, too, for credits against taxes in the country to which an income remittance is made. Unfortunately, there is little uniformity among these agreements, especially as regards the definition of taxable income. A draft convention[14] for double taxation on income and capital, drawn up by the OECD in 1963, which aimed to standardise terminology, has been largely ignored. And in any case compliance with it would require the re-negotiation of hundreds of existing agreements.

Methods for reducing a company's tax liability involve going into the intricacies of income tax assessments. But the geographical deployment of a multinational enterprise's operations also affect the tax position. The 'tax-haven' offers one way of maximising after-tax income on a world-wide basis (although it need not directly maximise returns to the parent company). A tax-haven company is established where a host country does not levy tax on dividends paid to non-residents or where tax is paid at a concessionary rate. Thus a holding company outside the tax-jurisdiction of countries where subsidiaries are operating can collect dividends from them and by definition earnings remitted to the tax-haven do not pay taxes. In this way the earnings of a subsidiary in one country (which could be Holland) would be preserved without paying tax in the holding company in a tax-haven (say Luxembourg[15]). Subsequently the funds could be transferred to yet another country to expand the activities of the multinational enterprise. Self-financed expansion can therefore be increased under this strategy.

As the number of multinational enterprises has increased, and as the intricacies of national tax policies have increased with various kinds of tax concession being introduced to attract foreign investment, especially by developing countries, so the number of tax-havens have been proliferating. In recent years many small and unknown, and almost unpopulated, islands have become 'homes' for the name-plates of international holding companies. Governments guard jealously the 'gaps' in their tax systems which attract foreign investments and financial operations and they are strongly inclined to oppose attempts to close them. In any case, unless tax rates and tax structures are harmonised new havens, in ever more remote parts of the world, seem likely to take the place of any that are closed and the initiative is likely to come, as before, from experts in financial centres like London, Zurich and New York.

There are thus several major issues in the field of taxation that are a source of conflict between national governments and multinational enterprises and also, between different governments. But apart from general differences there is much scope for conflict over details of tax rates and methods of assessment. Differences in tax systems influence the business decisions of multinational enterprises which determine real resource allocations between alternative uses in different tax jurisdictions. It is not even a question of direct comparisons between tax systems in two countries — say the investing country and host one. The intrusion of tax-havens on the part of third countries can affect a decision regarding the use of income earned in one of the first two countries — that is, real resource allocation — as well as the amount of tax revenue collected in one or both countries. Moreover, any transfer of funds between the two principal countries and the tax-haven involves foreign exchange costs. All this only relates to the problem of resource allocation within established tax systems. The prospect of changes in taxation which result in further resource reallocations over time has to be considered.

Once assessments have been made there is then the problem of collection. If a taxpayer is outside the jurisdiction of the levying authorities, in no legal way can he be forced to pay, given that governments do not generally collect taxes on behalf of other governments. It has been suggested that one way around this would be international co-operation and exchange of information. Presumably the difficulty here would be to induce governments in tax-havens to co-operate!

Awareness by governments that the investment decisions of multinational enterprises can be influenced by tax structures has caused them to use tax concessions as a policy measure to attract foreign investments. In advanced countries such devices as depreciation allowances are used as an element in regional development policies. Many developing countries, too, have sought to attract foreign capital by means of 'tax holidays' of fixed duration or by means of concessionary tax rates sometimes limited to earnings retained in the local subsidiary. As competition for investment has increased, the incentives to use holding companies in tax-havens have increased, almost correspondingly. A drawback to these schemes is that earnings are often repatriated to the investing country, which then taxes the parent according to its system of corporate taxation, or they are transferred to a holding company in the tax-haven. In either case, the country, usually a developing one, is foregoing tax revenue which in effect is transferred to the government or resident of a developed country. Effectively, therefore, high rates of corporate taxation in investing countries on repatriated earnings are encouraging the host countries to raise their taxes on remitted earnings to the same level, in order to maximise tax revenues. Perversely this must reduce the attractiveness of overseas investment. Conflicts over taxation policies need not be even directly apparent!

## Domestic Economic Policies

A survey carried out by the United States Tariff Commission showed that an important determinant of overseas investment by American-based multinational enterprises has been the tax-reliefs and other incentives provided by foreign governments. Indeed, in 1967 it was estimated that half of American direct investment in Western Europe, valued at $1,700m, benefited in some way or other from regional development subsidies, although the proportion has fallen since. These benefits included tax exemptions or postponements, special allowances, export subsidies, subsidised credits or rents and investment or development grant. Not satisfied with tax transfers and subsidies, many governments have also offered guaranteed markets through public procurement policies.

In effect the governments of Western Europe have been competing against each other to attract investment by multinational enterprises. Regional development policies in West European countries have become progressively more generous towards potential investors in their efforts to redistribute capital investment, and hence employment, within their countries. But the most 'foot-loose' investors have come from outside a particular country because they have no commitment to a particular area in the country through an established plant or other interest. In consequence, foreign investors have been able to make the most of regional incentives offered by governments and, too, to take account of such measures in initial investment decisions. Moreover, as governments have realised the growth potential provided not only by the inflow of capital, but also by the package of management, technology and marketing skills accompanying it, they have gone to even greater lengths to attract multinational enterprises, rather than see them go to neighbouring countries. United States multinationals have thus acquired valuable real resources from these transfer payments.

Competition between governments to attract investments from multinational enterprises has reached such a height that some reaction was bound to occur. It has taken two forms which both illustrate the conflicts between national policies.

First, the Commission of the European Community has been attempting to harmonise regional development policies. Incentives offered by some member countries have become so large that any positive return to the national economy can only be expected in the long-run — in ten years or more. Yet for a national government to opt out of the competition for foreign investment could result in irreparable losses, as France found in 1968 when Gaullist anti-Americanism reached such levels that, following the imposition of restrictions against United States investment in certain sectors, net investment in the country by American firms fell to zero. The measures were promptly removed! A common policy in the European Community on regional development is under discussion, and in 1971 the member states agreed to limit regional incentives to 20 per cent of capital cost in capital areas; no agreement was reached on peripheral areas.

The second aspect of the conflict of interests has been presented in the United States. Disturbed about the rapid decline of certain American industries and the large transfer of production to low-cost overseas plants, the labour unions — with wide political support — have been lobbying to restrict overseas investments by American corporations. Since, it is argued, American capital is attracted to other countries by tax concessions, and other government incentives (and this includes retained earnings as well as capital flows from the United States), the only way the United States can retaliate is by introducing compensatory taxes on earnings by overseas subsidiaries.[16] The Nixon Administration has imposed — under the Trade Reform Act of 1973 — a tax on overseas earnings, regardless of whether they are retained in the foreign subsidiary or not, which would be equivalent in value to the 'concessions' provided by the foreign government. Compared with the proposal in the so-called Burke-Hartke bill, which would impose the full tax rate on all earnings retained abroad in countries where tax relief or grants are given, the Nixon measure is moderate. In both cases overseas operations would become distinctly less attractice to American firms, because overseas earnings would be taxed twice — once locally and once in the United States.

Again the clash of interests between governments is the cause of the difficulties and multinational enterprises are likely to be squeezed in the middle. From an American point of view, policies of tax relief and other incentives in foreign countries appear to be causing a distortion in real resource allocations by United States multinational enterprises, which are against the interests of the domestic economy. The real costs and benefits to the United States economy will be difficult to determine. In the absence of clear understanding, however, and under pressure at home, the United States Administration has taken retaliatory action. It is action that contravenes existing double taxation agreements and so it is likely to provoke a major international response. Moreover, it is by no means certain what the overall effects of such a policy might be for the United States or the world economy, regardless of secondary effects from retaliation.

In summary, then, the use of government policies to attract foreign investment necessarily results in direct conflicts between governments. Multinational businesses can exploit these policies to their own benefit — for example, by moving plant out of a country at the end of a tax-holiday period and seeking a similar arrangement from another government. But real resource allocations can be distorted by these policies and competing policies might even result in net economic losses to countries. On the other hand, retaliatory action by a government that considers its national interest has been harmed by such policies could result in further losses, and it could cause severe problems for multinational enterprises with operations dispersed so as to optimise earnings under the previous system of policies.

**Make Haste Slowly**

Five problem areas affecting relations between national governments and multinational enterprises have been identified and described briefly. Examination of all five suggests that although multinational enterprises are targets for criticism from governments and various groups, in both host and investing countries the real source of conflict is often to be found in divergencies between national policies. Governments determine the environment in which business operates. When foreign-owned subsidiaries appear to be acting against the interests of the host country it is frequently the case that they are merely optimising their own position as between alternative systems provided by different governments. For their part, multinational enterprises — as a general rule — declare that they wish to conform to local laws and customs in the countries where they operate. There are obvious advantages in 'a quiet life'.

Very often, of course, it is not the causes of confrontations that are subject to criticism, but the means adopted by a multinational enterprise to implement a policy. 'Transfer pricing', for example, is a recurring and perplexing problem. Prices charged for materials or components traded between affiliated companies, or charges made for services provided by one subsidiary for another, can be manipulated to ensure that profits can be shown to be earned in one part of an enterprise rather than in another. By this means, multinational enterprises can exploit differences in taxation systems in countries where they have operations, or they can overcome foreign exchange controls by a hidden transfer of funds. An associated problem arises from 'leads and lags' in settling accounts between affiliated companies. This, of course, is a commercial practice of long-standing between independent companies, but such manipulations may be more difficult to pick up in transactions between affiliates, and less susceptible to regulation. The use of these and other related devices have consequences for the balances of payments of the countries in which the subsidiaries operate: beneficial in some cases, harmful in others. Hence governments are concerned about these devices. But, as stressed already, the source of the problem is usually to be found in policy differences between countries which a multinational enterprise is seeking to exploit.

As the operations of multinational enterprises extend to cover more and more sectors of the economy, and as their organisation becomes more centralised, the problems of conflict caused by divergent national policies will increase and the difficulties of managing multinationals will also grow. For this reason many multinational enterprises have declared their support for the more orderly and co-ordinated framework for their operations that is being demanded by some governments. A variety of proposals have been made for international agreements to ensure the 'good behaviour' of these transnational giants. They range from the creation of a body of supranational law under which the global parent would be incorporated, through to a kind of GATT for international investment (in other words an inter-governmental organisation) embodying a 'code of behaviour' for multinational enterprises, and down to *ad hoc* procedures for inter-governmental consultations. Finally there have been counter proposals to do nothing and leave the solving of any problems that arise to normal diplomatic processes. At present these various proposals are being discussed in United Nations agencies, in the OECD and, more narrowly, in the Commission of the European Community and in national governments.

It is quite clear from the earlier discussion of specific problems that it would be very difficult to get general agreement among the major countries on common principles covering areas such as taxation, balance-of-payments policies and domestic investment incentives. Thus the possibility of obtaining international agreement on a 'code of behaviour' seems remote. Adoption of a law of international incorporation would make even deeper inroads into national sovereignty: witness the difficulty in making progress with the plans for a European company law.[17] These proposals appeal to many commentators because they represent ideal solutions, but they do not seem to be practical objectives for the present. The main obstacles appear to come from the side of governments. For many multinational enterprises would welcome a clearly defined environment within which to operate. It is not certain though that such radical innovations would necessarily be economically to the good. Since little is really known about the operations of multinational enterprises, in spite of all the studies, it is impossible to know whether the consequences of a particular provision would be beneficial or not.

The Rey Report[18] for the OECD adopted a cautious approach to the problems of multinational enterprises. It declined to make recommendations on the grounds of too little information about this phenomenon and its reactions to changes in national economic policies. Precipitate action at the international level certainly has inherent dangers. But, on the other hand, if governments adopt sharply contradictory policies and begin to compete against each other to attract investments, then similar dangers are present. The new compensatory tax in the United States is evidence of these dangers and indicates the degree of feeling towards tax-incentive schemes in West European countries. Similarly, the British Government's action against Roche Products highlighted the equally sensitive problems of 'transfer pricing' and obscurities in parent-company accounts regarding uses of remitted earnings.

Another difficulty associated with achieving international agreement on a code of behaviour is that the problems between multinational enterprises and governments have been changing. As noted earlier, in the 1960s the Canadian authorites saw 'extra-territorialities' as the most important issue in their relationship with American-owned subsidiaries. Yet the passage of time has greatly diminished the importance of restrictions on trade with Communist countries by Canadian subsidiaries of American parents, and compromise solutions have been found to the differences that existed over anti-trust policies.

In the absence of international agreements on problems affecting multinational enterprises, concerned governments may find it worthwhile to seek action through agreements with those countries willing to co-operate to establish codes in particular areas. Several instances have already been cited where governments achieved com-

promises, or provided consultative procedures, to ease the difficulties of multinational enterprises faced with conflicting policies
from different governments. Double taxation agreements are an
obvious way to overcome some problems regarding tax reliefs and
other incentive schemes. If the OECD draft convention were employed in re-negotiated agreements it would also impose some
uniformity which would introduce a degree of multilateralism into
these agreements. Where certain governments are unwilling to
co-operate, others could exert pressure by requiring special information from foreign subsidiaries operating in their jurisdiction, and
possibly by applying penal tax rates to remittances sent to tax
havens. Co-operation between governments in this way could lead to
such agreements attracting new adherents.

One of the major difficulties concerns the legal position of a
subsidiary in a multinational group. Often a parent company owns
all the equity capital of its foreign subsidiaries, although debt capital
may be provided from a wider compass. (Many American companies
favour 100 per cent ownership of overseas subsidiaries.) As an
unquoted company, therefore, the subsidiary firm may have to meet
less stringent rules on disclosure of accounts than if there were local
equity participation. One proposal, then, is that any foreign-owned
subsidiary should permit local participation in the equity to a
minimum share, say 25 per cent. It could thereby be required under
company law to release specific information and to publish full
company accounts annually. The advantage of these proposals is
that they would increase the 'transparency' of multinational enterprises. Such requirements could be extended further to demand
certain information, too, about the operation of parent companies.
If all countries required the former, of course, the latter would not
be necessary. But as long as countries like Switzerland allow almost
complete secrecy to companies of particular kinds, this is the only
way that information on the use of remitted funds can be acquired.
(This was at the root of the Roche controversy in Britain.)

Straighforward nationalism and a fear of bigness seems to induce
a presumption that multinational enterprises represent some kind of
threat. When rationalised, these fears are mainly related to 'control'
being exercised over subsidiaries from abroad, which places them
outside the national legal system. As far as size is concerned, the
obvious solution is an adequate anti-trust policy or an effectively
enforced body of rules of competiton; this though is probably
desirable anyway from a purely national point of view. The multinational enterprise is a symbol of the international oligopoly that is
being established in many sectors of industry. But in many countries
the introduction of investments by multinational enterprises has

increased competition in the market rather than reduced it. What is needed is an appropriate and enforceable policy on competition. Recognition of this by the Commission of the European Community should accelerate the implementation of its competition policy.

Since the late 1960s the Commission in Brussels has been trying to draft a set of regulations governing the operations of multinational enterprises. So far such regulations have appeared piece-meal, in statements like the Colonna Plan, [19] and in programmes for the harmonisation of taxation and company law. They have been widely criticised on the grounds that they discriminate against non-European companies. The problems associated with drafting a special set of regulations for multinational enterprises in the presence of so many outstanding proposals for policy harmonisation are clearly illustrated in the document, *Multinational Undertakings and Community Regulations* which was published by the Commission of the European Community in Brussels in November 1973. This document contains a confused discussion of multinational groups and a statement of certain policy objectives for the European Community which are often contradictory. Following the theme of this article it is apparent that the Community's policy harmonisation could remove many sources of friction between multinational enterprises and national governments. But they will not eliminate the major problems, because divergencies will remain between the policies of the Community and those of outside countries, especially the United States. It is for this reason that it would seem to be advisable and profitable for the interests of third parties to be considered in conjunction with the formation of harmonisation policies. The only real contributions that the Commission document seems likely to make are in the compilation and exchange of information on the activities of multinational enterprises in the member countries and, as previously mentioned, by safeguarding consumer interests through the enforcement of rules on competition.

In conclusion, while it is unlikely that in the near future an international agreement can be reached on a 'code of behaviour' for multinational enterprises, and government policies towards them, there is considerable scope for governments to co-operate in their attitudes towards these agents of international economic integration. In view of the veil that hangs over many aspects of international business activities, and the way they respond to particular policy measures, it seems wise for the time being to proceed gradually rather than to establish a code of behaviour which may be impossible to implement, or which has gaps in its coverage that could very well be revealed as the real problems posed by multinational enterprises are uncovered by further examination and study.

## NOTES AND REFERENCES

1. See, for example, W.B. Reddaway, *Effects of UK Direct Investment Overseas* (Cambridge: Cambridge University Press, 1968); G.C. Hufbauer and F.M. Adler, *Overseas Manufacturing Investment and the Balance of Payments* (Washington: United States Department of the Treasury, 1967); John Dunning, *The Role of American Investment in the British Economy* (London: Political & Economic Planning, 1969); and M.D. Steuer *et al.*, *The Impact of Foreign Direct Investment in the United Kingdom* (London: H.M. Stationery Office, 1973).

For other studies on the operations of multinational enterprises, see Donald Brash, *American Investment in Australian Industry* (Canberra: Australian National University Press, 1966); A.E. Safarian, *Foreign Ownership of Canadian Industry* (Toronto: McGraw-Hill, 1966); Charles P. Kindleberger, *American Business Abroad* (New Haven: Yale University Press, 1969); Raymond Vernon, *Sovereignty at Bay* (London: Longmans, 1971); and Dunning (ed.), *The Multinational Enterprise* (London: Allen & Unwin, 1971).

2. United States Tariff Commission, *Implications of Multinational Firms for World Trade and Investment and for US Trade and Labour* (Washington: US Government Printing Office, 1973).

3. P.M. Goldberg and Kindleberger, 'Towards a GATT for Investment: a Proposal for the Supervision of the International Corporation', in *Law and Policy in International Business* (Washington: Georgetown University Law Centre, 1970).

4. Safarian, *The Performance of Foreign-owned Firms in Canada* (Washington and Montreal: Canadian-American Committee, 1969).

5. Herbert Gray, *Foreign Direct Investment in Canada*, Gray Report (Ottawa: Queen's Printers, 1972).

6. Fruehauf-France S.A. and Automobiles Berliet S.A., 1964, quoted in Goldberg and Kindleberger *loc. cit.*

7. See Gray Report, *op. cit.*

8. *Ibid.*, p. 391.

9. For an account of the Labour Party conference, see *The Times*, London, 3 October 1973.

10. A fuller discussion is provided in David Robertson, 'The Multinational Enterprise: Trade Flows and Trade Policy', in Dunning (ed.), *op. cit.*

11. In the United States, 'Voluntary restraints' on capital exports in 1965, then mandatory controls in 1968, caused substantial transfers of funds from Canada to America. As a result, the American authorities undertook, in March 1968, to exempt Canada from United States balance-of-payments measures affecting capital flows. In return the Canadian authorities guaranteed to police any attempts to use this undertaking to evade United States regulations against other countries.

12. Foreign Direct Investments Appeals Board, composed of officials from the United States Department of Commerce.

13. United States Tariff Commission, *op. cit.*, chap. 4.

14. *Draft Double Convention on Taxes on Income and Capital* (Paris: OECD Secretariat, 1963).

15. Luxembourg does in fact collect a small withholding tax on net income of holding companies.

16. Malcolm Crawford, 'Tax Threat to American Companies in Britain', *The Sunday Times*, London, 1 July 1973.

17. Dennis Thompson, *European Company Law* (London: Royal Institute of International Affairs and Political & Economic Planning, 1968).

18. High-level Group on Trade and Related Problems, *Policy Perspectives for International Trade and Economic Relations*, Rey Report (Paris: OECD Secretariat, 1972).

19. Commission of the European Community, *Industrial Policy in the Community*, Colonna Report (Luxembourg: Office for Official Publications of the European Community, 1970).

# CHAPTER 9

## General Principles for World Monetary Reform

### HARRY G. JOHNSON

The international monetary system has been in an increasingly unsettled state for more than a decade and discussions on its reform, at inter-governmental level, have been proceeding for about as long. The monetary crisis of August 1971, and the consequent Smithsonian Accord of December of that year, placed greater emphasis on the need to reach an agreement on a fundamental reform of the international monetary system within a short space of years. But, and only partly due to the collapse of the Smithsonian Accord in February-March 1973, the deadline set for agreement on specific reforms, namely the 1973 meeting of the International Monetary Fund (IMF), passed without any settlement being reached. And in fact the 'oil crisis' has since led to the IMF's Committee of Twenty to accept floating rates as a fact of current life.

Past experience with the evolution in the IMF of Special Drawing Rights (SDRs) suggests that there is little point in academic experts — or anyone else for that matter — devising detailed plans for reform, given that the measures actually adopted (if any) will be shaped by the circumstances of the time, and will be expressed in terms designed to free nations from the embarrassment of past bargaining positions. Such plans can only serve to illustrate principles and thus one might as well discuss the principles directly. The present paper is therefore directed at the question of defining the optimal solution to the problem of international adjustment. This is the central problem, judged by the experience of recent strains in the system and, too, by the theory of international monetary organisation.[1]

It is obvious from the outset that it is much easier to discuss non-optimum solutions, or the pessimum solution, than to discuss the optimum one. This comment, however, must be qualified. There would be no problem, and no need for a solution, if the world were so arranged that economic adjustments took place painlessly and automatically. The difficulties arise for several reasons. The more important ones are:

(a) that changes occur which are unforeseen and to which adjustment is painful;

(b) that the political process, acting through governments,

offers possibilities of palliating or reducing the pain — at least in the short run — by interfering in one way or another with whatever system of adjustment is generally thought to exist; and

(c) that these interferences tend both to create inefficiency in the operation of the economy and to aggravate the adjustment problem, first by impeding adjustments which might otherwise occur without too much difficulty and, secondly, by allowing disequilibria to accumulate. [2]

These difficulties apply to changes of any kind, not merely to those mediated through international trade and payments. This fact is important because it relates to the strong tendencies which exist in the modern world of nation states for governments to base their policies on two assumptions.

One assumption is that adjustments to changes transmitted through international trade and payments are especially damaging and difficult by comparison with changes emanating from the normal process of economic growth in the domestic economy. The result is to confer a special status on problems of adjustment to international change and to sanction methods of adjustment — or of resistance to adjustment — via international economic policy that would not be regarded as appropriate if applied to problems of adjustment to domestic change. Another consequence is to sanction methods of cushioning adjustment that are clearly second-best and which can only be justified by the fact that in some sense they can be argued to be directed against foreigners.

The growing understanding of these consequences of a wrong assumption has had an important influence on contemporary thinking about national policies concerning adjustment.

1. At the level of micro-economics, it is now perceived that public assistance for the adjustment of particular industries or sectors to economic change should not be linked to disturbances associated with changing comparative advantage in international trade, but should be focused on the problem of change itself.

2. At the level of macro-economics, the subject of this paper, it is increasingly recognised that the international monetary system should provide for as much automatic — or perhaps one should say 'non-politically-controlled' — flexibility as possible in order to minimise the possibility of using balance-of-payments disequilibria as an excuse for interventions in international trade and payments.

This introduces the second of the faulty assumptions — a notion that has a long history in economic policy and has been disposed of time and time again by economic logic, but which keeps being resurrected by successive generations of policy-discussants and policy-makers. It is that the burden of policies designed to resist adjustment can somehow be passed off on to other countries.

1. At the micro-economic level, it is assumed that the effects of trade restrictions designed to prevent a slow-down of adjustment to a loss of comparative advantage are mostly confined to discommoding the foreigner. This is true in the very short-run; that is, at the time of imposition of new restrictions. But in the longer run, the burden generally falls on the country's own consumers — in the form of higher prices, less efficiency and less growth than would otherwise be achieved.[3]

2. At the macro-economic level, it is assumed that forcing the foreigner rather than oneself to initiate adjustment measures transfers the burden from oneself to him. In fact, adjustment is a mutual and reciprocal process: a reduction in one country's deficit must mean a reduction in the other's surplus, with adjustment of production patterns on both sides. Thus the countries of the European Community were unhappy about the 1973 devaluation of the dollar. But would they have been happier if the United States had chosen a drastic deflation of its economy instead?

These remarks are intended to draw attention to a possibly insoluble problem in improving the mechanism of adjustment. The present system — if it can be identified very broadly with the structure that existed up until 1971 and which has remained the dream of restoration — is profoundly shaped by the prevailing concentration of international economic policy-makers on problems that are rooted in nationalist rivalries and which would be technically much more easy to solve were it not so. Consequently the improvement of the present system is to an important extent a problem of 'defusing' nationalist rivalries. But there is no purely technical way of resolving nationalist rivalries. It is almost certain, though, that technical changes in the system — particularly changes allowing much greater flexibility of exchange rate adjustments — could ameliorate or actually reduce the supercharging of problems which are, in economic terms, essentially easy to resolve.

## Problem in Historical-Theoretical Perspective

Over the past decade the theory of the international monetary system has come to distinguish three main problems of the gold reserve standard system on which the international monetary order was based until the *de facto* demonetisation of gold in 1971. These are the liquidity problem, the confidence problem and the adjustment problem. The questions of confidence has successively come to be known as 'the composition problem', the 'overhang problem' — a term initially, and mistakenly, applied in 1968 to gold and since 1971 to reserve and private holdings of dollars, probably equally mistakenly [4] — and the 'consolidation problem'. The question of 'consolidation' arises from the asserted need to consolidate gold, dollars and special drawing rights (SDRs) on the International Monetary Fund (IMF) into a single international reserve asset. This idea is usually coupled with the notion of de-liquifying a part of the total.

## Complementarity of Liquidity and Adjustment

The consolidation problem is one aspect of the liquidity problem, and hence neither of them falls within the scope of detailed discussion in this paper. It is an axiom of the theory of the international monetary system, however, that liquidity and adjustment problems are complementary and cannot really be separated. The usual simplistic formulation of this proposition is that the better (in the sense of effectiveness and speed of operation) the adjustment mechanism, the less is the need for international liquidity and *vice versa*.

But this proposition raises some difficult questions when the adjustment mechanism involves exchange-rate flexibility. For one consequence of greater exchange-rate flexibility, recognised more or less explicitly in the case for an acceptance of wider bands for exchange-rate variations around parities, is to shift some part of the burden of stabilising speculation in the exchange markets from official to private hands. This reduces the level of official reserves which it is necessary to hold, but implies an increase in the private holding of reserves, either directly or through the development of equivalent private credit facilities. [5] The former effect alone is generally taken into account in discussions on the need for international liquidity in relation to the adjustment mechanism; and it is sometimes carried to the extreme and absurd lengths of supposing that if and when greater exchange-rate flexibility became an accepted part of the system there might be practical implications, arising from the proposition of floating exchange-rate theory that floating rates would make official reserves unnecessary, for the international monetary system at its present level of liquidity. [6] Greater exchange-rate flexibility is likely to bring about a change in the locus of holding of international money quantitatively more important than any prospective change in the quantity of it required for the efficient working of the system. Among other things this implies — as has been recognised and pointed out by several experts — that if SDRs are to become the reserve base of a reconstituted international monetary system, a private market for SDR-denominated assets and liabilities will have to be developed.

There is another difficulty inherent in the simple view indicated by fundamental monetary theory that international liquidity and international adjustment are substitutes one for the other. In the background is the assumption (inherited from the international monetary collapse of the 1930s and from the earlier period of concern after World War I over the adequacy of international gold supplies) that there is a chronic shortage of international reserves which must be compensated for by the deliberate creation of credit substitutes for gold.[7] General economic theory suggests that the hypothesis of a secular disequilibrium between demand and supply is untenable. Monetary theory also indicates, first, that this is particularly so for an asset as fungible and with such close credit substitutes as commodity money. Secondly, it suggests that the proper indicator of reserve inadequacy or adequacy is not technical calculations involving ratios of one kind or another but the trend of world prices — which strongly suggests an excessive level and rate of growth of international liquidity since the middle of the last decade. And thirdly, monetary theory suggests that the misguided effort to make good an assumed shortage of liquidity by liquidity creation is likely to produce world inflation.

From the standpoint of coming to grips with the adjustment problem, the dynamic connection between, on the one hand, the rate of growth of international liquidity in relation to growth of aggregate demand for it and, on the other, the world price trend against which the adjustment problem occurs is far more satisfactory, in the writer's view, than the static (assumed-stable-price-level) framework of reasoning in which liquidity and adjustment appear as substitutes for one another. The main point that the more dynamic approach suggests is that there is a fundamental difference in kind, analytically speaking, between

> (a) an international monetary system of fixed rates (a term which we will use here very broadly to include systems with more or less flexibility short of complete flexibility) functioning in an environment of relatively stable prices, and
> (b) one functioning — or attempting to function — in an

environment of substantial but erratic price deflation or inflation.

This difference needs to be incorporated into the theory of the system and allowed for in recommendations for reform.[8]

## Exchange Rates under Unstable Price Conditions

In a regime of world prices which are, on average, stable, the exchange rate is not only a measure of the exchange value of a country's money in terms of other countries' currencies. It is also a measure of the purchasing power of the country's money over goods and services in the international market — with which the domestic purchasing power of the national money must remain in alignment if international equilibrium is to be maintained. Hence disequilibria in a country's balance-of-payments position reflect errors or divergencies in that country's domestic policies from those consistent with price stability and balance-of-payments equilibrium. They are signalled to the policy-makers by domestic indicators and can be corrected by domestic adjustment policies undertaken by each government on its own. Briefly stated, in such an environment each country can seek to behave domestically in a way which follows the parameter of stable world prices.

In an environment of falling or rising world prices, however, a country's price-trend and balance-of-payments position represents an amalgam of its 'real' position relative to other countries and the 'monetary' position of the world economy as a whole. In these circumstances domestic policy signals become confused and confusing. Moreover, the need for adjustment to a 'monetary' disequilibrium is likely to be shared by a group of countries, and possibly the world as a whole. Such a situation requires a co-ordination of national policies among countries used to 'exercising their monetary sovereignty' in independence.

The point may be illustrated historically by two successive and recent episodes in international monetary history. There is the case of the long and successful operation of the classical gold standard in the nineteenth century, followed by its collapse in the 1930s under strains that had been building up in the 1920s. And there is also the case of the near twenty-year period of reasonably successful operation of the successor IMF system, followed by increasing strains culminating in the *de facto* collapse of that system in 1971-73.

In the first case, the traditional gold-standard mechanism of adjustment via inflation in surplus countries and deflation in deficit countries proved unable to meet the strain of a general collapse of world liquidity. The collapse could have been averted by:

(a) a general rise in the price of gold in terms of all currencies or

(b) by the provision of sufficient supplementary credit to make up the difference, either through the existing channels of inter-bank lending developed in the 1920s or through the creation of a new form of international credit reserve.

Instead countries attempted to overcome the *general* monetary problem by the application of the traditional technique of deflation appropriate to an *individual* country. When this remedy became too painful they attempted to overcome the problem by managed downward floating of their currency or by devaluation. This was again a remedy appropriate for an individual country the exchange value of whose currency had got out of line with a (stable) world price level.

Being at most a second-best solution, it is not surprising that as a result flexible exchange rates got a very bad name among policy-makers, through guilt-by-association with crisis, and among economists. The latter were influenced by the arguments first that devaluation was unlikely to produce an improvement in the balance-of-payments of the devaluing country and secondly, that it was a 'beggar-my-neighbour' method of increasing domestic employment, which was thus bound to excite retaliation.

The IMF was intended to overcome these defects of the gold standard (a) by providing supplementary credit liquidity in the form of drawing rights, together with a reserve possibility of altering the international price of gold, and (b) by sanctioning the use of exchange-rate adjustments in cases of 'fundamental disequilibrium'. Its general orientation in the latter respect was a guard against competitive devaluation and 'deflationary bias' — according to the concepts developed in the 1930s in criticism of the gold standard. In fact, however, its actual operation came to place increasing emphasis on the gold standard mechanisms of domestic deflation and inflation.

In any event the IMF worked fairly well during its initial period, in which period the United States maintained relative stability in the purchasing power of the American dollar, in spite of the reluctance with which some West European governments became accustomed to the idea that the American dollar, and not gold, was increasingly the basic international reserve of the system.

But all this changed with the advent of a significant rate of inflation in the United States. For a complex dual element was introduced into the adjustment problem which now included the adjustment of non-dollar currency values individually relative to one another and collectively relative to the dollar. [9]

In these circumstances, the European central banks were faced with the necessity of extending their thinking beyond the role of an atomistic competitor in relation to a stable world price level — a role to which they were accustomed by their long historical experience of the gold standard and twenty years under the dollar standard. Instead, they were obliged to begin thinking about Western Europe as a whole in relation to the dollar. Such an extension in thinking was part of the motivation in the European Community for the establishment of a European currency (the europa). It was, though, only a minor part compared with the desire of the bureaucrats in Brussels to repair their failure to force European economic integration and policy harmonisation through *inter alia* the common agricultural policy. But the goal of creating a European monetary union has proved very difficult to realise and now seems to have become a pious hope. (The inherent reasons have already been outlined.)

Nevertheless, setting the objective of a European monetary union helped to paralyse any more modest efforts at the adjustment of European exchange rates against the dollar. As a result, in August 1971, the United States was finally exasperated into forcing an adjustment of European (and Japanese) exchange rates against the dollar by suspending gold convertibility and introducing a temporary import surcharge. The interpretations of experts differ as to what happened next.

> Either (a) the Americans got the appropriate realignment of rates in the 1971 Smithsonian Accord (reached at a meeting of the Group of Ten in Washington), and were then panicked by an idiosyncratic large-scale capital outflow early in 1973 into an unnecessary further devaluation of the dollar; or
> (b) they settled too easily at the Smithsonian discussions and took advantage of that capital outflow to enforce the exchange rate change they really wanted.

But on either interpretation, present evidence suggests a case of 'over-kill' — such that the European countries will have to adjust, in the 1970s, to a period of chronic dollar shortage like the one that prevailed in the immediate postwar period. If this is in fact the problem to be anticipated, it should be taken into account in any thinking about the optimum method of solving the adjustment problem.

## Importance of Liquidity in Relation to Prices

The more general conclusion to be drawn from this brief historical-theoretical interpretation is that not only the magnitude but the very nature of the adjustment problem depends crucially on what is done about the provision of international liquidity.

If international liquidity is provided over time in such a fashion as to be consistent with world price stability

— which in contemporary circumstances means a significantly non-zero rate of price inflation, but one that is fairly reliable and not too high for serious inconvenience to domestic and world economic organisation —

the adjustment problem will in principle be the relatively simple one of bringing back into alignment individual national economies whose price and/or aggregate demand levels have got out of line with the requirements of international equilibrium. With luck, most of the adjustments could be effected by fiscal-monetary policies along the lines of traditional gold-standard theory, with exchange-rate changes being few and far between and not requiring an atmosphere of international crisis.[10] Moreover, countries chronically deviant from the norm in one direction or another could be allowed to have floating exchange rates. On a broad view, these few accepted exceptions would be quite consistent with the general regime of fixed exchange rates, since the purchasing power of other countries' currencies over those countries' goods would be stable even though their exchange rates were steadily depreciating or appreciating.

The chief danger to the intent and purpose of the system of fixed rates would be the development of national syndromes of inflationary policies in which the adverse balance-of-payments implications of inflation were constrained by the cumulation of controls over international trade and payments, punctuated by stepwise devaluations accompanied by monetary-fiscal deflation, and followed (when successful) by the dismantling of controls previously built up. Even that would not be too serious if confined to a few countries. For in a generally prosperous and open world market for goods and capital the chief damage would be borne by the countries in question and not by their better-behaved neighbours.

If, on the other hand, international liquidity is so managed as to produce a pronounced inflationary trend in world prices, and still more if that trend has a large random element, the problem of adjustment would become far more serious. This would be because methods of adjustment would have to straddle both 'real' and 'monetary' disequilibria, and the question of the optimum solution to the adjustment problem would have to be answered with the possibility of both types of disequilibrium being kept in mind, together with the consequences of the interaction between them.

This poses a serious problem. For it is still doubtful what sort of international monetary framework will emerge from the contemporary post-IMF-system interregnum. All that seems certain is that the vast majority of countries or their officials and governments would prefer some sort of fixed-but-adjustable exchange-rate regime. And there is the likelihood, judging from past experience, that whatever provision is made for greater exchange-rate flexibility in the interests of facilitating adjustments, national policies will tend to drift towards using less than the full degree of flexibility provided.

The possibilities may be summarised briefly in the proposition that what may emerge is

(a) a no-reserve-currency system, (b) a one-reserve-currency system, or (c) a two-reserve-currency system;

that is, (a) an SDR-based system with consolidation of other reserve forms into the base, (b) an American dollar standard, or (c) a dollar/europa standard with flexibility in the dollar-europa exchange rate.[11]

Of these the first two would be tidier and perhaps one or the other would be the end result of experimentation with the last. The last has the appeal of seeming to provide an obvious way out of the major fundamental source of disequilibrium and tension in the international monetary system in recent years.

That source has been European resentment of the imposition on a reasonably well-functioning system of a prolonged spurt of American inflation associated with an unpopular American war, together with the somewhat inconsistent desire — which has accordingly arisen on both sides — that this tension should be eliminated by building a European currency capable of parity of importance with the American dollar. As already mentioned, however, the establishment of such a currency in the European Community would involve a major change in European national habits with regard to sovereignty in domestic economic management. Also, the recent trend of international economic and political relations suggests that, far from resolving recent tensions, such a system would promote the division of the world economy into rival economic blocs that would rapidly generate a deteriorating situation of inter-bloc economic warfare.

Assuming for simplicity that the major choice is between an SDR and a dollar system (since for the time being the effort to establish a common European currency would have to be grafted on to a better-established or more firmly prospective world system) each raises the question of whether, and how well, the growth of international liquidity would be managed under it so as to promote world price stability. Here there would seem to be a Hobson's choice.

The dollar standard has become increasingly suspect. This is due less to American inflation than to the explicit isolationist and Europhobic attitudes reflected in the Nixon Administration's policy actions of August 1971 and February 1973. In addition there is no reason to think that the dollar will not continue to be managed indefinitely with virtually exclusive orientation towards domestic policy considerations. Of these, the desire to maintain high employment clearly takes precedence over the desire to avoid inflation.

As for SDRs, as presently designed, they constitute a *very weak* base for controlling the growth of overall international liquidity — as has been amply demonstrated since the first distribution of them. To make them into an effective monetary base for the world financial system would, as previously suggested, require not only the consolidation of other reserve assets into them. It would require their establishment as a privately and widely used means of payment and unit of account for debt obligations or as a 'standard for deferred payments'. Neither requirement would be easily achieved. And in any case success might still not prevent the resurgence of a dollar or Eurodollar standard.

It would therefore seem necessary to consider the problem of the optimum solution to the adjustment problem on the hard-case assumption of continuing international monetary instability.

## Problem of the Optimal Solution

This section is circumspectly entitled the 'problem of the optimal solution' rather than 'the optimal solution' because the latter title would imply a definite plan that could be defended at every point. But the practical problem, and the only purpose a discussion of this kind can serve, is to concentrate attention — as explained at the outset — on certain general principles that should motivate concrete plans for institutional reform.

It may be taken as axiomatic among scientific economists, though not necessarily among 'political economists', that the purpose of the international monetary system is to promote as far as possible freedom of competition internationally among both goods and factors of different national origins; and further that to the extent that international monetary arrangements entail permission or necessity to resort to intervention in international trade and payments 'for balance-of-payments reasons' they are failing in their primary purpose.

This basic principle depends on a standard proposition of contemporary international trade theory, less well-known and consistently applied than it should be, that while there are conceptually in pure theory — and maybe quantitatively significant in reality — any number of cases in which competition fails to achieve the social welfare optimum and needs correction by government intervention, all such cases require permanent policies of intervention to be applied independently of the state of the balance of payments. The balance of payments provides an excuse. It does not provide an argument.

The proposition also depends, less incontrovertibly, on regarding as of secondary importance two assumptions that bulk large in popular consciousness and policy discussion.

One is that the private competitive process generates destabilising transient disturbances on a significant scale which need to be offset by temporary government interventions. On this assumption the same general observations apply as in the particular case of destabilising exchange rate speculation. The case for intervention implies that speculators are consistently losing money.[12] It assumes that the authorities have superior information or judgement which they will not — or cannot credibly — share with the private market. And it derives its plausible examples from cases in which government speculation on its own ability to manage things in the teeth of economic laws offers private individuals cast-iron opportunities to speculate against the government.

The other assumption is that there are frequently cases in which governmental action to slow down adjustment represents a social-welfare-maximising policy. The problem with this contention, as Milton Friedman pointed out many years ago, in criticism of James Meade in the context of exchange-rate flexibility,[13] is that there is no *a priori* reason for assuming slow adjustment to be better than rapid adjustment. There are also the questions (a) of whether it is rational and efficient to identify adjustment assistance with international change and to link it to commercial and payments policy, and (b) of how far the competitive market will in fact fail to make investments in slowing down change that would be socially profitable.

### Role of Fiscal/Monetary and Exchange-rate Policies

In the light of the basic principle just stated, it is clear that adjustment should in principle take place by use of the two general and non-discriminatory policies and corresponding policy instruments that, following the pioneering work of James Meade,[14] have come to be distinguished in the theory of international economic policy. These are fiscal/monetary policy and exchange-rate policy.

It should perhaps be remarked in passing that in the wake of considerable theoretical exploration in recent years, the use for exchange-rate adjustment as a policy instrument has to be associated with rigidity of wages and prices: in a downward direction for devaluations; and in an upward direction for revaluations. Otherwise price flexibility would eliminate price-level misalignments unless these were supported by fiscal/monetary policy. Thus, for example, it is easy to construct models in which the expansion of aggregate demand beyond the level commensurate with full-employment and balance-of-payments equilibrium raises the country's price level about the purchasing-power-parity relationship. Demand management would consequently be the only problem for macroeconomic policy-making. Furthermore, with sufficient international mobility of capital, demand-management policy boils down to fiscal policy, with monetary policy serving only the function of determining the level and rate of growth of the country's international reserves.

It should also be noted that while the need for exchange-rate adjustment arises from wage and price rigidity, the possibility of using it for policy purposes depends on the presence of money illusion. This is a significant point. For money illusion depends on belief in the stability of the value of money and this belief, and the ability to exploit it by exchange-rate changes, can be seriously damaged by experience. The experience one chiefly has in mind here is that of the inflationary consequences for domestic prices of either a large-scale devaluation of the domestic currency or a failure to appreciate the domestic currency when world prices are rising rapidly.

An important implication of this analysis is the desirability of small and fairly frequent exchange-rate changes in place of infrequent but large ones. This is because the price effects of the former are likely to be absorbed with other random changes in relative prices which are accepted as consistent with broad stability in the value of money.

It is desirable not only that exchange-rate changes should be small and frequent, but that they should be as automatic and apolitical as possible. The more politically discretionary the decision to change an exchange rate, the more likely is procrastination, cumulation of disequilibrium, resort to controls on trade and payments and eventual large-scale changes which inject a fresh disequilibrium into the system. For this reason, most economists who have studied the problem dispassionately, which would exclude 'political economists' who work directly or indirectly for governments and accept the fixed-rate system as a politically given part of the environment, have concluded in favour of completely freely floating exchange rates, confident — on the basis of both theory and historical evidence — that the various arguments against such a system lack foundation. This school includes myself.

Nevertheless, one has to recognise that central banks and treasuries are the institutions which hold power, and they are almost unanimously opposed to freely floating exchange rates. For purposes of discussion it has to be accepted that the most radical development one can consider in connection with potential international monetary reform is limited flexibility of exchange rates.

That being accepted, there is a case for the wider band as a means of providing more automatic exchange-rate flexibility, by making movements within the band a matter of technical management rather than political decision. This is in addition to the point mentioned in the previous section that more flexibility transfers some of the responsibility for conducting and financing stabilising speculation from the central bank to the private foreign exchange market.

The wider band, though, is primarily a device for providing greater exchange-rate flexibility around a parity assumed to be a sustainable norm. While it has the advantage from the authorities' point of view of enabling them to impose greater financial penalties on speculators who speculate against their ability to maintain the parity — an activity usually but wrongly described as 'destabilising speculation' — it provides for adjustments of the values of currencies in terms of the base money of the system

(a) only within the extreme limits of twice the band for adjustments of currencies relative to one another (the 'real' disturbance problem discussed in the previous section), and

(b) only within the extreme limits of the band itself (the 'monetary' disturbance problem).

*Gliding Parity: Solution to 'Real' and 'Monetary' Disturbances*

In coping with these two adjustment problems the 'crawling peg' device, recently re-christened the more gracefully-sounding 'gliding parity', offers the only effective solution. For currencies gliding differently in relation to the *numeraire* in terms of which parities are fixed can achieve any desired degree of adjustment relative to one another if sufficient time elapses, while gliding of all currencies in the same direction against the *numeraire* could in principle correct for any given monetary disequilibrium.[15] The problem remaining, however, would be that the disturbances might be too great to be solved by gliding at the top speed permitted by the gliding formula. (This last would be determined by the permitted band of variation about the parity and the length of the averaging period for determining the new daily parity, and expressible in a maximum percentage rate of change per calendar time period.) Deliberate politically-determined parity changes would consequently be required in such circumstances, in addition to the automatic changes effected by the gliding formula.

One might have expected, after the period of intermittent crises that preceded the devaluation of the French franc and the appreciation of the German mark in 1969, and the resulting interest of the major IMF members in increased exchange-rate flexibility —including the possibility of a period of (upward) flotation for undervalued currencies, which originated in practical experiment rather than academic analysis — that the resolution of the 1971 crisis in the Smithsonian Accord would have included provision for greater exchange-rate flexibility along the lines discussed above.

In fact, only the wider band was included in the new parity agreement: and the Europeans proceeded to narrow that degree of flexibility by the 'snake in the tunnel' arrangement. Subsequently, American thinking has continued to run largely along the lines of a fixed-rate system of the IMF type, but with new provisions intended to force exchange-rate adjustment in cases of 'fundamental disequilibrium' of either the surplus or the deficit variety. These provisions have taken the form of bands for the accumulation or decumulation of international reserves around a self-determined national reserve-holding target. The attainment of the inner band would serve as a warning signal and the attainment of the outer band would signify the need for positive policy action of some kind (not necessarily exchange-rate change).[16]

While this section of the essay has argued strongly for the gliding parity, such an arrangement would provide a useful backstop in cases where the gliding parity failed to provide enough adjustment, within a reasonable time: and it would be even more desirable in the absence of any gliding parity arrangement. But it would still, at least in the proposed form, not solve the adjustment problem in an optimal or near-optimal manner. For it would allow plenty of scope both for argument about the reality of the presumed need for some sort of adjustment policy, and about the possible use of interventional methods rather than exchange-rate changes. Even so, it would constitute a significant step forward from the situation under the

IMF system, as it existed before the August 1971 crisis. At that time there was agreement neither upon criteria for the existence or probable existence of disequilibrium nor upon whose responsibility it might be to take corrective action. Prolonged and inconclusive debate and recrimination were thus encouraged up to the point where a crisis forced some sort of action — which was not necessarily the action envisaged in the preceding debates.

The conclusions reached, then, are undoubtedly unsatisfactory to anyone only interested in optimal solutions. No novel ideas or concrete proposals have emerged. But, to repeat, that is probably not the most useful purpose for discussions of this kind anyway.

## Instruments of Intervention

One aspect of the optimal solution of the adjustment problem that has been touched on only briefly and peripherally in the paper, but which really deserves far more detailed exploration (if one accepts the virtual certainty that countries will continue to use interventions in international trade and payments as part of adjustment policy), concerns the relative merits of different methods and objects of intervention.

(1) While the IMF charter stipulates the use of quotas on imports rather than tariff increases for restrictive purposes, both theoretical analysis and administrative experience suggest that temporary tariff surcharges are both more effective and more efficient than quotas, not least because the administrative apparatus for imposing tariff surcharges is already in place.

(2) There is no obvious economic sense (only the possibility of avoiding violation of international treaties) in leaving merchandise account transactions free and concentrating restrictions (including the establishment of a dual rate system) on international capital movements.

(3) Finally, although this may be personal prejudice, it seems highly undesirable from the point of view of the personal liberty of the citizen to impose restrictions on foreign exchange available for tourism and foreign study if only because these items are not such as to entail ready possibilities of import substitution from domestic sources.

## NOTES AND REFERENCES

1. The essay was published earlier as Harry G. Johnson, *Neglected Principles in the Discussions on World Monetary Reform*, **Staff Paper No. 4** (London: Trade Policy Research Centre, 1974).

2. One of the worst offenders in this respect, in my considered judgement, is so-called 'regional policy', which has a strong tendency to pass the problem of chronic regional depression on from generation to generation. There is no law of economics to the effect that a piece of territory capable of supporting a certain population at a low standard of living should be capable of supporting the same, or a larger, population at a higher standard of living, even with substantial subsidies. But there is a law of political survival according to which people and not land have votes and a politician, in order to survive, must attempt to maintain the numbers of his constituency. If maintaining them involves maintaining them in relative misery, the resulting grievances are likely to rebound to his advantage.

3. The exception arises, of course, from the 'optimum tariff' argument, but this possibility is unlikely to be quantitatively significant for any single country other than the United States; and to the extent that the argument holds, it implies that the trade-restricting country has relatively little success in preventing domestic production from decreasing under the pressure of foreign competition.

4. For those with short memories, the view widely held in 1968-69 was that private purchasers had rushed into gold only in the belief that the dollar would be devalued, and once it had been convincingly demonstrated that the dollar and not gold ruled the roost the speculators would stampede out of gold and its price would crash. The 'dollar overhang' concept developed in 1971-72 was based on the same logic and, as Robert Mundell has consistently emphasised, ignored the fact that the considerable gap between the private-market and official prices of gold made existing official holdings of gold unusable as an international reserve asset. This misinterpretation undoubtedly played some part in generating the crisis of February-March 1973 and in producing the present system of dirty floating of exchange rates.

5. It is worth noting that the sharp distinction conventionally drawn between 'reserve assets' and borrowing rights or looser understandings about the availability of official credit in emergencies, together with the even sharper distinction between either the narrower or the broader concepts of international liquidity and other assets, rests on two artificial elements in contemporary international monetary arrangements which are of relatively recent historical origin, and are both carried over from domestic governmental financial management. One is the assumption that governments ought to be able to borrow at lower interest rates than even the most credit-worthy of private individuals (ideally, at a zero rate of interest internationally). The other is the assumption that governments ought not to be callable to account by foreigners for the uses to which they have put borrowings and intend to put new ones. One can readily conceive of an alternative system in which governments borrowed at commercially competitive rates in private international capital markets — as indeed they do in part at present through the offering of Treasury bills, and as Britain did in the early stages of financing World War I.

6. There is a contrary school of thought, identified with Oxford University, to the effect that floating rates will require more and not less official international reserves. This contention apparently rests on the typically 'Oxbridge' view that the market has no sources of information other than what the 'authorities' choose to give it, so that failing a government commitment to maintaining a limited range of rate variation private speculation will be unlimitedly destabilising and the authorities will have to perform all stabilising speculation themselves. My hunch is that this view is a pseudo-theoretical rationalisation of R.F. Harrod's misinterpretation of the relevant experience of the 1930s, during which the British authorities were seeking to maintain an undervalued exchange rate in order to build up a war chest of gold and dollars against the expectation of a coming war against Germany in which the United States would remain neutral. (As the recently-published Royal Economic Society volume on Keynes's activities during World War I amply documents, obtaining and conserving gold was at that time Britain's overriding wartime financial problem on the

international side.)

7. This assumption played an important part in the thinking and deliberations that culminated in the invention and implementation of SDRs, although that invention was in part motivated by the desire to find a safer substitute for gold than American dollars, rather than to augment international liquidity by providing extra reserves additional to the outflow of dollars.

8. Note the parallel between these two approaches to the international monetary system and the conflict in monetary theory between the Keynesian approach which assumes rigid wages and prices and unitarity elasticity of expectations, and the neo-quantity theory, which explicitly includes not only price trends but expectations about price trends as influences on monetary behaviour.

9. The perspective adopted here suggests a reinterpretation of the devaluation of sterling in 1967, which at that time seemed to be an outstanding example of how the International Monetary Fund system was intended to work, inasmuch as a major currency was devalued by an internationally accepted percentage that provoked no retaliatory devaluation by another major currency. The absence of retaliation could be understandable on the hypothesis that there ought to have been a general revaluation of European currencies against the dollar, and a devaluation of the pound relative to the other European currencies but not necessarily relative to the dollar. If the now fashionable view that devaluations take a long time to be effective is accepted, Britain's long travail since 1967 and her briefly healthy balance-of-payments position in spite of exceptional domestic inflation in the meantime can also be rationalised.

10. There is some reason to suspect that professional myopia has led both international monetary policy-makers and experts on international monetary organisation into overestimating the world welfare costs of international monetary crises, and also of sub-optimal adjustment policies. The cost of maintaining a class of officials capable of attending and obfuscating the proceedings of international monetary conferences, and of sending them to such conferences, is trivial. The inefficiencies created by controls, and the uncertainties generated by the imposition and administration of them, are probably quantitatively insignificant by comparison with the main forces that produce economic growth. It can be argued that so long as governments maintain reasonably full employment, or more accurately refrain from preventing the competitive system from doing so by gross monetary mismanagement, as they have learned to do after the disastrous policy errors of the 1930s, international monetary crises and international monetary changes and reforms are essentially froth — though highly visible froth — on the surface of the ongoing stream of world economic activity.

11. Some commentators have envisaged a three-reserve-currency system, the third currency being the Japanese yen. This vision seems to derive more from a holistic view of the attributes of economic power — as including a dependent monetary empire — than from a realistic appraisal of objective possibilities and of Japanese foreign economic policy.

12. What is generally misunderstood, in attempts to dispute the Friedman proposition on this point, is that the proposition relates to speculators as an aggregate. It is always possible to construct cases in which a small group of informed professional speculators profits from destabilising speculation at the expense of a larger group of amateur speculators, probably of shifting composition, who derive their finance from efficiency in some other activity.

13. Milton Friedman, 'The Case for Flexible Exchange Rates' in *ibid.*, *Essays in Positive Economics* (Chicago: University of Chicago Press, 1953).

14. J.E. Meade, *The Theory of International Economic Policy*, Vol. I, The Balance of Payments (London: Macmillan, 1951).

15. Thus, if there is an SDR standard and an excess supply of SDRs tending to

push up world prices in terms of SDRs, the nations in the system can collectively prevent an inflation of prices in terms of domestic currencies by contractionary demand-management policies that force their currencies to appreciate in terms of SDRs, and *vice versa*. Similarly, if there is a dollar standard and an excess supply of dollars, the other countries can prevent an inflation of prices in terms of domestic currencies by contractionary demand management, forcing an upward glide of their currencies in terms of dollar, and *vice versa*. In the SDR standard case, the authorities responsible for issuing SDRs would then have a signal to issue SDRs at a less or a more rapid rate. In the dollar standard case, the Federal Reserve in the United States would have a similar signal, to which it could if it wished respond with more alacrity. These observations suggest a modified interpretation of the famous 'n-1' or redundancy' problem: the extra degree of freedom could be used collectively by the n-1 countries to influence the inflationary or deflationary trend of prices in national currencies, and insofar as their exchange rate choices influence the rate of issue of the *numeraire* or reserve money, the trend of world prices in terms of the *numeraire* as well.

16. This scheme was actually first proposed by Donald B. Marsh in the late 1960s.

## Part IV

## ISSUES ON THE AGENDA

# CHAPTER 10

# Industrial Tariffs and Economic Spheres of Influence

HUGH CORBET

Almost straight after the international trade negotiations were opened in Tokyo in September 1973,[1] it did not seem too early to be considering what could happen if they came to grief, so tortuous had been the effort to get them started. The initiative for the negotiations was again largely taken by the United States, although for a variety of reasons, to do with both domestic politics and foreign diplomacy, the Nixon Administration had sought to lead from behind.[2] But it was the Johnson Administration which in 1968 embarked, after the successful conclusion of the Kennedy Round negotiations, on the thankless task of trying to maintain the international momentum of trade liberalisation.

Blame for the slow progress of events can be ascribed to several factors. When all is said and done, however, the nub of the problem has been the inability of political thought to keep pace with the rapid integration and growing interdependence of the world economy.[3] Now that the Tokyo Round negotiations are formally launched, to dwell on the consequences of their failure might help to strengthen the political will that, more than in previous rounds, is vital to their success — given the complexity, not to say enormity, of the issues they are meant to be addressing.

## Two Major Underlying Issues

The negotiations, which are being conducted in Geneva, are the seventh round under the General Agreement on Tariffs and Trade (GATT), the instrument by which the international commercial system has been governed for a quarter of a century. GATT rules and principles guided the restoration, in the 1950s and 1960s, of some semblance of order in world trade, following the disorders of the 1930s (and 1940s).[4] These last were characterised by protectionist excesses which led to autarkic and discriminatory policies (and worse). In the late 1960s, similar trends began to reappear and gather force, almost encouraged by the loss of impetus in the movement towards an open world economy.[5] Fortunately the monetary crisis of 1971 obliged governments to face up to the underlying tensions that have developed in the international system of trade and payments. Reforms are now being actively considered. This chapter concentrates on the trade aspects of the general crisis in international economic relations. But a prerequisite for a more liberal international trading system is a more liberal international monetary system.[6]

Essentially the GATT negotiations are between the United States, Japan and the European Community. Other industrialised countries and some developing ones will be involved to varying degrees. Indeed, the roles of the smaller trading partners could be significant, if only they realise as much.[7] The fact remains, though, unless the big three are able to agree there will be no overall agreement worth mentioning.

Two fundamental issues will need to be addressed constructively by the big three if the negotiations are not to founder and plunge them all in deeply troubled waters:

(1) One relates to the division of the free-enterprise world — for want of a better phrase — into economic spheres of influence. That prospect has developed because of the multiplying number of discriminatory trading arrangements that have been appearing on the world scene in recent years. It is at the heart of the question of what is to be done about remaining tariffs on industrial products traded among developed countries.

(2) The other issue relates to the isolation of commercial markets for temperate-zone farm commodities. For little or no impact has been made, either in the Kennedy Round or previous negotiations, on the rising trend of protection accorded to high-cost farmers in industrialised countries against the competition of low-cost producers in agricultural-exporting countries.

Neither issue is likely to be discussed in such bald terms. That is the way both are posed though by those, not only in the United States but also elsewhere, who are calling for the reform of the GATT system of international trade.

It is in the context of negotiations on the further liberalisation of international trade — dealing with more 'nitty gritty' questions — that the United States and others, including Japan,[8] expect to pursue reforms to the GATT system. That underlying purpose probably accounts for much of the Franco-British temporising which, combined with continuing monetary turmoil and the debilitating consequences of the Watergate affair, thwarted progress in the preparations for the negotiations. When the negotiations do begin in earnest, however, they are due to take two years to complete.

On this occasion the preparations for negotiations have been almost as important as the negotiations themselves. In that sense the negotiations began long ago. But by the same token they could take longer than expected to get thoroughly under way. This is because the negotiations as such will be very different from previous GATT rounds:

(a) Even on tariffs, it was agreed during and after the Kennedy Round marathon that the traditional mode of negotiation, based on reciprocal bargaining with 'concessions' extended unconditionally to all GATT countries on a most-favoured-nation (MFN) basis, had been played out and would have to be replaced by a new approach. [9]

(b) There is a second major departure in that the new GATT round is focussing in a concerted way on non-tariff interventions in international trade. By these are meant a wide variety of government measures which either by design or accident protect or favour domestic producers *vis-a-vis* foreign suppliers — at the expense of domestic consumers and tax-payers. [10]

(c) On all sides it is recognised,[11] although not necessarily accepted, that a serious attempt must be made to open trade in temperate-zone agricultural commodities. [12]

(d) Another important objective is to improve the present arrangements which are meant to provide safeguards against 'market disruption' caused by sudden surges of imports and yet provide security of access for new entrants to markets. [13]

On non-tariff interventions and 'safeguards' it appears that governments are at least on the same wavelength. Major points of controversy arise in both areas. But they are not likely to cause a breakdown in the negotiations.

## Non-tariff Barriers and Emergency Measures

Non-tariff measures include *inter alia* quantitative import restrictions and export constraints, customs valuation procedures, industrial standards, government subsidies and public procurement policies. Since the trade effects of such forms of public assistance are difficult, and in many cases impossible, to quantify it is accepted that for the most part they cannot be modified by reciprocal bargaining, in the way that tariffs have been modified in the past. [14] Governments accordingly envisage the principle of reciprocity being satisfied in a broad framework. Because it has been found that often several non-tariff measures serve to protect a single industry,[15] and more generally because of the high degree of substitutability between different categories of non-tariff protection, negotiations on them do have to be conducted over a wide range. Objectives must differ from category to category. Some non-tariff devices could be eliminated altogether. [16] It should be enough with others to remove trade-distorting side-effects.

With many non-tariff interventions, however, only an incremental approach seems feasible, involving initially an equal commitment by governments to general principles or rules of international competition, followed by a process of more or less continuous consultation and negotiation on their elaboration and implementation. Such codes of conduct might frequently amount to elaborations of existing GATT provisions. Codes have already been drafted on an *ad referendum* basis on industrial standards, customs valuation procedures and import licensing. This work commenced in the quiet period after the Kennedy Round negotiations. Work on further codes has been moving forward.

It has been proposed, as part of a broad strategy, that the present negotiations should be conducted on a *conditional* MFN basis, ensuring that only the parties to agreements can benefit therefrom. An equal commitment from all the major trading partners would thus ensure the application of the principle of reciprocity which is being stressed on all sides. [17] It should be explained that the principle of non-discrimination, a cornerstone of the GATT system, finds expression in the General Agreement's Article 1 which requires MFN treatment to be accorded *unconditionally* among all signatory countries except where, under conditions laid down in Article 24, a customs union or free trade association is being formed. [18] Another part of the proposed strategy was that the phased elimination of tariffs on industrial products traded among developed countries, with appropriate provisions for 'exceptions' and 'safeguards', should be one of the objectives of the negotiations. The conditional MFN approach would then be 'Gattable' in that the negotiations could be conducted under Article 24. This last concern has not bothered the European Community which, in its initial bargaining position, has proposed as a general rule, in relation to non-tariff problems, that 'the advantages which might derive from solutions comprising obligations that go beyond the GATT should be reserved for countries which in practice abide by these solutions'. [19]

Achieving the adherence of governments to rules of international competition will be no mean task. Proceeding on a conditional MFN basis could produce a strong incentive. The European Community has been worried that the Nixon Administration might not obtain from Congress sufficient authority to enable the United States to abide by negotiated agreements in the non-tariff field. On the other side American officials point out that the Brussels Commission, negotiating on behalf of the European Community, does not have an authority to negotiate on the non-tariff interferences that bother the high-technology industry of the United States, especially public procurement policies and government subsidies.[20] Industrial policy in the Common Market is still the perogative of national governments.

Indeed, there is concern in the United States[21] and Japan that when the European Community does set about agreeing on a common *industrial* policy, it might go to protectionist excesses in discriminating against external interests, much as its common agricultural policy has done. For that reason there is a strong interest in establishing, in respect of non-tariff measures, a framework of international obligations that would have to be observed by the new Europe in formulating a common industrial policy. This interest is not confined to exporters of manufacturers to Common Market countries. It is shared by many within the European Community.[22] Even so, some with a vested interest in Community preference and protection are liable to argue, perhaps invoking the cause of European unity to do so, that the Europe of the Nine should settle a common industrial policy before worrying about any international implications.

Action on non-tariff interventions is bound to touch the sensitive question — in terms of domestic politics — of 'national' sovereignty. That is inevitable if only because of the growing interdependence among nations. Non-tariff measures are further said to be intractable because many of them are instruments of industrial policy. But tariffs, too, are instruments of public assistance to industry. In domestic terms, commercial policy is concerned with the industrial structure of countries; internationally, it is concerned with the location of production where there are comparative cost advantages.[23]

The purpose of trade liberalisation is to bring about a better use of resources, both domestically and internationally, through greater specialisation on particular industries or on particular product lines within industries. Adjustment to changing market conditions, whether on the demand side or on the supply side, is a normal and continuous process in market-economy countries. It mainly takes place without the assistance of governments.[24] But in certain circumstances governments intervene to help industries adjust or to alleviate, at any rate, the social consequences of adjustment.

Now that tariffs have been reduced to very low nominal levels,[25] and non-tariff barriers are to be broached, it is widely argued that governments should put more emphasis on adjustment assistance.[26] If they do not it might be hard to induce support from firms and workers for the Tokyo Round negotiations. A clear distinction should therefore be drawn, maybe in a separate code, between 'fair' adjustment assistance to industry and 'unfair' feather-bedding of industry.[27] Dealing with non-tariff distortions, expanding the use of adjustment assistance and improving the safeguard mechanism are all bound up with one another in discussions on the reform of the GATT system.

Governments are generally agreed that temporary safeguard protection against sharp increases in import competition should be degressive according to a definite timetable, allied with a complementary programme of adjustment assistance and subject to multilateral surveillance.[28] The issue here is whether emergency protection should be applied on a discriminatory basis. The European Community is inclined to favour such a course where the source of abrupt 'market disruption' is confined to one or a few countries. In the past, however, insistence on escape-clause action being taken on a non-discriminatory basis has been self-defeating. For what has happened instead is that major trading powers with weak industries unable to cope with import competition have gone outside the GATT framework and negotiated 'voluntary' export restraints with the countries that are causing them difficulty. Yet the purpose of the principle of non-discrimination is to safeguard the interests of the small and middle powers in international trade. Their interest though, in cases of 'market disruption', is that emergency protection should be temporary. They should therefore support the consensus so far reached on a reformed safeguard mechanism.

What could be insisted upon is a new principle of multilaterality in situations where the principle of non-discrimination is relaxed.[29] In this way it might be possible to ensure multilateral surveillance in order to safeguard not only the interests of importing countries but also those of exporting countries. Japan may use her understandable preference for a non-disciminatory course as a bargaining counter in making sure that safeguards, while being made more liberally available, are applied under stricter conditions than before. There is a chance, also, that the same conditions might be applied to existing non-tariff devices, notably quantitative import restrictions and export constraints.

## Industrial Tariffs in Perspective

As governments, then, prepare to negotiate on non-tariff issues, adjustment assistance and safeguards it has been curious to find the

European Community still setting store by tariffs. Japan and the United States proposed as 'a working hypothesis' that customs duties on industrial products traded among developed countries should be substantially eliminated over a ten-year period — with appropriate safeguards and strict provisions for 'exceptions'. [30] Neither country pressed the proposition as hard as it might have done. Both have been distracted by other cares. Following the refusal of the European Community even to consider the substantial elimination of industrial tariffs, the Congress in the United States has placed limitations on the Nixon Administration's authority to negotiate on tariffs, ruling out their phased elimination. The negotiations have suffered a severe setback. What has been at stake?

In any attempt to put extant tariffs in perspective it is not enough to stress how low *on average* they are nowadays. Averaging tariffs conceals the high rates payable on certain products in the American, Canadian and Japanese schedules. And low *nominal* tariffs, particularly on semi-manufactures, can represent high *effective* levels of protection. It is plain that more needs to be said.

Political perceptions of economic needs tend inevitably to lag behind reality. Governments appear to be having much difficulty in placing what they perceive as commercial policy problems in an up-to-date context. For the way a problem is perceived and understood is influenced by experience. And the policy experience guiding governments as they prepared for the Tokyo Round negotiations derived from years of trading in an international system characterised by acute and growing exchange-rate disequilibrium. It is thus understandable that countries hope, and will probably attempt, to resolve through the negotiations many problems — which although experienced as trade problems — have been a reflection of exchange-rate disequilibrium that hopefully is now being corrected in the *de facto* reform of the monetary system.

Flexible exchange rates — fixed but adjustable rather than floating — have been written into a new monetary order.[31] They remove the balance-of-payments rationale for tariff protection. This is not to suggest though that tariffs no longer matter. Tariffs remain a distorting factor in the allocation of resources by affording domestic producers a price premium over foreign producers.

In this respect the tariffs of the European Community do not present a serious obstacle to the low-priced (and high-quality) exports of Japan or to the high-technology exports of the United States. Tokyo and Washington urged the phased elimination of substantially all tariffs as a means of overcoming the economic and political tensions being generated by the proliferation of the European Community's discriminatory tariff arrangements around the

Mediterranean, in Africa and even farther away. If the tariffs of the major industrial countries were to be phased out, there would be the prospect of preferential tariff arrangements being diminished over time, thereby easing tensions and restoring some credibility to the principle of non-discrimination.

But the very idea of phasing out the European Community's common external tariff fills some Europeans with foreboding. The fear, somewhat ill-defined, is that the Common Market will fall apart and, of course, that feeling is exploited by others more concerned with maintaining protection. Attention should also be drawn to the bureaucratic interest of the Brussels Commission in retaining a customs union to administer. In its 'overall' approach to the Tokyo Round negotiations, the European Community agreed that *inter alia* the customs union 'may not be called in question.'[32] If the common external tariff, however, is really a major unifying force in the European Community today, it says little for the spirit of European unity about which so much is made. It will say even less if tariff discrimination against the rest of the world is still a major unifying force in ten years time.

Part of the trouble has been psychological in that the European Community's common external tariff, its commercial agreements with 'outside' countries and its common agricultural policy have come to be regarded as symbols of European unity, proof to the world of the new Europe's virility.[33] Any criticism of these policies, whether from inside or outside the Common Market, is interpreted by some as an attack on the Common Market itself.[34] Yet the process of European integration must be pursued in harmony with the integration of the world economy as a whole if it is not to incur the hostility of countries which happen to be located elsewhere.

This is the spirit in which the European Community should be encouraged to pursue integration in the 1970s and 1980s. Policies must adjust to circumstances which have greatly changed since the 1950s. This means that Europeans must find a more constructive approach to unity than what is tantamount, in an age of increasing interdependence, to provoking economic conflict with the rest of the world. Such a Bismarkian approach to unity is something which Europe is meant to have learnt something about over the last hundred years.

There is thus a need in the European Community to develop a political consensus on the maintenance of international economic order that is responsive to the issues facing the world economy. Little headway will be made in that direction, however, if the Commission is allowed to get away with its obsessive and unfounded belief that tariff-free trade is impossible unless all conditions of competition are equalised. In the first draft of the European Community's initial bargaining position, the Commission asserted that 'tariff-free trade is impossible without international organisation and harmonisation of national policy considerations — for instance, taxation, social legislation and measures to stimulate economic development'.[35] The passage was among those eliminated from the document finally agreed by the Council of Ministers. But the Commission's obsession has since persisted in intruding itself into public discussion.[36]

No trade can take place if all competitive conditions are equalised. This is easily explained. International trade is based on cost *differences*. There is a wide gulf conceptually between (a) ruling out distortions to competitive conditions resulting from government interventions, which would come under the heading of one non-tariff measure or another, and (b) ruling out differences in competitive conditions resulting from varying taxation, social benefits and company laws. The first is a feasible and necessary part of any attempt to liberalise international trade. The second is neither feasible nor necessary among countries not aspiring to economic and political union.

## Erosion of Multilateral System

To consider the future of international economic relations, the Organisation for Economic Co-operation and Development (OECD) set up a special high-level group on 'trade and related problems', under the chairmanship of Jean Rey, the former President of the Commission of the European Community. In its report the Rey Committee identified three major areas of concern. The first of these, 'the weakening of the multilateral framework of trade and payments established twenty five years ago', has been the chief concern of this chapter.[37] The committee observed, as the present writer has done here and previously in several other essays elsewhere,[38] that 'the weakening of the system applies less to the mechanisms themselves than to the ways in which the general principles laid down by the GATT are applied.

'The system outlined in 1947/48 by the United Nations Conference on Trade and Employment, held in Havana, was based on multilateral trade liberalisation and the principle of non-discrimination. From the start these principles have of course been subject to exceptions, in particular for the benefit of the established trade partnerships between European mother countries and their former colonies, but these exceptions were clearly delimited and generally accepted . . . Over the past twenty years,' the Rey Committee continued, 'the proportion of international trade to which the most-favoured-nation clause applies has been considerably reduced, both by the creation of important regional groupings such as the European Community and the European Free Trade Association (EFTA) and by "association" and trade agreements concluded by the Community.'

What has been happening? First the European Community, then EFTA and finally the 'merger' between the two were sanctioned by Article 24, although its conditions were only broadly satisfied in each case. But a waiver of GATT rules was required for the 'association' agreements that the Common Market negotiated under the Yaoundé Convention with eighteen ex-colonies of the Six. Concern over the establishment of new preferential trade arrangements, falling far short of the requirements for free trade associations, was expressed by the United States and other countries, but high foreign policy considerations — to do with the promotion of European unity — prevailed in the end. Similarly the United States, and necessarily other countries outside Europe, went along with the extension by the Community of its 'association' agreements to four ex-colonies of what was then a non-member under the Arusha Convention.

More serious concern was expressed by the United States and others, however, when the Common Market negotiated at the outset of the 1970s another series of preferential trade arrangements with a number of non-ex-colonies around the Mediterranean, namely Spain, Israel and some North African countries, adding to those negotiated earlier with Greece and Turkey. By then high foreign policy considerations were having less influence on the American position. For the political justification for the Community's 'association' policy, the promotion of European unity, has been wearing thin where American eyes are concerned. Perhaps this has partly been because, as the Soviet threat to Western Europe has receded and as the countries of Western Europe have recovered their wealth and position, there has been a noticeable decline of public interest in Western Europe in a supra-national European union.

Meanwhile other groups of countries have also exploited Article 24 to negotiate preferential trade arrangements thinly disguised as free trade associations. There is the Latin American Free Trade Association, the Central American Common Market, a range of groupings in Africa and the New Zealand-Australia Free Trade Association besides others. Apart perhaps from the Anglo-Irish Free Trade Agreement, all of them, like their European predecessors, have failed to comply with all the conditions set out in Article 24.[39]

With the successful conclusion of the 'enlargement' negotiations, the European Community has negotiated another series of 'association' agreements with the EFTA countries which did not apply to join the Common Market. In addition, the Mediterranean, African and Caribbean members of the Commonwealth, as well as a number of island states in the Pacific and Indian oceans, have been offered the choice of 'association' or some other form of preferential trade arrangement. There will thus be centred on the European Community a trading block of around sixty countries accounting for over 60 per cent of world commerce.

Not surprisingly, preferential trade arrangements have become, as indicated earlier, a major issue in commercial diplomacy since it is thought they are progressively undermining the international economic order so painfully restored in the two decades after World War II. What is to be done about the principle of non-discrimination therefore has to be on the agenda of any meaningful negotiations on the reform of the international trading system. The larger questions will be difficult to avoid when the principle is discussed in relation to codes of behaviour on non-tariff interventions and to the application of emergency protection. If the principle is abandoned altogether the way could be opened to discriminatory trading arrangements all round the world between small groups of countries and in small groups of products. There is increasing talk of a world of trading blocks which nobody seems to want and yet everybody seems to encourage.[40] For the free-enterprise world appears to be polarising on the European Community, Japan and the United States.

Trends in this direction are noticeable already — some less formal than others. The United States and Canada have evolved a number of special bilateral arrangements, such as Canadian exemption from American restrictions on investment and 'overland' imports of petroleum, free trade between them in automotive products, matched tariff reductions on many products primarily traded between the two countries and consultative procedures on a number of economic policies.

While the mainstream of official thinking in Japan still favours a multilateral approach to economic problems, there is increasing interest in a regional approach, which has been encouraged by the tendency of the United States and the European Community to impose constraints on Japanese trade. Special economic relationships with Japan have not developed very far, but growing import requirements for raw materials and growing outflows of capital are being expressed in terms of, respectively, long-term supply contracts and joint business ventures. With Britain's incorporation in the European Community, Australia and New Zealand, if not Canada as well, have been obliged to look to Japan as a buyer of their agricultural exports.[41] Japan has recently proposed to Australia an organisation for economic co-operation in the Asian-Pacific region and this is now being actively studied in Tokyo and other capitals.

There is also increasing interest in an Asian yen market and a continuing discussion, at academic and business levels, of a Pacific trading community.

## Consequences of a World of Trading Blocks

There have been fairly clear economic and political reasons for regional developments in Western Europe and, for that matter, in North America and more recently in the Western Pacific. Movements towards greater regionalism in international economic relations were generally regarded early on as consistent with the 'universalist' principles of the GATT and the International Monetary Fund (IMF). They were believed to constitute a vanguard, as it were, for the further liberalisation of trade and investment on a multilateral or world-wide basis. Until the late 1960s events seemed to bear out this rationalisation. Since then, though, there have been reasons — apart from special relationships — for questioning whether the sequential movement towards more and more open markets on a multilateral plane will be maintained.

First, there appears to be developing a greater concern with internal (domestic or regional) economic and social problems, and correspondingly less willingness to accept external (or international) restraints on internal actions. Second, a smaller relative role for trade in the economic activity of progressively service-oriented countries, as reflected in employment statistics, is becoming increasingly evident. The trend here is tending to reinforce the priority being given to internal economic and social objectives. Third, the United States has been trying, particularly in recent years, to reduce its economic interdependence with Japan by restrictive trade arrangements in such industries as steel and textiles. Furthermore, the European Community is seeking to impose limitations on its trade with Japan, being possibly over-impressed by Japanese competitive strength. Fourth, there is evidence that the operations of some multilateral enterprises are carried out somewhat autonomously on a regional West European or North American basis, having once decided the overall corporate objectives and the allocation of resources. Fifth, and of most immediate significance, it is becoming increasingly evident that efforts to bring about a more flexible international monetary system could afford a further impetus towards regionalism. This is because, short of completely flexible exchange rates throughout the system, government intervention not only in the European Community but also in North America and in the Western Pacific would probably take special account of regional relationships.

The development of inward-directed blocks would run serious dangers:

(a) It could produce further pressures towards political isolationism and commercial protectionism in the United States, Japan and the European Community.

(b) It could result in discriminatory actions, especially in Western Europe, against American overseas investment, provoking retaliation in the United States.

(c) It could seriously undermine the effectiveness of international organisations formed on the basis of nation-states. This in turn could antagonise developing countries, and smaller developed ones, that rely heavily on multilateral institutions to express their interests in the international economic order.

(d) It could become a form of political as well as economic disengagement. This might encourage a political *rapprochement* between countries in Western Europe and Japan with Eastern block countries in a manner deemed by the United States to be inimical to its economic, political and strategic interests, producing tensions between the Western allies.

(e) It would probably generate pressures for certain developing countries to link, or to link even closer than at present, to a particular block — thereby extending economic spheres of influence.

(f) It could exacerbate old fears in South-east Asia of ambitions in Japan for 'a greater co-prosperity sphere'.

These are some of the possible implications of a continued movement away from the principles of non-discrimination that would need to be explored in any examination of GATT reform.

## Optional Negotiating Techniques

When the European Community is more familiar with these high policy issues, and with the technical difficulties also of dealing with remaining tariffs, it might be more sympathetic to the interest of the United States, Japan and others in reasserting the 'universalist' principles of the international economic order. It is to the technical difficulties of the optional negotiating techniques on outstanding tariffs that the discussion will now turn.

How low are industrial tariffs? Their average level, weighted by world trade and including duty-free items, is now 6.0 per cent for the original European Community (7.1 per cent for the United Kingdom), 6.2 per cent for the United States and 9.6 per cent for Japan.[43] Merely halving the tariffs that are outstanding, which was the objective of the last GATT round, might not be deemed worth the effort — as mentioned in Chapter 1. In fact, more so than in previous rounds, the Tokyo Round negotiations have needed to be motivated by a high objective. That objective had to be compelling enough to induce in the major trading partners a political commitment to the eventual success of the negotiations. This was another powerful reason for setting tariff-free trade as one of the major goals. Without a high objective the political drive has been weak.

What of the negotiating techniques that might be employed? Four options are being explored: (a) negotiations on traditional lines based on reciprocal bargaining and MFN treatment; (b) negotiations on the harmonisation of tariffs; (c) negotiations on a sector-by-sector basis; and (d) negotiations for an agreement on progressive, linear and automatic reductions over an agreed period on the lines of the European Community and EFTA.[44] These four options are not mutually exclusive. And there would probably be in each of them, to varying degrees, an element of item-by-item haggling. Indeed, strategies could be devised to combine two or more of the above techniques. But in order to sort out their advantages and disadvantages, they will be treated separately in the below discussion.[45]

## Significance of Extant Tariffs

Although considerably reduced, the tariffs that remain are by no means insignificant. In many cases they might be said to represent the 'hard core' of protection for the industries concerned. It can be argued that it is the high tariff rates that protect the really inefficient industries and that once tariffs have been reduced to very low levels the remaining inefficiency is small. What is overlooked here is that any tariff has a 'nuisance value', in affording protection to domestic industries, in terms of customs clearance and customs valuation problems. The reduction of tariffs to the last few percentage points does not eliminate this protective effect. What also needs to be remembered is that effective rates of protection, which takes into account the duties levied on material inputs, are inclined to be higher than nominal rates of duty listed in tariff schedules. Furthermore extant tariffs represent, in another sense, a nuisance tax on firms which are otherwise prepared to adjust production patterns to achieve a greater degree of specialisation in their international operations. This point is a growing concern of multinational enterprises.

After the years of depression and hostilities, order has been generally restored — if somewhat uncertainly — to the world economy, but the international trading system still discriminates against the interests of developing countries. Either as an automatic consequence of the bargaining process, or through the exclusion of sensitive items from negotiations, the tariff reductions agreed in successive GATT rounds have mainly been of interest to the developed world. Tariffs on goods of export interest to developing countries continue to be comparatively high. Moreover, where agricultural products are concerned there is considerable disarray in international trade and it bears heavily on the interests of developing countries, but more especially on the interests of a number of developed countries that are traditional exporters of temperate-zone foodstuffs. Trade in farm products has been accorded a 'special status' in GATT negotiations which has meant their exclusion, too, from the bargaining process. As a result no appreciable impact has been made in the post-war period on the growing protection that has been given to farmers in industrialised countries. The price and income-support programmes that have been implemented for their benefit constitute the most serious problem in the field of non-tariff distortions of competition. Non-tariff barriers, as they are more popularly (but less accurately) termed, have been increasingly exposed as tariff barriers have been lowered. GATT negotiators have not yet come to grips with them, but research and experience has shown that they are not a general problem; instead, they are a series of specific problems relating to trades in specific goods between specific countries—to repeat the phrase of the introductory chapter.

It is thus possible to identify certain criteria by which could be judged the various negotiating techniques on tariffs that might be adopted as the basis for the Tokyo Round negotiations. For a further endeavour to liberalise international trade to carry conviction it needs, to contain effective means for dealing with (a) outstanding tariffs on industrial products, (b) non-tariff distortions of competition, (c) agricultural-support programmes and (d) market-access for developing-country exports.

## Another MFN Round

The MFN clause, expressing the GATT's principle of non-discrimination, requires tariff concessions that have been negotiated between two or more signatory countries to be extended unconditionally to all adherents to the General Agreement. In the past it has therefore had the effect of limiting the progress of multilateral negotiations to the pace of the least willing participants. The Kennedy Round negotiations, based on linear tariff reductions, were designed to overcome resistance to progress posed by the traditional system, but on the 'sensitive' products in tariff schedules they in effect reverted to item-by-item bargaining. Before the completion of the marathon negotiations, which nearly broke down several times, it was recognised that a different approach would be required in any future tariff-cutting exercise.[46]

Even so, a second Kennedy Round could build, perhaps, on the success of the first. With fresh minds on the task this would seem a politically feasible possibility. Another MFN round would continue, moreover, the evolution of GATT negotiations and involve no radical departure from established bargaining procedures. Finally, a second Kennedy Round would be consistent, some still might argue, with a continuing need for consolidation. But against these advantages can be set a range of formidable drawbacks.

GATT experience suggests that new negotiating procedures are subject to diminishing returns in the short and medium terms. Only two out of the six rounds of GATT negotiations achieved substantial success, namely the first and sixth, each of which amounted to a fresh approach to trade liberalisation. As already mentioned, the Kennedy Round negotiations retrogressed significantly in the direction of item-by-item haggling, especially over politically sensitive items on national tariff schedules. They nearly broke down several times. With a repeat performance the chances of failure would be greatly increased. For 'hard core' tariffs are unlikely to yield to conventional approaches towards liberalising trade.[47] Stronger resistance can be expected from the vested interests protected by them. Another universal type of negotiation would thus probably be so encumbered with 'exceptions' that the effort required to reach agreement could well far exceed the will to do so.

Secondly, another multilateral effort along traditional lines would certainly have to be motivated by a high objective, as argued already. For governments to be galvanised into action the aims of a seventh MFN round really should include the total removal of extant tariff barriers. Yet, as already found, some of the leading trading nations are likely to balk at the finality of such a purpose.[48]

Thirdly, even if many governments are willing to proceed to tariff-free trade between industrialised countries, GATT procedure has in the past necessitated simultaneous agreement on the goals of a multilateral negotiation. Arriving at a 'common denominator' is difficult at the best of times. While some countries hope for unfair advantages — in terms of their balances of payments — from what might outwardly appear fair bargains, others have an opposite expectation and, at least in the initial stages, are very reluctant to negotiate. The MFN clause in the GATT has the effect, therefore, of limiting the progress of negotiations to the pace of the least willing participants — as preparations for the Tokyo Round have proved.

Among those with 'low expectations', when it comes to GATT negotiations, have been the temperate-zone countries which are established exporters of farm output, notably the United States, Canada, Australia, New Zealand, Argentina and Denmark. Over the last twenty years the liberalisation of trade in agricultural products has lagged far behind that in the industrial sector. Along with many developing countries, for whom agriculture also constitutes a vital source of foreign exchange earnings, they have been continually pressing for the situation to be remedied. Instead, with the implementation of the European Community's common agricultural policy, it has been worsening. And herein lies the fourth drawback to another multilateral MFN negotiation. For this approach has placed agricultural products in a special position considerably less amenable to bargaining than industrial products. What is more, the provisions for 'exceptions' have been used, in six previous rounds, to exclude from the bargaining process the labour-intensive and relatively simple products in which developing countries often enjoy a comparative advantage.

Lastly, if the momentum of trade liberalisation is to be resumed, a bold and imaginative initiative is required as an effective counter to the protectionist trends which have been developing in North America and Western Europe. From this point of view a seventh MFN round would be too dreary and prosaic.

## Sector-by-Sector Negotiations

Some inkling of what might be undertaken through the sector-by-sector approach can be obtained from an examination of the Kennedy Round negotiation on chemical products. An interesting precedent for such a strategy lies in the 'dominant supplier' authority of President Kennedy's Trade Expansion Act of 1962. This act empowered the United States Administration to negotiate tariff reductions of up to 100 per cent on those products in which the United States and the European Community together accounted for 80 per cent of free world trade.[49] The authority could be renewed to provide for the progressive extension of free trade through (a) expanding the definition of the countries to be covered by the basic statistic authorising negotiations and (b) reducing the percentage of free world trade required to qualify an industry for trade liberalisation.

Since the conclusion of the Kennedy Round negotiations, however, the case for the sector-by-sector approach has been concentrated on the concept of free trade in those sectors of industry in which the major trading nations have both a significant export and a significant import interest. Free trade in both directions would thus involve changes in the composition of specialisation. But no major industrial readjustments would be implied.

Three broad categories of products can be identified where the sectoral approach might be both desirable and possible: (a) products which have a high technological content; (b) products that are already internationally made and traded; and (c) semi-manufactured products or investment materials that are themselves the inputs of other industries.[50]

An attractive feature of the technique is that it would enable the negotiation process to be greatly simplified as only the countries chiefly concerned in each particular trade would be taking part in the discussion. With this approach it would be possible, too, to negotiate on all barriers to a particular trade, encompassing the non-tariff barriers which most hamper the export of sophisticated products. In addition, the approach, where applicable, could afford governments greater leeway in that it would divide protectionist forces on the home front and permit the exclusion of genuinely sensitive industries. Apart from other problems, a number of technical impediments to the approach have been revealed.

It is not easy to isolate clearly defined sectors of industry in which free trade could be amicably applied. Canadian officials have found this to be the case in their efforts to extend the Canadian-American automotive agreement to other products. Because of the input-output linkages between industries in a modern economy, the national participants in a sectoral negotiation would be put at an advantage, or at a disadvantage, by differences in tariff and other policies affecting their costs, while free trade in their products would affect the relative cost positions of user industries.[51] With the repercussions of liberalisation in one sector on other sectors differing from country to country, there could be extremely serious differences over the definition of sectors, which would be all the greater if the objective fell short of tariff-free trade in the industries concerned. Negotiations could well be deadlocked at the outset over such definitional problems (which may explain to a cynic why the sectoral approach is favoured in some quarters).

While it might be possible to cover them in a sectoral negotiation, non-tariff distortions of competition are far too complex to be broached in a piecemeal fashion, in the course of tackling tariffs. Non-tariff interferences in international trade need to be approached on a broad front. A general consensus has developed in favour of general codes of competition relating to the various categories of non-tariff protection underpinned by an institutional framework for more or less continuous consultations and negotiations with an effective complaints and arbitration procedure.

Research has not yet disclosed many industries in which the technique would be at all applicable. Serious doubts are therefore cast on the prospects for obtaining a sufficient degree of reciprocity among the major trading nations to render a sector-by-sector approach a worthwhile proposition as a basis for the Tokyo Round talks. That said, it is true that, in view of the large number of specifically sectorial problems, negotiations are likely to proceed at a certain stage and in certain areas by broadly defined sectors of industry. And it is also true that proponents of the sectoral approach have always envisaged it being combined with other negotiating techniques. But the problem of achieving reciprocity would remain difficult.

If the sector-by-sector approach were to be adopted, agriculture should be an early candidate for negotiation, but the first goal would heed to the harmonisation of domestic agricultural-support policies rather than free trade. There would be a temptation though to have such negotiations aimed at reaching international commodity agreements designed to raise and stabilise prices. Harry G. Johnson, of the London School of Economics, has argued that this temptation should be resisted. Concentration by UNCTAD 'on generalising the benefits of agricultural protection in developed countries through the intractable medium of international commodity agreements, instead of attacking the economic inefficiency and social immorality of protecting agriculture in the advanced countries at the expense of the incomes of competing producers in poor countries, has resulted in virtually no progress being made in the field of primary commodity trade'. [52]

The industries, however, in which the sectoral approach would be most applicable, at least theoretically, are the ones in which the industrially advanced countries have a commanding lead and the economically backward countries are at a comparative disadvantage. Not only would a strategy based on this approach tend to discriminate against the interests of developing countries. It would be seen to do so.

In a liberal climate of opinion, the flexibility of the approach might be regarded as an advantage, but that very flexibility would be a great disadvantage when protectionist forces are influencing the overall situation. [53] For in the latter circumstances more industries would be by-passed as 'sensitive' areas. But even in favourable circumstances, sector-by-sector negotiations would be painstakingly slow and subject, also, to possible default on the part of a major trading nation.

## Tariff Harmonisation

For much of the period of the Kennedy Round negotiations, the issue of 'tariff disparities' was pursued, mainly by the European

Community. It was argued that disparities between high and low rates of duty in different countries on certain items made it impossible to apply the linear method of tariff reduction. In the end, the negotiations were successfully concluded, although they had to resort to item-by-item bargaining.

After the implementation of the Kennedy Round agreement, the United States, Canada and Japan have relatively more items bearing rates of customs duty above 15 per cent than does the European Community. The disparities issue was therefore raised again in the preparations for the Tokyo Round negotiations. But the chances of inducing the United States, never mind other countries with high rates in their tariff schedules, to make unrequited concessions for the sake of achieving 'tariff harmonisation' are as remote in the 1970s as they were in the 1960s. For the very idea implies a rejection of the principle of reciprocity. It is suggested that a lesser number of high rates could be greatly reduced in return for a greater number of low rates being reduced by small amounts. But a slight lowering of already low tariffs holds few attractions for large industrial exporters not greatly troubled by tariffs anyway.

Apart from there being little economic point in having tariffs in line from country to country, the basic premise of tariff harmonisa- tion, namely that the most protective element of a tariff is to be found in the last few percentage points, is not borne out by theoretical or practical testimony. There is the point made earlier about the protective effect of para-tariff barriers. But it is more plausible to expect the early cuts to generate more additional trade than cuts eliminating the last few percentage points of a formerly high tariff. [54]

During the early 1950s low-tariff countries were concerned that in bilateral negotiations (and multilateral negotiations in the GATT are in fact a complex of bilateral exchanges with all concessions negotiated being extended to all contracting parties on an uncon- ditional MFN basis) they were at a disadvantage because they had little compensation to offer in return for major or worthwhile concessions from high-tariff countries. Two sets of proposals there- fore received serious consideration. [55]

1. *Low Tariff Club*: In the Council of Europe, the low-tariff countries proposed the imposition, over a three-year period, of a ceiling on tariffs, so that those on trade among countries ad- hering to the agreement would not exceed (a) 25 per cent on finished industrial products and food items, (b) 15 per cent on semi-finished goods and (c) 5 per cent on raw materials. The Low Tariff Club was designed as a step in the integration of

Western Europe; all the same, the possibility of non-European countries adhering was not excluded.[56]

2. *French Plan*: With a view to harmonising tariffs rather than reducing those at high levels, the French proposed a plan which, in its revised form as the GATT Plan, would have required participating countries to reduce the average unweighted incidence of their tariffs by 10 per cent in three successive years. While governments would have been fairly free to chose the items for reductions, ten broad sectors of traded goods were chosen where the 30 per cent reduction had to apply, in order to ensure that adherents to the agreement did not concentrate the reductions in a single area. Furthermore, the full reduction would not have been required where tariffs in a given sector were below an agreed 'ceiling', and no reduction at all would have been required where tariffs were below an agreed 'floor'.[57]

What attracted political support for the GATT Plan was its attempt to substitute a formula of automatic reductions for the uncertainties inherent in reciprocal bargaining. It represented an attempt to overcome the disparities issue, but, more important, it also anticipated the problem of lists of exceptions — of industrial products deemed to be sensitive to import competition.

The majority of contracting parties to the GATT supported the plan. It was blocked, though, by the opposition of the United States and Britain. In the end, the success of the European Community and EFTA, in reducing internal tariffs by an automatic formula similar to the French proposals, strengthened American interest in an across-the-board approach to tariff reductions. This was reflected in the Trade Expansion Act of 1962 and in the Kennedy Round negotiations which followed.

## Progressive, Linear and Automatic Reductions

Since then the idea has been receiving even more widespread attention. Moreover, serious consideration has been given to the elimination of substantially all industrial tariffs, perhaps within ten years, as an objective of American trade policy. That was a major recommendation of President Nixon's Williams Commission as it has been of several reports from liberal trade quarters in the United States.[58] Indeed, as argued earlier, it remains difficult to envisage future multilateral negotiations making progress unless they are motivated by such a high objective.

An agreement on the progressive, linear and automatic reduction and elimination of tariffs on industrial products traded among developed countries, involving a treaty commitment, might be visualised as an extension of the GATT Plan of the 1950s or of the technique successfully employed in the Common Market and EFTA in the 1960s. It would enable countries interested in global free trade to proceed towards that goal without being detained by others not yet ready to advance that far. In any case few developed countries would abstain from an agreement which embraced the United States, Japan and an enlarged European Community.

What such an agreement would offer is an assertive and inspiring counter to protectionist forces in North America and Western Europe. Yet as a fresh approach to trade liberalisation on a world-wide scale it would avoid the diminishing returns of a second Kennedy Round exercise.[59]

By contrast to another MFN negotiation, the proposal itself would not require all, or most, leading industrial countries to agree on the desirability of global free trade before discussions could begin. The pace of negotiations would therefore be decided by the most eager and not by the most reluctant. Nor would those prepared to lower trade barriers be obliged to give a 'free ride' to countries unwilling to reciprocate if only those countries which adhered to the agreement were allowed to benefit from its arrangements. The GATT's inter-pretation of the principle of non-discrimination in international trade would not be infringed because the strategy could be authorised under the article of the GATT which provides for exceptions from this general rule.[60]

By contrast to the sectoral approach, an automatic formula for progressive and linear tariff reductions would eliminate prevarica-tion and present, instead, a clear and over-riding objective for trade policy. The set timetable, along with the pre-arranged goal of zero tariff positions, would make it very difficult to exclude protectionist strongholds from the system. A treaty commitment to eliminate all, or substantially all, tariffs would indeed be a powerful instrument for overcoming 'hard core' tariffs.

If the developed countries could agree on an all-embracing strategy governing trade among themselves, they should also be able to agree on how to embolden the less developed countries to exploit the opportunities of world trade rather than indulge, as they often do, in uneconomic import substitution. Whether it is to be by aid or trade, or a combination of both, an international solution to the problem of the poor depends upon agreement among the rich. A tariff-free trade arrangement among developed countries could provide for a self-eliminating scheme of non-reciprocal tariff pre-ferences, encouraging less developed countries to penetrate indus-trial markets.[61]

In the United States the question of 'fair competition' is well to the fore. There have been proposals that governments should develop international rules of competition, or codes of conduct, for dealing with 'unfair trade practices' including techniques by which governments are thought to enhance the ability of their products to penetrate the markets of other countries by indirect subsidies, either for their manufacture or for their export. By providing a treaty commitment, an agreement to eliminate tariffs according to a pre-arranged schedule could probably provide a more effective institutional framework for 'harmonising' non-tariff distortions of international competition than have the *ad hoc* procedures of GATT experience.

Tied to the agreement there could be, as there is in the Stockholm Convention, the EFTA constitution, an undertaking to consult and negotiate on those policies and practices which have the effect of frustrating the benefits expected from free trade. The agreement could, indeed cover adherence to rules of competition covering such difficult issues as restrictive business practices, rights of establishment (a serious bone of foreign contention with Japan), public procurement policies, anti-dumping measures and government aids to industry.[62]

When it comes to non-tariff barriers the trade in temperate-zone agricultural products is the most sorely affected. Solving the complex problems relating to this trade, given the social and political issues posed by the farming communities of protectionist countries, will necessitate considerable patience and goodwill whatever policy option is adopted. Through the commitment to consult and negotiate, it should be possible, however, to devise as part of a broad trade agreement a programme for harmonising support policies (as may, in any case, be required in a seventh MFN round or under a sector-by-sector strategy). The longer-run purpose of the programme should be the elimination of protective devices that distort and disrupt without achieving appreciable domestic benefits.

## Consequences of Aiming Low

If, then, the substantial elimination of extant tariffs by the developed countries was after all one of the objectives of the Tokyo Round negotiations, it would involve securing agreement on a timetable of linear and automatic tariff reductions spread over a number of years, together with an agreement on criteria by which industries could be excepted, perhaps only temporarily, from the general movement towards tariff-free trade among industrial economies. It might be necessary to divide the timetable in two with the second part requiring a renewed mandate from governments and/or legislatures. Such a negotiation would anyway be relatively straight-forward and would accord to tariffs a degree of attention that corresponds to their reduced significance in a world of flexible exchange rates. The resources of commercial diplomacy could then concentrate on the items on the agenda which are economically more significant, namely safeguards against market disruption, non-tariff intervention and agricultural protection.

But if the tariff objective falls markedly short of 'substantial elimination', as seems almost certain at the time of writing, governments will have to find agreement on an alternative approach. It is generally acknowledged, as intimated earlier, that another Kennedy Round type of negotiation is out of the question. That leaves, of the negotiating techniques which have survived public scrutiny, the proposals for a harmonisation of tariffs or an industry-by-industry approach (or a combination of them). Both provide considerable scope for bureaucratic differences over technical questions. With the former there would be the problem of determining the appropriate level to which tariffs should be 'harmonised'; and with the latter there would be the problem of defining industries, each country's view being influenced by its international competitivity on the border between one industry and another. In the final analysis, neither approach offers much scope for reciprocity, which is plainly vital to the bargaining process.

There is accordingly a strong likelihood of the preparations for negotiations on tariffs getting bogged down in a morass of technicalities. Such a development would be extremely serious. For it could sap what political will there is to see the overall negotiations through to a successful conclusion. At the very least it would divert energies away from negotiations on the other, more substantive, issues of international concern. But there is another set of possible interactions which need to be borne in mind.

It will be recalled that the American and Japanese interest in tariff negotiations is to obtain an agreement which would guarantee the eventual elimination of preferential tariff arrangements, not because of their economic impact which is minor, but because of the political tensions they are generating and, more fundamentally, because they are undermining the international economic order.[63] Strictly speaking the principle of non-discrimination is an instrument of tariff policy. Under the GATT, however, it applies to non-tariff policies and practices and, also, to the implementation of emergency protection. Again the analysis is too technical to be pursued here.[64] But if the American and Japanese interest in gradually reasserting that principle in respect to tariffs is frustrated, it could be extremely difficult to persuade the United States and Japan to accept the relaxation of MFN treatment in respect to non-tariff interventions and emergency protection, which is what the European Community appears to want.

Differences between the major trading powers do not have to result in a breakdown in the negotiations to reinforce the trends towards a world of trading blocks. They only have to result in deep disappointment and an even greater sense of frustration. In the frustrated countries, the long-term direction of policy would be bound to change, whatever might be superficially agreed for the time being. If none of the major trading powers were prepared thereafter to champion the GATT system it would be difficult to contain the further loss of confidence in the international economic order that would ensue.

In the light of what is at stake in the Tokyo Round negotiations, the major trading powers need time for them all to acquaint themselves at all levels — legislative, executive and public opinion — with the issues involved, both tangible and intangible. Little irretrievable should be lost by political delays provided the technical analysis of problems can and does proceed. But a technical grasp of the issues will not be enough. What will be needed in the end is statesmanship.

### NOTES AND REFERENCES

1. In this chapter are combined two articles. The bulk of the chapter reproduces Hugh Corbet, 'Division of the World into Economic Spheres of Influence', *Pacific Community*, Tokyo, January 1974. The discussion of negotiating techniques draws on Corbet, 'Industrial Tariffs and Spheres of Influence', *The Round Table*, London, April 1973.

2. Much of the political background is discussed in Corbet, 'Australian Commercial Diplomacy in a New Era of Negotiation', *Australian Outlook*, Melbourne, April 1972.

3. This point was developed in Corbet, 'Role of the Free Trade Area', in Corbet and David Robertson (eds.), *Europe's Free Trade Area Experiment* (Oxford and New York: Pergamon Press, 1970). See Richard N. Cooper, *The Economics of Interdependence* (New York: McGraw-Hill, for the Council on Foreign Relations, 1968).

4. Those interested in the background to the GATT might read: W.A. Brown, *The United States and the Restoration of World Trade* (Washington: Brookings Institution, 1950); and Gerard Curzon, *Multilateral Commercial Diplomacy* (London: Michael Joseph, 1965).

5. A brief discussion of the situation was provided in Corbet, 'Global Challenge to Commercial Diplomacy', *Pacific Community*, October 1971, reproduced in the *Congressional Record*, Washington, 16 December 1971, pp. E 13590-93.

6. This is not to say that the latter should be achieved before the former can be embarked upon. Negotiations on both can proceed in parallel. An attempt is made to clarify the issues involved in *British, European and American Interests in the Negotiations on International Monetary Reform*, Staff Paper No. 2, and in Harry G. Johnson, *Neglected Principles in the Discussions on World Monetary Reform*, Staff

Paper No. 4 (London: Trade Policy Research Centre, 1974).

7. In this connection, see Corbet, *The Interests of Developing Countries in the Tokyo Round Negotiations*, Staff Paper No. 5 (London: Trade Policy Research Centre, 1974).

8. Japan's interest in the reform of the international trading system was emphasised by Hideo Kitahara, the Japanese Ambassador to the GATT, in an address to the European-Atlantic Group, London, 22 October 1973.

9. New approaches are analysed in Corbet and Johnson, 'Optional Negotiating Techniques on Industrial Tariffs', in Frank McFadzean *et al.*, *Towards an Open World Economy*, Report of an Advisory Group (London: Macmillan, for the Trade Policy Research Centre. 1972).

10. Robert E. Baldwin, *Non-tariff Distortions of International Trade* (Washington: Brookings Institution, 1971). Also see Gerard and Victoria Curzon, *Hidden Barriers to International Trade*, Thames Essay No. 1 (London: Trade Policy Research Centre, 1971).

11. Recognition of this point by the European Community was expressed by Sir Christopher Soames, as the Commissioner for External Trade, in his address to the European Parliament, Luxembourg, 4 April 1973.

12. An extensive analysis of the issues in international agricultural trade is provided in D. Gale Johnson, *World Agriculture in Disarray* (London: Macmillan, for the Trade Policy Research Centre, 1973). See, in addition, Hermann Priebe, *Landwirtschaft in der Welt von morgen* (Düsseldorf: Econ Verlag, 1970); and Michael Tracy, *Japanese Agriculture at the Crossroads*, Agricultural Trade Paper No. 2 (London: Trade Policy Research Centre, 1972), which has been published in Japanese by the Agricultural Policy Research Committee, Tokyo.

13. On this subject, see Jan Tumlir, *Proposals for Emergency Protection against Sharp Increases in Imports*, Guest Paper No. 1 (London: Trade Policy Research Centre, 1973), and also Robertson, 'Provision for Escape Clauses and Other Safeguards', in McFadzean *et al., op. cit.*

14. For an attempt to formulate a method of measuring the impact of non-tariff measures, see Hans Glismann and Axel Neu, 'Towards New Agreements on International Trade Liberalisation — Methods and Examples of Measuring Non-tariff Trade Barriers', *Weltwirtschaftsliches Archiv*, Kiel, Band 107, Heft 2, 1971.

15. The 'multi-stacking' of non-tariff measures is pointed out in Ingo Walter and Jae W. Chung, 'The Pattern of Non-tariff Obstacles to International Market Access', *Weltwirtschaftliches Archiv*, Band 108, Heft 3, 1972.

16. It might be noted here that the gradual elimination of tariffs would remove para-tariff barriers.

17. The conditional MFN approach was proposed in McFadzean *et al., op. cit.*, pp. 30-34, as part of a broad trade strategy for dealing with both tariff and non-tariff barriers to trade.

18. Two other exceptions are also provided for in the GATT. One is for preferential trade arrangements which existed at the time of the General Agreement's signature in 1947. The other, agreed in the New Part IV of the GATT, is for generalised preferential tariffs introduced for the benefit of developing countries.

19. *Overall Approach to the Coming Multilateral Negotiations in GATT*, Document I/135 e/73 (COMMER 42), Commission for the European Community, Brussels, Chapter III, para. 8.

20. This point has been made several times by William Eberle as President Nixon's Special Representative for Trade Negotiations.

21. C. Fred Bergsten, 'Crisis in US Trade Policy', *Foreign Affairs*, New York, July 1971.

22. Such an interest was expressed by Theodore Hijzen, the European Community's Representative to the GATT, in an address to the European-Atlantic Group,

London, 22 October 1973

23. Geoffrey Denton and Seamus O'Cleireacain, *Subsidy Issues in International Commerce*, Thames Essay No. 5 (London: Trade Policy Research Centre, 1972).

24. In both the European Community and EFTA, industries adjusted to internal tariff-free trade without experiencing serious problems.

25. The average level of tariffs on manufactured and semi-manufactured products, weighted by world trade and including duty-free items, is now 6.0 per cent for the original European Community (7.1 per cent for the United Kingdom), 6.2 per cent for the United States and 9.6 per cent for Japan — as noted later in the text.

26. See, for example, Presidential Commission on International Trade and Investment Policy, *United States International Economic Policy in an Interdependent World*, Williams Report (Washington: US Government Printing Office, 1971), pp. 45-64.

27. A code on adjustment assistance was proposed in Curzon and Curzon, *Global Assault on Non-tariff Trade Barriers*, Thames Essay No. 3 (London: Trade Policy Research Centre, 1971).

28. General agreement on safeguards was reflected in the report of the High-level Group on Trade and Related Problems, *Policy Perspectives on International Trade and Economic Relations*, Rey Report (Paris: Organisation for Economic Co-operation and Development, 1972).

29. Tumlir, *op. cit.*, p. 9.

30. This course was proposed by the United States and Japan, with the support of Sweden, at the 1972 ministerial meeting of the GATT.

31. Positions vary somewhat as to how adjustable fixed exchange rates should be in future.

32. *Overall Approach . . . op. cit.*, explanatory note, para. 6.

33. The common agricultural policy and the common commercial policy were also declared by the Council of Ministers of the European Community, in its initial bargaining position, to be beyond questioning. The 'fear' earlier mentioned seemed to be expressed in Günther Harkort, 'A Concept for an Open World Economy', *Intereconomics*, Hamburg, No. 4, 1973, reviewing McFadzean *et al.*, *op. cit.* The former State Secretary of the Ministry of Foreign Affairs in the Bonn Government wrote: 'Nowhere (in the report) is it made clear that the EEC has been launched by a legal instrument containing important articles which for some time have to be left essentially unchanged if the existence of the EEC is not to be put at risk.'

34. Typifying the defensive attitude of European leaders, President Pompidou, in an interview on French television, interpreted American efforts to obtain changes in the management of the common agricultural policy as 'tending to weaken it — that is to say, make it disappear'. See *Le Monde*, Paris, 24 December 1971.

35. Document COMM(73) 556, Commission of the European Community, Brussels, 4 April 1971.

36. Hijzen, *op. cit.* The extent to which it is necessary to harmonize policies in order to preserve the economic benefits of tariff-free trade is explored, both theoretically and empirically, in Victoria Curzon, *The Essentials of Economic Integration: Lessons of EFTA Experience* (London: Macmillan, for the Trade Policy Research Centre, 1974).

37. Rey Report, *op. cit.*

38. Corbet, 'Global Challenge to Commercial Diplomacy', *op. cit.*

39. Kenneth W. Dam, *The GATT Law and International Economic Organization* (Chicago and London: University of Chicago Press, 1970), pp. 274-95.

40. Theodore Geiger, 'Towards a World of Trading Blocks', *The Atlantic Community Quarterly*, Washington, Winter, 1971-72.

41. This point was elaborated upon in Corbet, 'Commercial Realignments and Commonwealth Relations', in Paul Streeten and Corbet (eds.), *Commonwealth Policy*

*in a Global Context* (London: Frank Cass, 1971).

42. The remainder of the discussion in this section owes much to discussions with Ernest Preeg, *World Economic Blocs and US Foreign Policy* (Washington: National Planning Association, 1974).

43. It will not be until 1975 that the British tariff will have been aligned with the common external tariff of the enlarged European Community.

44. The phrase describing this last option is the one used by Olivier Long, the Director-General of the GATT, although it forms the core of a variety of "free trade treaty" proposals of recent years. See Long, 'Towards Better Trade Relations in the 70s', Address to the Trade Policy Research Centre and the Foreign Affairs Club, London, 24 January 1972.

45. The following discussion of negotiating techniques is based on Corbet and Harry G. Johnson, 'Optional Negotiating Techniques on Industrial Tariffs', in Frank McFadzean *et al.*, *op. cit.*

46. Sir Eric Wyndham White, 'International Trade Policy: the Kennedy Round and Beyond', Address to the Deutsche Gesellschaft für Auswärtige Politik, Bad Godesberg, 27 October 1966. Also see *The Times*, London, 16 May 1967.

47. This point, and others relating to this policy option are discussed in Curzon and Curzon, 'Options After the Kennedy Round', in Johnson (ed.) *New Trade Strategy for the World Economy:* (London: Allen & Unwin, 1969), pp. 56-59.

48. See Johnson, 'Challenges Confronting Commonwealth Countries', *International Journal*, Toronto, Winter, 1969.

49. The secondary authority under the Act provided for tariff reductions of up to 50 per cent on any products that entered world trade and it was this which was exercised in the Kennedy Round negotiations.

50. For a fuller discussion of the sectoral approach see Curzon and Curzon, *op. cit.*, pp. 59-68.

51. The point is closely analysed in Edward English, 'Tariffs and Trade', in Canadian Tax Foundation, 1968 Conference Report (Toronto: Canadian Tax Foundation, 1969), quoted in Corbet *et al.*, *Trade Strategy and the Asian-Pacific Region*, *op. cit.*, p.17.

52. Johnson, 'Challenges Confronting Commonwealth Countries', *loc. cit.*

53. Curzon and Curzon, *op. cit.*, p. 72.

54. Tumlir, 'Trade Negotiations in the Field of Manufacturers', paper given at a conference on Trade and Development sponsored by the Cambridge Overseas Studies Committee, Cambridge, 27-29 September 1972.

55. The two proposals are discussed in Dam, *op. cit.*, pp. 64-68.

56. *Low Tariff Club* (Strasbourg: Council of Europe, 1952), pp. 25-26.

57. *A New Proposal for the Reduction of Customs Tariffs* (Geneva: GATT Secretariat, 1954). The GATT Plan is also briefly discussed in Curzon and Curzon, *op. cit.*, pp. 28-31.

58. Presidential Commission on International Trade and Investment Policy, *United States International Economic Policy in an Interdependent World*, Williams Report (Washington: US Government Printing Office, 1971), pp. 10 and 304.

59. For a succinct comparison of the results of six rounds of GATT negotiations, see Curzon and Curzon, *op. cit.*, p. 57.

60. The position of MFN in future trade negotiations is discussed in Corbet, 'Position of MFN Principle in Future Trade Negotiations', in McFadzean *et al.*, *op. cit.* .

61. The possibilities of linking to a general trade liberalisation agreement a system of generalised tariff preferences in favour of developing countries are examined in David Wall, 'Opportunities for Developing Countries', in Johnson (ed.), *Trade Strategy for Rich and Poor Nations* (London: Allen & Unwin, 1971).

62. A general discussion of non-tariff barriers and rules of competition can be

found in David Robertson, 'Scope for New Trade Strategy', in Johnson (ed.), *New Trade Strategy for the World Economy, op. cit.*, pp. 287-89; Curzon and Curzon, *Hidden Barriers to International Trade*, Thames Essay No. 1 (London: Trade Policy Research Centre, 1970); and Harald B. Malmgren, 'Negotiating Non-Tariff Barriers: The Harmonisation of National Economic Policies', in *US Foreign Economic Policy for the 1970s, op. cit.*, pp. 79-109.

63. In the United States this attitude even applies to the generalised tariff preferences which the Nixon Administration proposed to the Congress in its Trade Reform Bill. For it was proposed that the scheme should only be authorised for ten years. The position of the United States on preferential trade arrangements has been summarised from various sources in *Toward a New World Economic System: the Goals of US Policy* (London: United States Information Service, 1973).

64. See, respectively, Curzon and Curzon, *Global Assault on Non-tariff Trade Barriers, op. cit.*, and Tumlir, 'Proposals for Emergency Protection against Sharp Increases in Imports', *op. cit.*

# CHAPTER 11

## Strategies for Modifying Non-tariff Distortions

### PETER LLOYD

One of the principles underlying the General Agreement on Tariffs and Trade (GATT) when it was drawn up after World War II was that countries should rely exclusively on tariffs for the control of imports. Various articles of the General Agreement outlawed measures such as quantitative import restrictions and, on goods going the other way, export subsidies, and laid down the permissible scope and operation of such measures as customs valuation procedures and anti-dumping and countervailing duties. Exceptions were made for the use of quantitative restrictions for balance-of-payments reasons and for trade in agricultural commodities; but it was intended that these should be used infrequently.

Unfortunately, as tariffs have been reduced through six rounds of multilateral negotiations, the GATT has not prevented the marked growth over recent years in the use of non-tariff trade-distorting measures by its signatory countries. This failure has been due partly to the 'grandfather clause' (The Protocol of Provisional Application) which permitted countries acceding to the General Agreement to continue all pre-existing practices. Consequently Part II, covering non-tariff measures, has hardly operated at all. Another contributing factor has been the lack of any effective enforcement procedures.[1] What is more there has been no GATT regulation of certain non-tariff measures. Government purchasing, industrial standards and restrictive business practices (such as territorial market sharing and price fixing) are not specifically covered in the General Agreement.

### Significance of Non-Tariff Measures

The growing significance of non-tariff barriers has caused concern for two main reasons. First, an increase in the use of non-tariff interferences threatens to thwart the greater freedom of trade that has resulted from the tariff reductions achieved in six post-war rounds of multilateral GATT negotiations. One example of the substitution of non-tariff devices for tariff barriers is the spread amongst the developed countries in Western Europe and North America of 'voluntary' export restraints and import quotas restricting shipments of textiles to these countries and Asian sources.

Second, non-tariff interventions could become important in the increasing division of the world economy into trading *blocs*, with the accompanying danger of 'trade wars' between *blocs*.[2] During 1972 there was concern in the European Community, in particular, over the introduction in the United States of tax deferments to exporting corporations and with the pending regulations prepared by the Treasury for the enforcement of the Anti-dumping Act. The United States Congress has refused since 1967 to ratify the GATT Anti-dumping Code (on the grounds that the Administration was not authorised, under the Trade Expansion Act of 1962, to negotiate on non-tariff matters). Following the earlier Mills Bill, the Burke-Hartke Bill threatened, among other measures the use of import quotas. At the same time, however, the United States, Japan, Australia and other countries became increasingly concerned with the restrictions on exports to the European Community after the British decision to accede to the Common Market.

Now that a new round of GATT negotiations is under way there is a third reason why non-tariff barriers are important. The exports of some countries are much more severely restricted by non-tariff barriers in their major potential export markets than are the exports of other countries. The two groups of countries which are probably harmed the most are the developing countries and the exporters of temperate-zone agricultural commodities — cereals, dairy products, fruit and meats and so on. These countries stand to gain less than the European Community and Japan from another round of negotiations that results chiefly in further reductions in tariffs on manufactures and semi-manufactures.

If the negotiations on tariffs on industrial products do aim at (a) substantially tariff-free trade in industrial products among the developing countries or (b) take the form of a harmonisation of tariffs at a common level of say 10 per cent or (c) set about a general linear reduction in industrial tariffs,[3] the developing and agricultural exporting countries would be required to make greater reductions in their tariffs on average than would the European Community in particular. Average tariffs for the United States have been estimated at more than 10 per cent, compared with an average of about 6 per cent for the original European Community,[4] although some bases of comparison put them closer together. Average tariff levels are higher in other developed countries. In Australia, for example, the Tariff Board calculated that the average nominal tariff on the output of the manufacturing sector in 1967-68 was 28 per cent, since when there was no basic change until the Whitlam Government unilaterally reduced tariffs by 25 per cent in 1973. While it is notoriously difficult to compare average tariff levels between countries, in the sense of comparing the degree from country to country to which tariffs restrict imports, there is no question that substantial differences in *measured* average tariff levels do indicate important differences in the protection afforded by tariffs.

It is quite understandable and reasonable therefore for those countries which make greater concessions in reducing tariffs on industrial products to expect that they will benefit from greater concessions on the part of the European Community in reducing the levels of protection which it accords to its farmers through the common agricultural policy. This issue resembles the issue of 'tariff disparities' which divided countries and prolonged matters in the Kennedy Round of GATT negotiations.

The exclusion of any major groups of products or instruments of protection from the negotiations would have seriously reduced the desire of some countries to participate. This is an obvious implication of the fact that the particular exportable products which are restricted, and the instruments which restrict them, differ significantly from country to country. One of the dangers concerns agricultural commodities. The United States is seeking greater access to the European Community for its exports of grains and other farm commodities. One eminent American international trade expert has predicted that the comparative advantage and export competitiveness of the United States in manufactures would continue to decline and that increased agricultural exports would be vital to cover the growing American demands for energy and other imports. [5] Agricultural commodities are one of the fields where non-tariff restrictions on imports into the major world markets in North America and Western Europe are often more important than tariffs. [6] Negotiations on agricultural trade, however, are discussed in Chapter 12 below by D. Gale Johnson, of the University of Chicago.

## Nature and Scope of Non-Tariff Barriers

Before the negotiation of reductions to non-tariff barriers can be discussed it is necessary to clarify the meaning of the term. It has crept into popular usage since the last GATT round, but it is commonly misunderstood, even by ministers. 'Non-tariff barriers' is an omnibus term for the set of government policy instruments and practices which operate deliberately, or sometimes only incidentally, to restrain imports or distort exports. It is conventional to exclude from the broad meaning of the term only exchange-rate changes and other monetary and fiscal measures which affect all export and import-competing goods and are designed, moreover, to maintain external balance rather than to give selective protection.

The range of non-tariff instruments is broader than is commonly thought. A GATT inventory listed over 800 non-tariff complaints which have been subsequently classified into thirty categories. First, the term includes para-tariff practices which are usually regarded as tariff instruments; for example, dumping and countervailing duties, customs valuation procedures and administrative discretion in determining the tariff classification or rate of duty. Secondly, the term includes all quantitative restrictions, both on exports and on imports. Thirdly, government procurement policies, selective subsidies on exports and production, other aids to industry (such as regional policies, public services on concessionary terms and 'adjustment assistance' policies) are included when the use of these instruments does give public assistance to particular exports or import-competing industries. Assistance which goes to producers whose output is sold on the domestic market as well as to producers whose output is exported, may nevertheless give the exporters a substantial competitive advantage in third markets over the exporters of other countries, and over the local suppliers. Similarly, a subsidy on production granted to an import-competing producer discriminates against imported substitutes as does a tariff. Although they are intended for other purposes such forms of assistance as regional development grants or adjustment assistance also protect the local producer from import competition. Fourth, the term includes industrial standards laid down for safety, health, environment or other social purposes. [7]

In some cases, as mentioned earlier, the protective effect of a 'non-tariff barrier' is genuinely unintentional, but in the others it is deliberate. In either case foreign competitors may regard subsidised competition as unfair. The principle has long been recognised in the GATT through the provision for countervailing duties, but it is difficult and time-consuming to show, and measure, the effect of subsidies or other public assistance on the export price of particular products; and as a result few countervailing duties are imposed. It is recognised that the growth in subsidies and the growing interdependence of the industrial economies make these forms of non-tariff barriers important. [8] One major difficulty with any GATT examination of non-tariff measures such as government subsidies or regional policies is that they are, visibly, instruments of industrial policy, which governments have traditionally regarded as purely domestic matters. [9]

The term 'non-tariff barriers' is not an apt expression because some practices result in a lowering of protection for particular industries and lead to over-importing rather than under-importing; or, on the export side, lead to over-exporting rather than under-exporting. For example, the 'escalatory' structure of the tariffs in most industrial countries admits unprocessed materials like raw rubber and cotton at zero or low duties. While these low rates increase imports of these materials, they at the same time increase the *effective* protection of domestic industries which use the materials. [10] This is one of the chief complaints of manufacturers in developing countries. On the export side export subsidies lower the market price of the exports to the detriment of the producers (but not consumers) in the import market and the producers of third countries. The term 'non-tariff intervention' or 'non-tariff distortion' is more accurate.

The multiplicity of non-tariff instruments, along with the large degree of administrative discretion and variation in their use in each country, create special problems for multilateral negotiations. They often render it extremely difficult even to identify the products whose prices are distorted by non-tariff measures. When the products can be identified it is still very much more difficult than it is with tariffs to measure quantitatively the extent to which they restrict or distort international trade. There is no schedule of non-tariff instruments conveniently arranged by tariff items as there is with tariffs in most countries. The extent of the protection against imports by non-tariff barriers must be obtained by a direct comparison of the landed duty-free price of imports for each product affected, on the one hand, with the domestic prices to producers and consumers of the locally-produced substitutes, on the other. (Such comparisons have been made in different parts of the Common Market, where internal tariffs have been abolished, and the prices of the products compared have differed by much more than any reasonable allowance for transport costs.[11])

It is not surprising, then, that few measurements have been made anywhere of the effects of non-tariff instruments. The few estimates that have been made mainly relate to import quotas and other quantitative restrictions.[12] No quantitative measurements have been made in any country, as far as the present writer is aware, of many apparently important non-tariff instruments including anti-dumping practices, industrial standards, disciminatory features or public purchasing or unfair customs valuation practices.

In view of the paucity of information on non-tariff interventions, an international programme of studies was mounted in 1970, co-ordinated by the Trade Policy Research Centre in London and the Brookings Institution in Washington. It covered most of the major trading countries of the world.[13] To make them comparable, the studies were confined to the same six categories of non-tariff barriers: namely, quantitative restrictions, customs valuation, anti-dumping duties, public procurement policies, government aids to industry, and industrial standards. They confirmed the widespread use of all six categories of non-tariff instruments for protective purposes.[14] The studies also confirmed that the relative importance of each category varies considerably among the countries. The United States, for instance, probably makes relatively more use of restrictions on government purchasing. Japan makes more use of quantitative restrictions; and Australia, of the administrative features of tariff provisions.

There are other aspects of non-tariff interventions which have important implications of the strategy of negotiations. One notable characteristic is that non-tariff devices are largely concentrated on the same few groups of industries in each country. In a study of non-tariff protection in 15 developed countries, Professor Ingo Walter and Dr J.W. Chung, of New York University, found: 'sectors which emerge as particularly heavily subject to non-tariff barriers are processed foods, beverages and tobacco products, certain chemicals, pharmaceuticals, starches and allied products, cotton and synthetic textiles, electrical and electronic apparatus, motor vehicles and clothing'.[15] This similarity across countries in the incidence by industry of non-tariff interventions reflects the greater competition in world markets for the products of these industries. Sometimes this competition comes chiefly from the major developed countries, as in the case of chemicals, and sometimes from the developing countries, as in the case of textiles.

In the author's contribution to the TPRC-Brookings programme, on Australian non-tariff barriers, the same essential pattern was found. Non-tariff measures tend to be concentrated in a few areas of the tariff classification. These are the 'trouble areas' which generally enjoy high levels of protection by tariffs, in addition to non-tariff methods of protection, and they are the areas which are subject to frequent review of their levels of protection by the Tariff Board. In Australia the two main industries subject to non-tariff protection are the textile and chemical production.[16]

Another related feature is that the products which are subject to one non-tariff instrument tend to be subject to multiple non-tariff instruments.[17] The author has analysed in some detail several cases of multiple non-tariff measures on the same product in Australia. As an example consider the production of butter and cheese. The producers of butter and cheese in Australia are assisted by almost the whole gamut of non-tariff instruments. They receive subsidies on production, on inputs of fertiliser, tractors and credit, on exports of processed dairy products, and they received compensation for the devaluation of sterling in 1967. In addition, there are prohibitions on imports of margarine substitutes, unless they are coloured pink! Then there are 'voluntary' restraint agreements with New Zealand producers as well as quarantine regulations which prohibit imports of butter from most other countries. There is a five-year stabilisation plan, which equalises the pay-out to farmers from the domestic sales and the lower priced export sales, and a dairy farms reconstruction scheme. All of this goes to an industry which is undoubtedly efficient by the standards of the European Community and North America. The worst problem in the industry in the next few years and the principal reason for continued subsidisation and rural adjustment is that Australian butter will be largely excluded from its previous principal export market in Britain following British membership of the European Community. With all this assistance the Australian exporters have little hope of overcoming the multiple combination of non-tariff barriers used in the European Community, especially the variable import levy and quota provisions — unless the European Community allows it. The Australian prices are much less distorted from the prices at which butter and cheese are traded on free world markets than those of the Common Market.

**Strategy of Negotiations**

How can the reduction of non-tariff interference with international trade be negotiated? One immediate thought has been to treat them in the same way as tariffs and try to negotiate multilateral reductions on a reciprocal basis. As a general approach this is not a practical possibility. Note has already been taken of the large number of non-tariff devices, the diversity among countries in their form and relative importance, their hidden nature and the scope they permit for administrative discretion, besides, the extreme difficulty in measuring the restrictive effect of them. All these features mean that international comparisons of levels of non-tariff protection cannot be made. No country can make a linear reduction in all of its non-tariff barriers to imports without fairly precise measures of the levels of protection which each barrier implies. For the same reason exchanges between countries of offers of reductions in disparate lists of non-tariff barriers — as in earlier GATT negotiations on tariff barriers — are not possible.

Although non-tariff interventions do not lend themselves to modification and elimination through a multilateral process of reciprocal bargaining, certain categories of non-tariff protection could be broached directly — that is, eliminated as part of a wider agreement. Many interferences with trade associated with the administration of customs duties could be tackled in this way and the incidence of para-tariff barriers would be substantially overcome with any agreement to phase out tariffs on products traded among developed countries.

The difficulties of achieving multilateral modifications in non-tariff distortions were illustrated during and since the Kennedy Round of GATT negotiations. In the early stages of the Kennedy Round it was decided that the negotiations 'should deal not only with tariffs but also with non-tariff barriers' and one of the four principal sub-committees of the Trade Negotiations Committee dealt with non-tariff barriers and a second with agricultural problems.[19] An early attempt to devise general standards was abandoned as negotiations proceeded in favour of the barrier-by-barrier approach that the GATT has followed in the non-tariff field since the Kennedy Round was concluded in mid-1967. In the end the only agreements on non-tariff barriers reached among the contracting parties were the GATT Anti-dumping Code, elaborating on Article 6 of the General Agreement, and the 'package' in which the United States agreed to abolish the American Selling Price (ASP) method of customs valuation, applied to benzenoid chemicals and a few other commodities entering the American market, in the return for tariff reductions in chemicals and the abolition of the road taxes in some Common Market countries which discriminate against higher horse power vehicles from the United States. The package lapsed because the United States Congress refused, for the reasons already mentioned, to press legislation abolishing ASP.

The barrier-by-barrier approach is thought to hold considerable promise over the long run. The GATT Committee on Trade in Industrial products has completed drafts of three codes of conduct for specific categories of non-tariff interference: on industrial standards, customs valuation procedures and import licensing. The basic purpose with codes is to secure general agreement among the signatory countries on permissible methods and uses of non-tariff instruments and, therefore, institute a process of more or less continuous consultation and negotiation on their elaboration and implementation. Such codes would outlaw certain practices, as did the GATT Anti-dumping Code, and perhaps put limits on the uses of them. The Organisation for Economic Co-operation and Development (OECD) has been drafting a code of good conduct for public procurement which specifies certain tendering procedures as well as the derogations and exceptions that should be permitted. The codes already drafted are likely to be endorsed in the 'Tokyo Round' of GATT negotiations. But the time taken to draft them suggests that it could be difficult to negotiate other codes in the time available.

Other methods of negotiation will in any case have to supplement the code approach. An industry-by-industry, or sector-by-sector, approach has been suggested. This would be particularly suitable if the negotiations of tariffs proceeded, at least in part, on the basis of sectoral negotiations, but this seems less likely than the use of some across-the-board method of tariff reduction. Nevertheless, this method deserves consideration, if only because of one feature of non-tariff barriers noted above. The occurrence of multiple non-tariff barriers on many products means that success in negotiating reductions or eliminations of some types of non-tariff instrument may be frustrated if there are other instruments applying to the same products which can be increased to compensate the affected producers. This is a distinct possibility because countries will offer reductions in tariffs or other non-tariff devices where they are redundant. A tariff or import quota, for example, may be eliminated as a result of negotiation and the domestic producer may not be harmed if industrial standards or quarantine regulations already preclude the foreign supplier from competing effectively on the market.

Because of the 'multi-stacking' of non-tariff measures, and more generally because of the high-degree of substitutability between different categories of non-tariff interventions, there have been proposals for a comprehensive approach to the problem, most notably those of an advisory group sponsored in 1972 by the Trade Policy Research Centre in London. The proposals in the McFadzean report were based on a number of studies, particularly one by Gerard Curzon and Victoria Curzon, of the University of Geneva.[21] They involve four aspects.

The first step in a logical and 'incrementalist' approach to the non-tariff problem should be the negotiation of a set of criteria, an international code, covering adjustment assistance to industry. The criterion for judging whether one form or another of public assistance to an industry is defined in broad terms by the Professor and Dr Curzon in the following way: 'If it serves to perpetuate the need for assistance, it is negative and is to be condemned. If, on the other hand, it is designed ultimately to remove the need for assistance, it is positive and is to be commended.'

Since the GATT already contains adequate rules on some non-tariff interventions it would be a wasted effort to repeat them in an adjustment code or elsewhere. As noted at the outset, however, these provisions have been rendered nugatory by the 'grandfather clause' which has allowed signatory countries to derogate from the rules where pre-existing legislation contradicts Part II of the General Agreement (which contains the bulk of the rules theoretically governing world trade). The McFadzean report accordingly proposed as a second step that the Protocol of Provisional Application should be terminated.

A third step would be to negotiate on a conditional MFN basis general rules of competition to cover, where appropriate, the categories of non-tariff intervention not covered by part II of the GATT. The initial purpose would be to secure an equal commitment. Later these general rules could be elaborated upon, and adherence to them sought, in a process of fairly continuous consultation and negotiation.

The fourth step would be the development of an effective complaints and arbitration procedure.

Commodity agreements may reduce the non-tariff barriers obstructing international trade in certain farm products. Some commodity agreements may emerge from the Tokyo Round. The emphasis in commodity agreements, however, is usually on stabilising prices or incomes, not in liberalising trade. Such agreements as those for sugar and grains provide existing illustrations that commodity agreements do not remove many of the barriers to free trade and fair competition for efficient producers.

The key to a successful and large-scale reduction in non-tariff barriers to imports lies in providing appropriate adjustment assistance to the producers who will be adversely affected by these reductions. Adjustment assistance is even more important for the modification and elimination of non-tariff barriers than for tariffs because countries have chiefly resorted to non-tariff barriers in areas of production where their domestic producers are less competitive. International trade specialists have almost universally recognised the harm which is caused by non-tariff interventions. The essence of the problem is that they have not so far been able to persuade governments and politicians that they should be reduced. The latter are conscious and properly so, of the temporary dislocations of industry and unemployment that would inevitably result. Adjustment assistance is essential to encourage the movement of resources into uses where their contributions to national output and world output are greater.

These developments show that non-tariff barriers can be reduced but it will take more effort and more goodwill at the negotiating table to achieve the same average reduction in non-tariff barriers as in tariff barriers to world trade.

The discussion of non-tariff measures focuses on imports. But there was a sudden growth of prohibitions and quotas on exports from the United States and other industrial countries during 1973 and 1974. These have arisen as attempts to contain the accelerating rate of inflation by preventing the diversion of supplies from home markets into more profitable export markets. In 1973 the Organisation of Petroleum Exporting Countries also showed dramatically how export quotas used by export cartels can push up the world price of a raw material and restrict world trade.

## NOTES AND REFERENCES

1. The GATT's enforcement procedures are mostly limited to discussing a complaint without it being dismissed or upheld. Article 23 of the General Agreement authorises the withdrawal of concessions' which were granted in return for others which have been subsequently nullified or impaired by the action of another signatory country. This provision, however, has only been exercised on a few occasions.

For a brief review of the GATT and non-tariff barriers, see Gerard and Victoria Curzon, *Hidden Barriers to International Trade*, Thames Essay No. 1 (London: Trade Policy Research Centre 1970).

2. Theodore Geiger, 'Towards a World of Trade Blocs', *The Atlantic Community Quarterly*, Washington, Winter 71-72.

3. These three options, plus the proposal for sector-by-sector negotiations, have been the subjects of public discussion for several years. See Curzon and Curzon, *After the Kennedy Round*, Atlantic Trade Study (London: Trade Policy Research Centre, 1968); and Harry G. Johnson and Hugh Corbet, 'Pacific Trade in an Open World', *Pacific Community*, Tokyo, April 1970. They were the options advanced by the High-level Group on Trade and Related Problems, *Policy Perspectives for International Trade and Economic Relations*, Rey Report (Paris: OECD Secretariat, 1972). The advantages and disadvantages of all four options are analysed in Corbet, 'Industrial Tariffs and Economic Spheres of Influence', Chapter 10 in this volume.

4. Rey Report, *op. cit.*, p. 44.

5. Lawrence B. Krause, 'The US Economy and International Trade', a paper given at the Fifth Pacific Trade and Development Conference, Tokyo, 9-13 January 1973.

6. For a survey of the situation, see D. Gale Johnson, *World Agriculture in Disarray* (London: Macmillan, for the Trade Policy Research Centre, 1973).

7. Curzon and Curzon, *Hidden Barriers to International Trade*, *op. cit.*

8. The lack of coherence in the increasing use of government intervention in international trade was noted in a paper given at the 1968 conference, in Montreal, of the International Economics Association: Goran Ohlin, 'Trade in a Non-Laissez-Faire World', in Paul A. Samuelson (ed.), *International Economic Relations* (London: Macmillan, for the International Economics Association, 1969).

9. For a theoretical discussion of this topic see Geoffrey Denton and Seamus O'Cleireacain *Subsidy Issues in International Commerce*, Thames Essay No. 5 (London: Trade Policy Research Centre, 1972).

10. The concept of effective protection accorded to a particular product takes into account the nominal protection — that is, the duties as listed in the tariff schedule — accorded to the materials used to manufacture the product.

11. Curzon and Curzon, *Hidden Barriers to International Trade*, *op. cit.*, p. 00.

12. For an effort to measure the protective rates of protection afforded by a selection of non-tariff instruments in Britain and the United States, see Robert E. Baldwin, *Non-Tariff Distortions of International Trade* (Washington: Brookings Institution, 1970), ch. 7. Also see Hans Glismann and Axel Neu, 'Towards New Agreements on International Trade Liberalisation: Methods and Examples of Measuring Non-Tariff Trade Barriers', *Weltwirtschaftliches Archiv*, Kiel, No. 2, 1971, and Peter Lloyd, *Non-tariff Distortions of Australian Trade* (Canberra: Australian National University Press, 1973), Ch. 10.

13. The countries covered by the programme were Australia, the Benelux union

(Belgium, the Netherlands and Luxembourg), Canada, Italy, Japan, the United Kingdom, the United States and West Germany, with a study also covering measures of the European Community.

14. Summaries of the national studies and a discussion of negotiating strategies, is to be published in H.G. Johnson and Stanley D. Metzger (eds.), *International Negotiations on non-Tariff Barriers to Trade* (London: Allen & Unwin, forthcoming).

15. Ingo Walter and Jae W. Chung, 'The Pattern of Non-Tariff Obstacles to International Market Access', *Weltwirtschaftliches Archiv*, Kiel, Bd. 108, 1972, pp. 122-34.

16. Lloyd, *op. cit.*, ch. 10.

17. Walter and Chung, *loc. cit.*, observed what they called the 'multi-stacking' of non-tariff instruments in several product groups.

18. Lloyd, *op. cit.*, ch. 10.

19. The treatment of non-tariff barriers in earlier stages of the Kennedy Round negotiations is reviewed in Craig Matthews, 'Non-tariff Import Barriers and the Kennedy Round', *Common Market Law Review, London*, March 1965, pp. 403-419.

20. Frank McFadzean *et al.*, *Towards an Open World Economy*, Report of an Advisory Group (London: Macmillan, for the Trade Policy Research Centre, 1972).

21. Curzon and Curzon, *Global Assault on Non-Tariff Trade Barriers*, Thames Essay No. 4 (London: Trade Policy Research Centre, 1971).

22. McFadzean *et al.*, *op.cit.*, pp. 17-21.

# CHAPTER 12

## Impact of Farm-support Policies on International Trade

### D. GALE JOHNSON

There has been little, if any, liberalisation of trade in temperate-zone farm commodities during the past two decades. Many of the quantitative restraints on agricultural trade that were imposed during the Great Depression or after World War II were removed in the 1950s. But other barriers, nearly as restrictive, have been put in their place. Moreover, the creation of the European Community, with its common agricultural policy has caused a substantial amount of trade diversion and uneconomic expansion of production of some farm products behind very high protection. The enlargement of the Common Market has significantly increased the protection of agriculture in Western Europe and has resulted in a further loss in export markets for countries outside the Community.[1]

The blame for the continuing trend of agricultural protection does not rest entirely on Western Europe. The three major exporters of temperate-zone farm products — the United States, Canada and Australia — have made no significant concessions to freer trade in farm products where they would be affected adversely by increased imports; and each has, at one time or another, continued to use export subsidies and pay subsidies to domestic producers of commodities that they export. All three countries have their 'sacred cows': literally in their protection of dairy production; and figuratively in the case of sugar, tobacco, peanuts, rice and wool in one or more of them.

### Why Agricultural Protection?

Agricultural protection is not new in the history of the world. In fact, free trade in farm commodities has been the exception rather than the rule throughout modern history. Only Britain among the major industrial countries followed a policy of free trade for more than two or three decades. And she, alas, gradually abandoned her commitment to free trade over the past few decades and has now committed herself to a high degree of protection for agriculture by joining the European Community.

Why have most countries isolated, to varying degrees, their agricultures from international competition? There is no simple answer even for a single country. It may perhaps help in trying to answer the question, however, if it is acknowledged that the interferences with trade in agricultural commodities in recent decades have not been the result of conscious and deliberate decisions forming part of general trade policy. In fact it has been widely recognised that the regulation of trade in farm products has been inconsistent with the general trade policies of the industrial countries. Trade interferences have been the consequence of decisions made with respect to domestic farm-support policies; quite frequently, they have incurred only after it was clear that the cost of operating farm-support policies would be too great or that the policies would be ineffective in meeting their objectives.

Difficulties arose most directly when price-support policies were the chosen course to maintain farm incomes and internal prices were established above world market prices. Without direct control of imports, the national market would be flooded and, if the product involved was one that was normally exported, such a price-support policy would result in a decline of exports and an accumulation of stocks. Thus export subsidies were required if exports were to be maintained at any level. Such subsidies were often justified on the grounds that they were required to obtain a nation's 'fair share' of the export market.

What, then, have been the major objectives of the farm-support policies that have required varying degrees of interference with trade? Historically the objectives of farm policies have included one or more of four major concerns:

(a) national self-sufficiency, or autarky, for food or some raw material that is considered to be of crucial importance;
(b) reducing balance-of-payments difficulties;
(c) benefits to consumers in the form of an assured source of supply and stable and reasonable prices; and
(d) benefits for the farm population in terms of higher incomes, stable prices or greater employment opportunities.

The first of the concerns — self-sufficiency in food — had its origins in the vulnerability of a nation in time of war, especially in countries that imported a significant proportion of their food requirements.

Turning to the second objective, the use of agricultural policies to solve balance-of-payments difficulties can be viewed as either quite old or quite new: quite old if one considers it a feature of mercantilist policy; quite new if one relates it to the monetary difficulties of the last half century and particularly of the last quarter of a century. British agricultural policy after World War II was strongly influenced by the fear that the immense amount of foreign exchange required to import about half Britain's food supply would create continuing and not readily solvable balance-of-payments problems. The severe restrictions on imports of farm products by several of the major West European countries during the 1950s were both justified and excused on balance-of-payments grounds.

As for the third objective of benefiting the consumer through an assured source of supply and stable and reasonable prices, it can only be taken seriously, as far as recent experience in the industrial countries is concerned, in the United Kingdom. Until mid-1971 such an objective was met for a major part of the British food supply. There were exceptions — horticultural products and sugar, for example — but in the main the British consumer has had reasonable access to most of his food at prices that approximately reflect world market conditions. When one reads, though, that one of the three main objectives of the sugar programme of the United States is to 'assure American consumers of a plentiful and stable supply of sugar at reasonable prices', or that one of the important objectives of the common agricultural policy of the European Community, as stated in the Treaty of Rome, is 'to ensure reasonable prices in supplies to consumers', one can easily imagine that he is accompanying Alice through Wonderland.

The fourth concern has to be treated more extensively. For recent years the primary objective of domestic farm-support policies has been to improve the income of the farm population or to prevent any anticipated decline in such income. Most, if not all, of the industrial countries have what can be called a farm-income problem. This is true, in part, because agriculture tends to be a declining sector of an economy as real income increases. because most farm products are necessities, the demand for food and other agricultural products increases at a slower rate than the demand for all other goods and services. [2]

The point has now been reached in Western Europe and North America where a 10 per cent increase in real per capita income results in no more than a 1 to 5 per cent increase in the demand for food at the farm gate. While the demand for food grows slowly, agriculture's capacity to increase output is of roughly the same order as the growth in real national output. And since the average product of labour in agriculture in the industrial countries has increased at least as rapidly as in industry, the absolute level of employment in agriculture has declined over several decades past. In most industrial countries the decline in employment each year has been substantially larger than the number of retirements and deaths of farmers and hired workers. Thus if *no* young farm people stayed on the land, it would be necessary each year for some who are actively engaged in farming to seek employment elsewhere. Farm people are continuously faced with important and difficult adjustment problems and it is hardly surprising that governments make efforts to minimise or ameliorate them.

Although labour must and does leave agriculture, this is not generally true of other resources. In industrial economies, agriculture is continuously adding to its stock of farm machines and expanding its use of such non-farm inputs as fertiliser, protein supplements, herbicides and pesticides and petroleum products. To a large degree such resources are brought into agriculture because of the profitability of finding substitutes for labour, whose real value has been increased steadily and significantly. Nor is there any reason to believe that economic growth has resulted in adverse effects upon the return to land. While the current return to land is often quite low, the low return is largely if not entirely offset by anticipated (and realised) increases in the price of land. In most industrial countries, land returns and prices since World War II have behaved like growth stocks.[3] Thus of labour, capital and land the only resource used in agriculture that may earn a lower return than a comparable resource earns in the rest of the economy is labour.

The incomes of farm people can be low, not only because one or more resources earns a lower return than comparable resources earn elsewhere, but also because farm families own fewer resources than families in the rest of the economy. The major source of the discrepancy between farm and non-farm family incomes is the difference in resources — human and non-human — owned by the two groups. And it is primarily limited human resources that are responsible for the lower average level of resources. On average, it is probable that farm families own more non-human capital than the average non-farm family, although the distribution of such capital among farm families is highly unequal. Hired farm workers have little non-human capital and the same is true of most farm families operating small farms.

The primary reason for the limited human resources in agriculture is the difference in educational attainment of farm and non-farm workers. In some countries this differential is now being eliminated for young people, but the effects of past discrimination will linger on for many years because such a large fraction of the current farm labour force received their education twenty years or more ago. In countries with very different types of educational finance and control — United States, France, and the Soviet Union — the farm population that is now forty-five years or older received not only fewer years of schooling but attended schools that offered a relatively poor quality education.[4]

## Farm Policies Don't Benefit the Poor

While it is true that the average incomes of farm families are below those of town families, even after adjustments are made for differences in cost of living, family size and taxes, the policies that have been employed by the industrial countries to improve the welfare of farm families have been marked by a failure to eliminate income differentials. Most of the expenditures or costs of the policies have gone on higher farm prices or subsidies closely related to the level of farm output. This approach does nothing to eliminate the inherent disadvantage of limited resources. Nor does it reduce to any significant degree the differential between returns to farm and non-farm labour. The benefits that have accrued to the farm population have gone primarily to the relatively large farmers and to those who own farm land. There can be no doubt that land values have increased by such policies. But what has never been fully considered is the impact of continuously rising land prices upon future generations of farm families, especially those who must purchase part, or all, of their farm land in order to engage in farming. In the large majority of industrial countries the income benefits, which are small compared with the total cost, go to farm families that already have quite satisfactory levels of income. In the United States, for example, the fifth of the farm families who sold almost four-fifths of all farm products in 1971, had incomes that were substantially higher — by nearly half — than the average family incomes of the whole country.[5] Where the instrument of the policy has been relatively higher farm and consumer prices, income has been transferred from relatively low-income urban families to relatively high-income farm families — from poor people in the towns to rich people on the land.

Farm support policies have done little or nothing to reduce income discrepancies within agriculture. In fact, it is quite possible that in most countries income differences within agriculture have been exacerbated by the emphasis that has been given to high crop prices, especially grain, and the relatively low degree of protection provided for livestock production. On average, farms that specialise in grain production are larger than other types of farms. The smaller farms tend to specialise in livestock production and have been forced to pay high prices for most of their feed.

Denis Bergman, of the Institut National de la Recherche Agronomique in Paris, has pointed out that, in 1969/70, 80,000 French farmers, out of the 1.7m altogether, sold almost two-thirds of all grain marketed. [6] While the majority of the rest of the full-time farmers produce grain that is fed primarily to their livestock, especially dairy cattle, the major use of their labour is hardly protected at all. In fact, the high prices for livestock products, made necessary by high feed prices, have restricted consumption and reduced employment opportunities on the farms that depend upon livestock production as their major source of income.

T.E. Josling and Donna Hamway, at the London School of Economics, have made estimates of the distribution of farm income in the United Kingdom under three assumptions — no support, the deficiency-payments system of farm-support as of 1969, and the import-levy system of the European Community. [7] If there were no support, the highest income quartile of farm families would have received 41 per cent of farm income. Under the British farm-support policy of 1969 such families received 48 per cent of farm income. If the United Kingdom had been in the European Community — subject, that is, to the common agricultural policy — in that year such families would have received 50 per cent of farm income. The lowest income quartile would have received 13 per cent of farm income, either with no support or under the 1969 policy. If Britain had been in the Common Market the relative income of this group would have been increased to 15 per cent of the total. The second quartile (next to lowest income group) would have received 25 per cent of all farm income with no support, but only 17 per cent in 1969, and only 10 per cent under the Common Market system. The data for the second quartile does not mean that such families had lower incomes in 1969 than they would have had with no support because net farm income was increased by the policies then in effect. What the data do show is that 'those who have get'; the incomes of high-income farm families are actually or potentially increased by support policies, both in an absolute and relative sense, while low-income farm families lose relatively and gain rather little absolutely.

## Costs to Consumers and Taxpayers

With the very large costs that have been imposed upon consumers and taxpayers in Western Europe, North America and Japan — more than $26,000m annually in recent years [8] — and the relatively small and unequally distributed benefits realised by farm people, it is surprising that farm-support policies continue to persist. When these costs are added to the damage that conflicts over the trade effects of such policies have caused, and are causing, in the international relations of friendly countries the surprise becomes even greater.

Several factors may be responsible for the persistence of costly and largely ineffective farm-support policies. First, even with very substantial governmental intervention the reduction of the farm labour force in the industrial countries is occurring at a rapid rate — often 4 to 6 per cent annually. Thus it is assumed that if high support prices and subsidies were eliminated, the farm labour force would decline even more rapidly, and might reach a level that would result in very substantial dislocations in both rural and urban communities. Second, since it is generally believed that farm incomes are even now, under existing policies, lower than non-farm incomes, the elimination of these policies would result in a disastrous fall in farm incomes. In the European Community, for example, the costs of farm-support policies to consumers and taxpayers is at least half that of the value added by agriculture. It is feared that the elimination of the common agricultural policy would result in economic disaster for farm families. Finally, it is feared that freer trade would result in political unrest, to varying degrees, in rural areas. Since World War II few democratic governments in industrial countries have had firm and substantial majorities. Even though farm populations have become rather unimportant as a percentage of the total voting population, and are declining almost everywhere, they often represent a large enough block of voters to have an effect on national elections. [9]

It is not improbable that the seventh round of negotiations under the auspices of the General Agreement on Tariffs and Trade (GATT), launched in Tokyo, will founder because of failures to accomplish meaningful reductions in the barriers to trade in farm commodities. If such should be the case the long-run harm to the cause of trade liberalisation will be very great. It is perhaps unfortunate that in the United States the major supporters of trade liberalisation are certain farm groups. Protectionist sentiment, which is just below the surface in the United States, has been greatly strengthened since the late 1960s because of the defections of some large labour unions from the ranks of liberal trade supporters. If farm groups are once again disappointed, as they were in the previous two GATT rounds of trade negotiations, the major vocal and politically important opposition to further trade restrictions in the United States will itself look inward and press for farm policies that minimise the importance of international trade.

## Approaches to Negotiations

It has not been clear what approaches will be made to international negotiations on agricultural products. While negotiations were planned to begin in 1973, very little has been said publicly by the United States, the European Community, Japan or any other participants about either objectives or approaches.[10] In preparing to negotiate they have had considerable difficulty agreeing on anything specific. It is quite clear that the major temperate-zone exporters are hoping for substantial reductions in barriers to trade — in the short run, at least enough to offset the trade diversion due to the enlargement of the Common Market, and looking further ahead a substantial liberalisation over a decade or so. What is not yet apparent is what these exporters will offer in return for concessions on agricultural products. The United States, Canada and Australia have some agricultural sectors that are heavily protected and their trading partners can rightfully seek concessions in those areas, either for their own benefit or for the benefit of developing countries.

**Proposals of the Rey Group**

One can only speculate about possible approaches to multilateral negotiations for expanding commercial trade in temperate-zone farm products. The report of the High-level Group on Trade and Related Problems, set up within the framework of the Organisation for Economic Co-operation and Development (OECD), probably gives a picture of the broad range within which various governments are likely to posture themselves.[11] While the members of the High-level Group (chaired by Jean Rey, formerly President of the Commission of the European Community) participated as individuals, this does not mean that there was any hesitancy in reflecting the official views of the nations of which they were citizens.

The chapter on agriculture begins as follows: 'As was to be expected, it was the examination of agricultural problems which gave rise to the longest discussions within the Group. This is not surprising. As is known, this subject has been debated for years both within the Organisation and in the other international bodies, without it having been possible so far to reconcile fully the divergent points of view held. The present examination revealed that it is still not possible to reconcile these differences.'

The High-level Group suggested three types of approaches to the negotiations, ranging from modest changes in current agricultural and trade policies to the establishment of longer-term global objectives and principals that would lead to fundamental policy reforms and a long-term reduction in the protection of agriculture to the level provided for industrial products.

The most modest of the set of proposals for negotiations called upon governments:

(a) to alter the relationship between prices resulting from government policies to promote better adjustment of supply to demand by encouraging production of products for which there is a strong demand and slowing down or reducing the production of those that have unfavourable market prospects;

(b) to avoid introducing further protection;

(c) to avoid abuses in the use of export and production aids that disrupt world markets and to seek to regulate, by bilateral and multilateral understandings, the use of such aids that disturb other countries;

(d) to carry out a stock-building policy to counteract sudden fluctuations in supply and demand and prevent disruption of world markets;

(e) to limit official aid for market support for surplus products, requiring producers to share in the costs of holding stocks and subsidising exports;

(f) to try to control production in extreme cases where overproduction exists;

(g) if small farmers would suffer as a result of the adjustments and changes described, to provide for compensation by direct payments of tax relief; and,

(h) for some products where there is a problem of imbalance between supply and demand, to arrive at international arrangements to make markets more orderly and stable.

Some members, who agreed that the measures described above were desirable, felt that such measures constituted only a first step in a more far-reaching effort. Recognising that 'governments wish to maintain — within certain limits — their national agricultural production' it is argued that international trade makes it possible to limit the financial burden on the economy and to provide low priced products for the benefit of consumers. 'The primary aim of these efforts should be to develop a better division of labour within the agricultural sector, including those countries that want to maintain a certain level of agricultural protection. Another aim should be to arrive at a stable equilibrium between supply and demand both geographically and over time, on the one hand by ensuring that markets are regularly supplied, and on the other by reducing existing production surpluses and preventing the development of new structural or occasional surpluses. Domestic adjustment efforts should be intensified and import regimes made much more flexible and there should be a substantial reduction in exports aids in order to 'leave market forces freer to play their part'.

With respect to negotiations, these members suggested that the concept of support levels should be made use of so that 'in each country support levels that are relatively high should be progressively lowered . . . ' If the reduction of support levels resulted in farm-income losses, direct support should be used that would have little effect upon output. It was then stated that the negotiations should give particular attention to products in which efforts to promote trade were urgently needed — cereals together with live-stock-feed, meats, dairy products and sugar.

A still smaller number of members felt that the two other approaches represented steps that should be taken, but believed that significant further modifications were required, specifically funda-mental policy reforms. Ultimate objectives that would guide the negotiations were considered to be essential. These objectives should include a substantial expansion of trade, a far greater market-orientation for agriculture and bringing agriculture over time into line with other sectors of the various national economies. 'In the view of these members, there is a danger, if countries cannot consider these more fundamental questions now and go further, that the scope and significance of agricultural trade may hamper more general progress in trade policy and trade relations.'

These three approaches to negotiations can perhaps be sum-marised as follows:

1. The basic principles and objectives of the agricultural policies of the industrial countries should be accepted, but governments should commit themselves (a) to take no actions that would further increase protection, (b) to accept respon-sibility for stock holding when supply exceeds demand and (c) to try to limit the use of export and production aids that dis-rupt world markets.

2. Governments should consider reducing support levels that are relatively high and accept a responsibility for assisting in achieving a balance in world supply and demand.

3. There should be fundamental reforms of agricultural policies with the long-run objective of reducing protection to agriculture to the same level as in industry.

The differences between the three approaches, and especially the first and third, in terms of the liberalising of trade in farm com-modities are very great indeed. The first envisages efforts that would put some restraints upon further changes in farm-support policies, but holds out little hope for significant trade expansion, while perhaps preventing a deterioration from the present situation. This may be too gloomy an interpretation of what was intended. Even so, since no significant change in average degrees of protection was implied, it may be a fair prediction of what the outcome would be.

The third proposal calls for a major reformulation of agricultural policies, substantial trade liberalisation and, consequently, a significant expansion of economically justified trade in farm commodities.

## Two Other Possibilities

Two other negotiating approaches have been proposed from time to time. One is that agriculture should be covered in the course of a general round of GATT negotiations. The other is that commodity agreements should be attempted again. These two possibilities bear some comment.

The previous two rounds of GATT negotiations were singularly ineffective in reducing interferences to trade in agricultural products. Some of the important reasons for the failures are historical: the negotiations came at critical times in the creation and development of the European Community. The first negotiations came just as the Community was being established; the Kennedy Round was underway while the Community was trying to digest and extend its common agricultural policy. At the time of the Kennedy Round it was perhaps too much to expect that the European Community would significantly modify its system of agricultural protection so soon after the painful internal negotiations that resulted in its creation.

Unfortunately the passage of time has not significantly improved the prospects of success in reducing interventions in agricultural trade through a general round of GATT negotiations. Apart from the fact that trade liberalisation for agricultural products would benefit the producer interests in only five of the major industrial countries (United States, Canada, Australia, New Zealand and Denmark) and adversely affect such interests in many more, the basic framework of GATT trade rules is inadequate for the task of agricultural negotiations.

To a very considerable degree the United States is responsible for this state of affairs. American responsibility goes back to the origins of GATT and American insistence upon exceptions from the general trade rule that 'no prohibitions or restrictions other than duties, taxes or other charges' on either exports or imports were to be permitted. Exceptions were authorised for other types of restrictions when required for the enforcement of government programmes in agriculture that restricted domestic production or marketings or removed a temporary surplus through a domestic two price system. In addition the United States, as well as certain other countries, refused to endorse an absolute prohibition against export subsidies. Still further, the United States has not abided by the prohibition against the use of import quotas for farm products that applies when there is no governmental programme to limit domestic production: American use of import quotas on dairy products is a flagrant violation of this GATT rule. The fact that exceptions have been granted by GATT members is of little or no consequence.

Of course, it might be possible to renegotiate the GATT rules as they affect agricultural trade, but this hardly seems possible within the framework of a new round of GATT trade negotiations. Such a renegotiation, it seems to me, would have to be a separate enterprise and has to involve general consideration of all aspects of agricultural policy.

International commodity agreements for agricultural commodities represent a possible framework for liberalising agricultural trade. It is possible to include a wide variety of features within a commodity agreement — access arrangements, minimum and maximum prices, output or marketing limitations, surplus disposal, restraints on domestic subsidies, the degree of protection whether by tariff, variable import levy or import quota. The concept has sufficient flexibility; the problem is to realise these potentialities in actual negotiation. Since World War II international agreements have been negotiated for only five commodities — wheat, coffee, sugar, tin and olive oil and of these the last is not now in operation. It would take the proverbial Philadelphia lawyer to determine if the International Grains Arrangement (the wheat agreement) is still in effect.

Commodity agreements do not represent an effective approach to the problems of liberalising agricultural trade. I do not reach this conclusion because of the historically limited success of such agreements:

(a) First, the commodity agreements that have been negotiated have not had trade liberalisation as an important objective. Primary emphasis has often been upon limiting price variations; while this may be a worthy objective, the contribution to trade liberalisation is generally very limited.

(b) Second, commodity agreements, while theoretically possible for all commodities, seem most applicable to commodities with relatively low storage costs.

(c) Finally, the trade problems that face agriculture are nearly universal with respect to the commodities involved. It is difficult to imagine the negotiation of many commodity agreements simultaneously. The negotiation of a small number of commodity agreements for certain major farm products is likely to shift production adjustment problems to other commodities. For example, assume that it was possible to obtain a wheat agreement that guaranteed access to the European Community for a specified fraction of Community consumption but that no agreement could be reached on feed-grains. The probable effect would be that more wheat would be denatured for use as livestock feed and the feed-grain import market would be further restricted.

An OECD Group of Experts in 1965 concluded its discussion of international commodity agreements as follows: 'Experience to date with international agreements suggests that they can play a useful role in promoting short-term stability. A danger exists, however, that they can be used to inhibit long-term adjustments required to bring overall agricultural resource use into line with market requirements and to promote appropriate international balance of resource use.'

Commodity agreements have normally not concerned themselves with the degree of protection provided by importers or exporters. Thus as noted by the OECD Group of Experts, such agreements have not contributed to an appropriate international balance of resource-use and it is quite unlikely that this defect can be corrected.

## Farm Policies in the Negotiations[12]

If the seventh GATT round is to achieve a substantial liberalisation of trade, governments must be willing, either directly or indirectly, to negotiate on the nature of their farm-support policies. Put another way, governments must be willing to accept a degree of discipline with respect to their policies, a discipline that up to this time has been largely absent. This does not mean that there need to be negotiations about the merits of variable import levies or export subsidies or import quotas. Such discussion would almost certainly be largely ideological and fruitless. While retaining considerable freedom with respect to the form of protection, governments should negotiate on the gradual reduction of the average level of protection afforded agriculture. Within this framework, the Common Market could retain its variable import-levy system; and the United States, its payments to producers who withhold land from production. But each would make a commitment that over time the amount of protection that would be provided to agriculture would be reduced by stages to an agreed level.

Negotiations could also be used to reach agreement on certain forms of income support that would not be considered in the measurement of protection. Liberal or even free trade does not require that all types of income transfers be abandoned. The critical question concerning any form of income transfer relates to its impact upon production and consumption and therefore upon trade.

There are many measures that would help to alleviate economic distress in rural areas that have minimal impacts upon production and some that would assist in facilitating production adjustment. Therefore payments for early retirement, payments to low-income farm families that are not associated with the level of production, or even rather general payments made to offset the income effects of lowering support levels, can be devised to have minimum effects on production. If price supports were reduced and payments were made on the basis of past levels of output or inputs (hectares of land or number of dairy cows), for example, the current output effects would be small and perhaps small enough to be ignored entirely. There are many ways of transferring income to farm people; unfortunately, the policies of most countries tie the transfers to current output, either through higher prices, deficiency payments or input subsidies, and thereby significantly distort production decisions.[13] A substantial reduction in protection for agriculture would be much easier to achieve if there were prior agreement on measures that governments could use to soften the income effects of reducing the degree of protection.

Governments have been unwilling to discuss such measures because of the presumed interference with the domestic farm-support policies. What is here implied is that no government would be asked to accept any particular measure of income support, but each government could adopt measures that it would know in advance would be accepted by others as having acceptable small effects on production, consumption and trade. If the countries had agreed to staged reductions in the degree of protection, income support measures that had been agreed to have acceptably small effects on trade would not be counted in the measurement of protection. Governments could accordingly agree to lower levels of price support, without being precluded from effective measures to prevent sharp and unacceptable changes in farm income.

### Adequate Preparation for Negotiations

Negotiations on agricultural trade will be both difficult and complex. Yet relatively little, if anything, is being done adequately to prepare for them in the seventh GATT round. In the past, when the negotiations were primarily concerned with changes in tariff rates and the major concern, aside from a few sensitive commodities, was in a balancing of offers in terms of approximate equivalence of imports and exports, relatively limited advance preparation was required. Any significant degree of success in the seventh GATT round will require, at least over time, substantial changes in price-support levels and methods of income support for farmers.

It must be said that governments are woefully ignorant of the effectiveness of their existing farm-support policies in meeting their objectives and have generally been unwilling to consider how the same objectives might be met by alternative policies that resulted in minimal impact upon trade in farm products. Governments do not know the answers, with any reasonable degree of reliability, to the following questions:

1. How much have agricultural policies increased net farm income?
2. What effect have agricultural policies had on farm output and on domestic consumption of farm products?
3. How much do agricultural policies cost taxpayers and consumers?
4. How are the economic benefits of agricultural policies, distributed between high and low income families in agriculture?
5. What part of the total costs borne by consumers and taxpayers actually accrues to farm people as additional income?

Given the enormous costs imposed upon consumers and taxpayers, it does seem reasonable that governments would be willing to devote a few resources to trying to answer such questions. Yet there seems to be no inclination to do so.

Equally depressing, there appears to be little or no attention given to the analysis of measures that do not depend upon high price supports and subsidies tied to output, but which would attack more directly the income and adjustment problems of farm people. Such failure to consider alternatives to present policies is not for a lack of such suggestions. For example, *A Future for European Agriculture*, prepared by a panel of experts for the Atlantic Institute in Paris, makes a number of suggestions for a gradual transition from high price supports to measures that would minimize the reduction in farm incomes, especially for moderate and low-income farm families, and would not encourage uneconomic production.[14]

Another way of posing the issue of adequate preparations for the negotiations is to ask this question: What would happen to the level and composition of farm output and to farm employment in the European Community if there were (nearly) free trade in farm products? In the United States? In Australia? No one, and least of all the appropriate governmental officials, know the answer to this question and few have even made an effort to imagine what the answer might be. There is a clear presumption, widely held in Western Europe, that agriculture must be highly protected if it is to survive in competition with the supposedly more efficient agri-cultures of North America and Oceania. But there is evidence that much of Western Europe, especially the European Community, is a relatively efficient producer of dairy products, compared with the United States and Canada (although not with New Zealand and Australia), and in pork and probably could be in cattle feeding with appropriate relationships between the prices of grain and fed cattle. It is exactly these sectors though that are being adversely affected by the high protection of grain production by the common agricultural policy.

Policy makers who are concerned, and perhaps properly so, with the rapid rate of decline in farm employment in agriculture are following policies that penalise the labour-intensive sectors — namely livestock — and protect the labour-extensive sector — grain. If the policy makers meant what they say — or understood the implications of what they are doing — they would encourage the production of livestock products rather than penalising it by induc-ing high feed prices and high consumer prices that restrict consump-tion and consequently restrict the amount of production. The author has estimated very roughly that a 10 per cent increase in livestock production in the European Community would result in an increase in farm employment greater than the decline in employment that would result from a 25 per cent reduction in grain production. And under free trade, livestock output could well increase substantially more than 10 per cent — more probably by double that after a period of time. If minimising the decline in farm employment is a serious objective, farm-support policies are often in conflict with that objective.

The report of the High-level OECD Group included the suggestion that studies be undertaken to determine the effect of farm policies upon production, consumption and trade. This was not the first time such a suggestion has been made; nonetheless at the time of writing there has been no decision by the OECD or any other international organisation to sponsor such a study.

## Concluding Comment

The sharp increases in the price of farm products that occurred in 1973 and 1974 have not diminished the desirability of trade liberalisa-tion. The gains from trade are not a function of the level of prices except as some types of trade barriers, such as variable levies or specific duties, are less restrictive at high prices than low prices. Unfortunately, the post-1972/73 levels of international prices of farm products and the record high levels of trade may well lead some exporters to minimise the importance of the agricultural negotiations and, at the same time, permit importers to maintain that there is little or no need for liberalisation since no exporter is lacking for a market.

The interferences with the exports of farm products that occurred in 1973 and 1974, including the limitations on the exports of soybeans from the United States, will almost certainly cause the major importers to press for greater assurances on the availability of supplies. The large stocks of grains in North America served as the world's reserves for the past two decades. But these stocks are gone and there is a real reluctance among farmers and policy makers in North America to deliberately rebuild them. Thus there is a real need for serious consideration of the responsibilities of both importers and exporters for the maintenance of reserves and agreement on rules concerning interferences with and limitations on the availability of exports.

There may be numerous reasons why governments are willing to enter a seventh GATT round totally unprepared for negotiations on agriculture. Whatever the reasons, the failure to consider alternatives to the present and enormously expensive farm-support policies will almost certainly doom the negotiations to failure. The cost of the failure may well be much greater than the continued uneconomic use of such a large fraction of the world's agricultural resources. The cost could be a major trend toward trade restrictions generally which would almost certainly generate political tensions in international relations.[15]

## NOTES AND REFERENCES

1. This chapter is based on the author's article, 'Obstacles to Agricultural Trade: Need for New Perspectives', *The Round Table*, London, April 1973.

2. The points in this paragraph are developed in D. Gale Johnson, *World Agriculture in Disarray* (London: Macmillan, and Fontana (paperback), for the Trade Policy Research Centre, 1973), chaps. 4 and 5.

3. *Ibid.*, pp. 209-10.

4. *Ibid.*, pp. 210-12.

5. In 1971 the average family income, from farm and non-farm sources, of the top fifth of farm families was $21,750 which compared with a national average family income of approximately $15,000.

6. Denis Bergmann, 'European Agricultural Policy: a French Viewpoint', in Hermann Priebe *et al.*, *Fields of Conflict in European Farm Policy*, Agricultural Trade Paper No. 3 (London: Trade Policy Research Centre, 1972), p. 28.

7. T.E. Josling and Donna Hamway, 'Distribution of Costs and Benefits of Farm Policy', in Josling *et al.*, *Burdens and Benefits of Farm-support Policies*, Agricultural Trade Paper No. 1 (London: Trade Policy Research Centre, 1972), pp. 76-77.

8. Johnson, *World Agriculture in Disarray*, *op. cit.*, pp. 44-51.

9. In the United Kingdom 'the farm vote' counts for very little with less than 2.5 per cent of the working population engaged on the land. But in the rural constituencies which overwhelmingly return Conservative members to Parliament, the organisation

of the Conservative Party is highly dependent on farming interests. On the other hand, the Labour Party, with its strength in urban constituencies, has been far from conspicuous in safeguarding the consumer interest in farm-support measures.

10. The position of the United States appears to have been worked out more fully than that of the other major participants. See Assistant to the President for International Economic Affairs, *Agricultural Trade and the Proposed Round of Multilateral Negotiations*, Flanigan Report (Washington: US Government Printing Office, for the Senate Committee on Agriculture, United States Congress, 1973). For earlier expressions of the American interest, see the agricultural chapter, and the technical papers on agricultural trade, in the Presidential Commission on International Trade and Investment Policy, *United States International Economic Policy in an Interdependent World*, Williams Report (Washington: US Government Printing Office, 1971).

The negotiating position of the European Community was agreed by the Council of Ministers on 26 June 1973.

Accounts in English of Japanese agricultural policy are rare. The reader might be referred to Michael Tracy, *Japanese Agriculture at the Crossroads*, Agricultural Trade Paper No. 2 (London: Trade Policy Research Centre, 1972).

11. High-level Group of Trade and Related Problems, *Policy Perspectives for International Trade and Economic Relations*, Rey Report (Paris: OECD Secretariat, 1972).

12. The ideas developed briefly here are more fully presented in Johnson, *World Agriculture in Disarray, op. cit.*, chap. 12.

13. In the paper by Jan Horring, 'European Farm Policy: a Dutch Viewpoint', in Priebe *et al.*, *op. cit.*, p. 44, a striking comparison is made between production and price developments in the 1960s in Denmark and the Netherlands, countries whose agricultures share many similarities. In the Netherlands farm prices were higher than in Denmark by 18 per cent in 1960-61, 31 per cent higher in 1964-65 and 48 per cent higher in 1968-69. Between 1960-64 and 1967-69 farm production increased by only 2 per cent in Denmark and 24 per cent in the Netherlands.

14. Bergmann  *et al.*, *A Future for European Agriculture* (Paris: Institut Atlantique, 1971).

15. Sir Christopher Soames, the European Community's commissioner for External Affairs, warned as much when introducing the Commission's proposal for the Common Market's negotiating position in the GATT negotiations. See *The Times*, London, 5 April 1973.

# CHAPTER 13

## *Access for the Exports of Developing Countries*

### SIDNEY GOLT

It is with misgivings that the phrase 'developing countries' is used in the title of this paper.[1] Not only has this expression forced itself, by repetition, into common currency. It is generally accepted as implying a definable and recognisable group of countries. This implication has obscured rather than clarified thought and has played a significant part in distorting international policy.

A number of variant categorisations of the groups concerned are referred to as 'less developed countries', 'agricultural countries', 'primary producers' and 'the poorer countries', on the one hand, and 'major trading powers' and 'industrial countries' on the other. This paper does not attempt to unravel cross connections and over-lappings between these different groupings. But some of the confusion of thought arises from disregard of these complexities of categorisation.

There are different degrees of development among the countries of the world, and it is possible to recognise some particular countries as being relatively more and some as relatively less developed (though it seems unrealistic to try to establish any sort of equivalence between the degree of development and a norm to which the inhabitants of every country should aspire). Certainly there are a comparatively small number of countries which, by the weight of their own wealth in relation to the rest of the world, are bound to exercise, through the economic and international commercial policies which they adopt, a substantial influence on the economic activity and the fortunes of much of the rest. Inevitably, the policies of those countries will be at the centre of discussion, and will almost certainly attract criticism and often resentment. Where there are conflicts among these major countries, the conflicts in their turn will have significant effects throughout the world.

### Post-war Developments and the GATT

Since the end of World War II there has been a good deal of change in the relations of the major countries both among them-selves and in relation to the rest of the world. These developments need to be looked at as the setting for the present situation. The outstanding characteristic of the entire period has been the deliberate and conscious effort in the world as a whole to establish international consultative procedures and institutions as venues for negotiation and discussion, not only for international action, but also, to a much greater degree than ever before, for internal domestic actions and policies which affect other countries. This does not mean that countries have been willing to subject their domestic decisions, even on matters of vital concern to others, to international jurisdiction or control. But it has meant that there has been among the major countries — perhaps with different degrees of whole-heartedness — an acceptance of a basic principle of the post-1945 international trade arrangements.

This principle maintained that there must be a set of rules designed to prevent a repetition of the troubles of the inter-war period. In particular, the rules were to prevent, as far as possible, what was seen as a particular evil of the 1930s: the proliferation of bilateralism by which strong countries were seen to exercise their superior bargaining strength — by virtue of sheer economic power and, even more objectionably, political power — to impose their desired pattern of trade on weaker trading partners. Moreover, these rules were reinforced by an international framework aimed at creating a system and, perhaps even more important, a habit of multilateral consultation, discussion and, to some extent, surveil-lance. It is probably fair to say that in the framework of the General Agreement on Tariffs and Trade (GATT), in which these arrange-ments were embodied, there was no trade matter of interest to two countries which was not directly or indirectly of interest to all and could not be made the subject of discussion by all.

Within this system, the main rules were designed first to prevent the emergence of new preferential systems through clauses requiring non-discriminatory trade through the operation of the most-favoured-nation (MFN) or equal treatment. Secondly, they were to limit to the customs tariff the *method* by which domestic industries might be given some measure of protection, and to promote through multilateral tariff negotiations the progressive reduction of the *level* of such protection. Thirdly, they were to lay down a body of ancillary regulations to protect the bargains arrived at in such negotiations from being undermined by other non-tariff devices, and to provide arrangements for the orderly discussion of disputes. Finally, the system's institutions — and especially the regular sessions of the contracting parties to the GATT — provided a forum for discussion of general problems of international commercial policy and for the initiation of new policies.

It is worth noting that from the very beginning the representatives of many countries outside the major trading and industrialised countries — countries now among the developing countries — were closely concerned in the creation of the GATT and, indeed, played distinguished parts in the whole process of establishing the post-war monetary and commercial arrangements. At the United Nations Conference on Trade and Employment in Havana there was a Mexican, a Uruguayan and a Lebanese among the chairmen of committees. And it is of some interest that the concept of a free trade area, as an addition to the article which allowed the creation of customs unions to override the non-discrimination provisions, was based on proposals by Syria and Lebanon. Equally, from the very beginning, the formal provisions of the GATT incorporated a recognition that the rules of protection might call for modification in the interests of development, and that in some cases quantitative restrictions might be more appropriate than tariffs to assist developing industries. Similarly, there was always ready acceptance of the view that less developed countries might need an easier resort to import restrictions for balance-of-payments reasons.

More generally, the prevailing style of participants in the GATT was always to look less closely at the practices of the smaller partners in world trade than at those of the major ones. One example of this has been the successive efforts to contain and control the use of export sudsidies. When, eventually, a declaration on this subject was agreed, it was made a matter for voluntary acceptance, and the major countries agreed to operate it as soon as all of them had accepted. It was not felt necessary to await the acceptance of the smaller countries to be bound in the same way.

Not all the smaller and less developed countries joined the GATT in spite of these and other manifestations of its flexibility and adaptability. But a considerable number did so; and by the end of the 1960s there were some seventy-five members, of whom by far the greatest number were outside the group of major trading countries. Indeed, such mandatory provisions as the GATT contained could have been enforced by these countries, who certainly had a two-thirds majority by number. It has been one of the virtues of the GATT, however, as a piece of international machinery, that formal voting has never been a significant element in its processes and its contracting parties have throughout aimed at conciliation and accommodation. Nor is it purely cynicism to say that any other attitude would have been self-destructive. For the smaller countries to have tried by majority voting to coerce a major country might have endangered the whole fabric. The fact is that, especially in the first decade of its existence, the GATT was a strongly civilising influence in the conduct of international commercial policy.

Of course, not all the differences of view, even among the major countries, had been effaced by the Havana debates on international trade and by the conclusion of the GATT. The most significant element of potential conflict was between the Americans, who stood on the principle of non-discrimination in its purest and most rigid form, and the French, who remained attached to a considerable measure of discriminatory action in the organisation of international trade. This reflected also the greater desire of the United States to rely on the operation of market forces, while the French, internationally as well as in their internal domestic arrangements, were by tradition, as well as by what they felt necessary in post-war circumstances, interventionist and *dirigiste*. One special target of the United States in the debates had indeed been the preferential systems of the Europeans, primarily the British system of Commonwealth preference — much the most important and significant set of mutual trading arrangements in the world at the time. Britain herself was also deeply devoted to the MFN non-discriminatory principle — which, in her own nineteenth century period of dominance in world trade, she had effectively imposed on the world — provided that the Ottawa system was allowed to survive.

In the event, the GATT embodied the MFN principle as its basic foundation. Existing preferential arrangements were permitted to continue, but strong limitations were placed on their extension or intensification. The reason for their continuance was on the basis that the progressive reduction of MFN tariffs, through the negotiation process, would reduce *pro tanto* and perhaps eventually eliminate the preferential margins. The GATT also included provision, under fairly strict conditions, for the future creation of customs unions and free trade areas (which, it seems, were thought of as a more suitable potential line of development for smaller, less developed countries).

## Dominance of Major Trading Powers

However conscious the founding fathers of the GATT may have been of the problems of less developed countries, it must be accepted, and indeed it was inevitable, that both the main objective of the General Agreement, and its main practical effect, have been to govern the conduct of the major trading countries in: (a) their trade with each other; (b) in their competition with each other in third countries; and (c) in the way in which third countries could behave towards their major trading partners in relation to that competition. The direct interest of their own, which smaller countries certainly had in the pattern of world trade, was a secondary set of considerations.

A number of factors contributed further to this process. Perhaps the most important was that, although the GATT made no formal distinction in its rules and its application between manufactured goods and agricultural or other primary products, the facts of the real world imposed such a distinction upon the General Agreement. It had long been the case for agriculture that in virtually all countries the practice of governments, even of those most deeply committed to theories of the supremacy of market forces, leaned strongly towards the sort of interventionism which, as the French had always argued, could not easily be accommodated within the firmly market-based philosophy of the GATT.

In the event it was the United States in the early 1950s who effectively removed trade in agricultural products from the governance of the GATT. The Americans sought and secured a waiver from the rules which would have illegitimised a great deal of their domestic agricultural policies at that time. It is only fair to say that over the intervening period there have been changes in American practice which make that waiver very much less relevant. But the American waiver gave cover to similar practices elsewhere, almost to the point of making the GATT applicable only to manufactured goods, and of making countries who had a major interest in agricultural exports (Denmark, New Zealand and Australia outstandingly) bitterly doubtful about its value for them. The British interest here, as in so many other instances, was ambivalent. Britain was virtually the only market in the world substantially open to agricultural imports, and she was in fact a beneficiary of other people's subsidy-created surpluses; but she still hankered after some reasonable body of international law in this field. One British civil servant is remembered as saying that what was needed for agriculture was a separate little GATT of its own — a 'Gitten', as he suggested it should be called!

The mechanics of the tariff bargaining process still further concentrated the area of GATT concern on those goods entering international trade which were of interest to the major traders. Reciprocity in negotiation means that a bargain can be struck only, or at any rate primarily, among those who have something to offer and think they have something to gain. Or sometimes, as may have been the case with the United States in the earlier post-war negotiations, a country may be prepared to forego the full value of its 'concessions'. Overwhelmingly and inevitably the centre of the bargaining stage was occupied by the major countries. A successful outcome depended on their ability to fill out mutually satisfactory packages. Only on the basis of these central bargains was it possible to embrace interests on the periphery.

This is not to say that the smaller countries derived no benefit from the existence of the GATT or from tariff negotiations. The truth is indeed the reverse. They derived very great benefit indeed compared with the pre-1939 (that is, pre-GATT) position. It was after all within the framework of the post-war monetary and trade settlements (the creation of the GATT, the International Monetary Fund and the International Bank for Reconstruction and Development) that throughout the 1950s and most of the 1960s the United States was able to pursue the policies, sometimes of high altruism, which so rapidly and so massively facilitated the restoration of the economies of Western Europe after the war. On the basis of the subsequent great growth in activity and trade so fostered, the trade and the activity of the rest of the world also grew very substantially. Nor was this trade subjected to the more execrable practices which had arisen from the bilateral treaties, which were indeed *Diktats,* of the 1930s. The 1950s and 1960s did not see Britain imposing clearing arrangements on Argentina, as she had done in the 1930s, in order to secure bilaterally balanced trade. Nor did Germany, in the manner of the Third Reich, force her neighbours to accept imports they did not want. If anything, the boot was on the other foot, as is evidenced for example by the long and patient efforts of what came to be called the Hague Club to make it possible for Brazil to move out of the strait-jacket of her self-imposed bilateralism. Moreover, even if the GATT's bargaining techniques (before the attempt to widen them in the Kennedy Round negotiations to linear tariff reductions) narrowed the field, they still provided the machinery and some incentives for the smaller countries to participate in the process. They strengthened the permanence of bargains once struck, and extended the benefits of the tariff reductions arrived at through central bargains to all members of the GATT (and as far as most of the major countries were concerned to the world as a whole) without too exacting a search for strict reciprocity from the smaller countries.

Nonetheless all this could not alter some basic elements in the GATT situation. An agreement dealing with world trade could hardly fail to be dominated by the world's major traders. In a world giving birth to a host of newly independent states, which had but yesterday been colonial dependencies of those major traders and which for the most part were extremely poor, such a system could hardly fail to look anything other than a rich man's club. And beyond any doubt, although the primary producing countries had shared in the increasing world trade, they had certainly not done so to anything like the same extent as the producers of manufactures. The really significant growth had in fact been among the industrialised countries themselves, rather than between manufacturing and primary producers.

Rich man's club or not, the GATT began, before the end of the 1950s, to direct its attention to the special problems of the less developed countries. Following the Haberler Report[2] in 1958 a number of points were raised calling for action by industrialised countries. Broadly speaking these points called for special efforts, beyond the limits of any kind of reciprocal bargaining, to ensure that the interests of less developed countries were given full consideration in the commercial policies of the industrialised ones.

The efforts made by the industrialised countries were to ensure the following:

(a) standstill provision on new tariff or non-tariff barriers;
(b) elimination of outstanding quantitative restrictions on imports;
(c) duty-free entry for tropical products;
(d) elimination of tariff barriers to exports of semi-processed products;
(e) progressive reduction of internal fiscal charges; and
(f) revenue duties on products of special interest.

There was envisaged a regular procedure for reporting on progress made and, in addition, a proposal to urgently consider the adoption of other 'appropriate measures' to facilitate the efforts of less developed countries to 'diversify their economies, strengthen their export capacity and increase their earnings from overseas sales'.

Some of these concepts were to be embodied in 1965 in a new chapter of the GATT which sought to define the duties of the more developed countries to the less developed countries. But in the transition from the language of debate to the legalities of treaties, there were 'hedges' and qualifications which made these new clauses very much a matter of generalised aspirations rather than binding obligations. Moreover, there still lay not very far below the surface, the rift within the major trading countries — in this case, between the British, laying stress on access to markets, and the French, still arguing that organisation of markets, at any rate for selected products, would be more positive and more fruitful.

## United Nations Conference on Trade and Development

Meanwhile other events seemed to suggest that the whole GATT debate was irrelevant and outmoded. First, within the machinery of the GATT itself, special measures were being taken in the Long Term Arrangement on Cotton Textiles, not in order to give unrestricted opportunities for the less developed to expand their exports, but to provide a means of containing the rate of increase. The

Agreement could, in its original form, be reasonably defended as intended to provide an orderly mechanism for abolishing existing import restrictions. In the event, it has proved to be a weapon for retaining and, in some respects, extending them.

But, far more important, a whole new forum of debate was being opened up outside the GATT in the United Nations. The Soviet Union had long been pressing the United Nations for a new world conference on trade. This pressure was reinforced by the emergence of the newly independent African and Asian nations. They were supported by the Latin Americans. The objectives shifted from the problems of East-West trade to the problems of trade, aid and investment in relations between, on the one hand, the Western industrialised countries and the Soviet Union and its associates and, on the other, what were now called 'the developing countries' (though without any precise idea of which countries were intended to be covered by this term).

The West agreed to a conference on this basis. It was thus that the United Nations Conference on Trade and Development (UNCTAD) came into existence. The Conference began with a full session of some 120 countries in 1964 and the outcome was the establishment of UNCTAD as a permanent new institution within the United Nations family. Without going too deeply into the institutional debates of the first Conference, it may be said that the Western countries rejected the proposition that the whole structure of international trade was wrong; nor did they accept that the GATT was an inappropriate instrument for putting it right. But they acceded to the pressure for the creation of this new permanent body as a means of satisfying the claimant countries that the unfinished debate could continue in an institution of *their* own choosing. For their part, the developing countries saw the new institution as their own instrument, where they would have an unassailable majority of votes (with no nonsense about vetos by privileged permanent members of an inner Security Council) and the political leverage to compensate for their lack of bargaining power. Moreover, they counted on the institution having a Secretariat which, collectively and to a very large extent individually, was committed to their own objectives, and would be under the direction of a Secretary-General (Raoul Prebish) who was the most able, forceful and articulate proponent of their needs and aspirations.

A number of preliminary meetings before the first UNCTAD, both inside the United Nations (in the preparatory committee) and outside in informal consultative discussions, had foreshadowed the emergence of an organisation of the countries which felt they had claims for better treatment in world trade. By the time the Conference began this set of interests had to some extent crystallised into a group of 75 countries. But the basis of its membership, and its central role, was still inchoate and somewhat arbitrary. On the one hand, there were some clear political biases which might have been thought irrelevant for a grouping related to economic criteria. On this account Cuba and Israel, for example, were excluded, but Yugoslavia became a leading member and spokesman of the group. On the other hand, it was still possible at this stage for New Zealand — whose discontent with the GATT has already been noted — to participate. It was also still quite possible, even in the early stages of the 1964 session, for policy discussions to be pursued between individual developed countries and individual developing countries in the hope of finding mutually acceptable formulas. Such discussions, about for example improved tariff treatment, came near to presenting a formula which might have been put forward by a dozen or so countries across the whole spectrum.

Midway through the session, however, there emerged what has become known as 'the Group of 77' who formalised and solidified the earlier *ad hoc* arrangements and retained its previous political slants. But the Group of 77 also aimed to impose an internal discipline on its members in a way which virtually inhibited informal discussion across 'group' boundaries (and also made New Zealand's continued membership impossible). Further, it imposed on the institution a continuing 'adversary' procedure between the Group of 77 and the rest which meant the permanent stereotyping and, in the end, the virtual stultification of debate. The countries outside the Group of 77 (to which most of the post-1964 newly independent countries adhered, although in a few cases rather half-heartedly) were in their turn obliged to adopt much more formal arrangements and work out more tightly agreed conclusions than would otherwise have been the case. The artificial tri-polar group structure (the Group of 77, the developed market-economy countries and the socialist countries of Eastern Europe) imposed a further rigidity and a more extreme polarisation. In each case, the need to achieve a common position tended to produce, on the one side, the most widely spread collection of demands and, on the other, the least liberal offer of concessions.

The Group of 77 arrogated to themselves the description 'the developing countries' (much as the original six, and now the nine, of the European Community have appropriated 'Europe'). In doing so they both included and excluded countries whose claim for special consideration was at least open to debate. It seems highly probable that on this ground alone the concept of the developing countries, in the form in which it has emerged from the essentially political rather than economic decisions which created the Group of 77 in 1964, has been on balance self-defeating.

The transfer of the main centre of the debate on development, as far as trade was concerned, from the GATT to UNCTAD did not necessarily make the GATT irrelevant. But it went a long way towards sealing the fate of still-birth which might have, in any case, been the outcome of the GATT Action Programme. With one exception, that of preference schemes for manufactured products which are discussed in more detail below, the Tokyo Round of GATT negotiations, with the postures of the different groups of countries and the issues between them, were not formulated very differently than the negotiations of a decade ago. There have, though, been very substantial changes over the period in many other ways: (a) in the balance of commercial bargaining power and the pattern of world trade; (b) in the role of the United States in the world; (c) in the emergence of substantial new participants in trade, including one country which has become a major force in the world, namely Japan; (d) in the consolidation and enlargement of the European Community; (e) in the evident signs that a growing number of countries have carried their export potentiality to a point which still further vitiates the identification of developing countries with membership of the Group of 77; and (f) in the change in world attitudes and atmospheres in relation to trade liberalisation and protectionism.

During the 1970s the big increase in the prices of many primary commodities, and the possibility of considerable shortages, became significant factors. In particular the economic power of the oil producing countries has dramatically altered the world situation.

So far the institutional background to the present situation has been spelt out at some length as it does throw into some relief the issues which now face the negotiators in the Tokyo Round negotiations. But before turning to the substance of these talks, preferential treatment schemes for exports from developing countries, the so-called Generalised Preference Schemes, which have been one of the few concrete policy developments to be ascribed to the ferment of discussion of the last ten years, should be at least briefly mentioned.

As we have seen there had been some approach to the discussion of preferences for less developed countries, or some form of special tariff treatment, in the GATT before the first UNCTAD session. Britain was well placed to play a leading part in those discussions. By far the major part of exports of manufactures from countries other than the industrialised countries of Western Europe, North America and Japan, originated in countries within the Ottawa preference arrangements; and Britain was far and away the major trading partner of these countries. The very substantial measure of industrialisation of these countries had taken place with a considerable inflow of British investment, but also within a system which provided access to the British market, both duty-free and without quantitative restrictions. Up to 1931, of course, these same conditions had applied (with exceptions for a small number of products) to the whole world. The Ottawa Agreement meant the preservation of these conditions for the independent countries of the then Commonwealth and, too, for the then colonial possessions of the United Kingdom. The imposition of tariffs on the rest of the world meant that, in effect, the Ottawa Agreement countries had a preference against the rest. But it was always foremost in the minds of British administrators of commercial policy that what was the important element in the situation — in relation both to the consequences for British domestic industry and to the opportunities for Commonwealth country exporters — was free entry, not preference.

When British industrialists felt threatened by competition from Hong Kong, what they complained of was not that Hong Kong had a preference against other suppliers, but that domestic producers had no tariff or other protection against Hong Kong. And what, in the event, gave the Asians their chance in the British market was not the preference as such, but the opportunity to compete on equal terms with domestic industry. It seemed perfectly obvious to the British that the right way for industrialised countries in general to help development elsewhere through the promotion of manufactured exports was to generalise this pattern. No doubt it did not escape their attention that this might incidentally take some of the pressure of these exports off the British market and perhaps lighten the corresponding pressure on the British Government to take protective measures in Britain against Commonwealth imports. Moreover, it seemed possible to present a proposal on these lines in a way which seemed reasonably compatible with, or at least less repugnant to, GATT principles rather than a proposal for preferences as such. What was suggested was that free entry should be accorded to imports from less developed countries at an early date as an advance instalment, so to speak, of the *eventual* achievement of the general elimination of tariffs, which in theory should be the logical outcome of further rounds of tariff negotiations.

Finally, a formulation of this kind would have made it clear beyond doubt that whatever special treatment was given for the benefit of particular countries, no grounds were given for inhibiting the general advance in tariff reduction among the industrialised countries as the occasion arose. Unfortunately, the glamour which attached itself to the idea of 'preferential treatment' in UNCTAD debates, swamped the strength of these arguments; and the 'generalised preference schemes' which emerged suffer from many defects. These schemes are quite substantially circumscribed in scope and in almost all cases incorporate exceptions and mechanisms of safeguard and control. These exceptions and safeguards are sufficient to lend considerable colour to the accusation that they are designed to make sure that competition can be cut off or at least deprived of any encouragement as soon as it threatens to become effective or significant.[3]

It is certainly arguable that even if the original British proposals had been accepted, the general mood of the world at the time of implementation might have meant that the same limitations would have been imposed. Exceptions for products such as textiles and limitation by quota could have been applied just as easily in the one case as in the other. If free or freer entry, rather than preference, for developing countries had been accepted it might very well have been easier for the United States to join in the arrangements than proved possible initially. And it certainly would have removed the possibility of misunderstanding about whether any contractual element, in the special tariff treatment of the less developed, limited the room for general world tariff manoeuvre. As things are, it is deeply discouraging that the European Community's agreed initial bargaining position for the Tokyo Round negotiations subscribed to the theory that 'a margin of preference for developing countries is a desirable thing to preserve.

Against this historical and institutional background this paper will now turn to the trade negotiations which were inaugurated in Tokyo in September 1973. In the context of the subject of this paper there is perhaps a powerful symbol in the venue of that occasion. Japan might be seen as a classic instance of a country emerging from a 'developing country' status to that of one of the major world trading countries. And this has been achieved without any special privileged status and, indeed, often in the face of discrimination. It would not be inappropriate for Japan to inherit the role played successively by Britain and the United States during their commercial heydays; that role which cast them as the champions of non-discrimination and the MFN rule, of the commercial rights of small countries and of multilateral tariff bargaining and commercial policy negotiation.

This brings us to the heart of the problem. Some of the shortcomings of the post-war settlement of world commercial policy have been touched upon. Would the developing countries be better off if it were now to be abandoned? There has been much speculation, especially since the changes in American circumstances in the late 1960s, brought to a head by President Nixon's speech of 15 August 1971, about a coming trade war or the emergence of a system of trade blocs as an alternative to the multilateral system. Is this, perhaps, a better future prospect for developing countries?

This is one of the major points at which the concept of a unified group of developing countries, exercising a beneficial influence on the interests of all and imposing, through political pressure and the power of sympathetic progressive world opinion, trade policies promoting the development of all, breaks down. The fact is that the nearer one comes to trying to assess the significance of particular policies, the more apparent it becomes that differences of circumstance, history, attitude, geography, climate, natural resources and human capability are more important than the essentially negative basis of categorisation which has lumped some hundred countries together as the developing countries. Similarly, of course, the statistics assembled by combining the national statistics of these hundred odd countries must be altogether valueless as a tool of policy.   An immense amount of time and energy has gone into work of this kind which might have been better used in a more thorough examination of the particular problems of particular countries or areas. Nor does it seem that a further example of negative definition, a sort of double negative, contained in trying to identify and seek special measures for the least developed of the developing countries is at all an advance in thought. On the contrary, it compounds the original error. A better line of advance might be to recognise, as a first step, the very severe limitations of trade policy in any form in relation to the problems of some countries which have emerged due to the political changes of the last thirty years. It must be accepted that in many cases trade policy is certainly not a sufficient engine of development and may very often be a quite irrelevant consideration. There is also, at the other end of the spectrum, a number of countries who regard themselves as developing countries and are members of the Group of 77, but whose natural resources (as in the case of the oil producers) or present state of industrialisation make it difficult to suggest that they have a greater claim for special privilege than do those who are expected to provide the privileges.

For all these reasons, it is virtually impossible to make categoric judgements about the effect of different possible commercial policies on the fortunes of the developing countries as a totality. But it does seem reasonable to assume on the basis of past experience that world prosperity would not be improved, and in the long run would almost certainly deteriorate, if there were to be a prolonged period of anything like a trade war between the major trading countries, or a division of the world into mutually conflicting economic blocs. It is just possible to conceive the existence of a tightly organised, highly protectionist and inward-looking Euro-African bloc, with a set of internal commodity markets which might, in the short term, appear to provide some benefits for some African producers. But it is difficult to see such a Euro-African empire as a permanent element in a world of rapidly developing technology and communications, or to ascribe to it any long-term political viability. Nor can one look with any equanimity on a world in which there was a proliferation of such north-south groupings. One has to assume that there is still enough economic sanity in Washington and in Brussels, as well as in Tokyo, to make sure that the current resurgence of protectionism will stop short of destroying the liberal international economic order which is the legacy of a quarter of a century of international co-operation.

It looks, therefore, (always with diffidence about the generalisation) as if the interests of long-term world prosperity and, as part of this, the prospects for development generally, will best be served by the successful outcome of the larger negotiations. There have already been a number of declarations within the Tokyo negotiations that an attempt will be made to overcome the difficulties referred to earlier. How can this be done?

As regards trade in manufactures, the first area for attention will no doubt be the existing preference schemes. Provided that it were made clear — as it was at the outset in UNCTAD — that these schemes still contain no contractural obligation, there are clearly a number of things which could be done to bring them nearer to the original concept. There are exceptions which must be eliminated. More products could be brought in, especially processed raw materials and processed agricultural products, and the quotas to which the preference schemes apply could be enlarged. There is no certainty though that such progress will be made. There will always be difficulty, particularly between the Community and the United States about the equality of national schemes. And following the oil crisis American opinion against preferential treatment is more than likely to harden. Indeed, on all counts it would be a better line of advance if, instead of concentrating on the preference scheme, a real effort were to be made to reduce tariffs generally on a number of items of interest to less developed countries which would not otherwise enter into the negotiations. This aspect will assume especial importance indeed if the pattern of negotiations otherwise follows the line which the Community has postulated — that is, that there should be consideration of reducing tariffs by industrial sectors with reciprocity as far as possible in each individual sector. [4] It would be an admirable return to sanity, for example, if there were a general lowering of tariffs on the semi-processed products of tropical agriculture and of raw materials of which the Asians, Africans and Latin Americans are the principal producers.

The extent to which agricultural products can be effectively brought into the negotiations may well turn out to be the crucial factor in the success or failure of the negotiations as a whole. For this is one of the main potential elements of conflict between the European Community and the United States. Clearly, unless a satisfactory bargain can be struck between these two, no bargain can be struck at all. This mainly affects temperate products. Although there is a wider world interest in these (and especially in cereals), the main interest in the present context lies in tropical products and in the special case of sugar produced in both tropical and temperate zones. There appears to be widespread agreement that on all counts there is a strong case for the reappraisal of sugar policy so as to remove some of the more glaringly discriminatory distortions of the market. As regards other commodities, immense time and effort has been expended over the years in UNCTAD and elsewhere on the theory of, and on conferences aiming at, international commodity agreements. The participants have not always agreed on whether the objective was (a) to reduce the degree of fluctuation around a middle open-market price, (b) to stabilise prices at agreed levels acceptable to both producers and consumers or (c) to establish prices at levels higher than would prevail in an open market (which has been described as 'taking money from the poor in rich countries to give to the rich in poor countries'). But this disagreement has not been the only, or even the main, element in the paucity of the results achieved. Even the most fervent advocates must surely now begin to acknowledge that there is not much juice to be squeezed out of this lemon. More, indeed, might accrue to the producers of these products through much less complex operations if some West European countries were to get rid of a portion of their revenue taxes on some tropical products, and much more accrue if the buying and internal price policies of the Soviet Union and other East Europeans were changed.

Apart from tariffs and agriculture, the negotiations are also concerned with non-tariff barriers. It is indeed regrettable that recent years have seen a reversal in this respect and that, directly or indirectly, quantitative import restrictions or persuasion of exporting countries to restrict exports, have increased and are increasing. This, like some of the other policies mentioned, is an aspect of the new mercantilism. It will be one of the tests of the negotiations to see what happens in this area, and whether the major countries will undertake to refrain from new restrictions of this kind and will contain and reverse the present tendency.

All in all, the policy prescriptions outlined would, if set out in full, bear a remarkable family resemblance to the GATT Action Programme of 1963. That this should be so may perhaps answer the question as to whether there has been value and effectiveness in the concept of the developing countries as an engine of political pressure. Much of the UNCTAD debate has been often directed to the right ends, but by the wrong means and with the wrong arguments, at any rate as far as trade questions have been concerned. Governments of major trading countries, however, seem to have been only a little less inept in the 1960s in ordering their relations among themselves than they have been in their relations with the rest of the world, including the developing countries, however that may be defined. Perhaps, even at this late date, they may recall the splendid dictum of Benjamin Franklin — 'no nation was ever ruined by trade'.

## NOTES AND REFERENCES

1. This paper is a revised version of one given to the economics section of the British Association for the Advancement of Science, Canterbury, September 1973.

2. Panel of Experts, *Trends in International Trade*, Haberler Report (Geneva: Gatt Secretariat, 1958).

3. See Richard N. Cooper, 'The European Community's System of Generalised Tariff Preferences: a Critique', *Journal of Development Studies*, London, July 1970. Also see Peter Lloyd, 'The Australian Tariff Preference Scheme for Developing Countries', *Journal of World Trade Law*, London, June 1970.

4. See paper by Hugh Corbet in Chapter 10 above.

# CHAPTER 14

## Adjustment Assistance to Import Competition

### GERHARD FELS

One of the main objectives of development policy in the 1970s has been to increase the level of manufactured exports from developing countries. The rationale of this policy derives from the insight that the foreign exchange shortages as well as the mass unemployment from which many developing countries suffer are linked with the lack of sufficient participation by these countries in the international division of labour. While the highly industrialised countries benefit mutually from a rapidly increasing volume of international trade, the developing countries are faced with a low and declining share in world markets. Their exports consist largely of primary products for which demand has expanded only moderately. Sharp price increases and shortages of oil and other raw materials have aided some, but harmed the bulk of the developing world. This situation could be remedied by a re-specialisation towards exports of manufactured goods which are on the dynamic side of the world market. The necessary improvement, however, is not easily attainable. It requires new thinking in the field of trade policies and a restructuring of industries in both developing and developed countries. One means of facilitating this process in the case of the latter is of course by way of adjustment assistance in favour of those who are adversely affected by restructuring. [1]

The first part of this chapter will deal with the trade problems of developing countries and the restructuring operations which have to be launched in order to solve them. Special attention is given to the preference schemes recently introduced in a number of developed countries to favour manufactured imports from developing countries. The second part is concerned with the philosophy of adjustment assistance and the nature of the process of adjustment in developed countries to enlarged exports from the developing world. Finally the additional policies which seem to be necessary to encourage restructuring, and to improve the international division of labour, shall be discussed.

So far as reorientation in the developing countries themselves is concerned this chapter will only touch on the problem. The shift towards a manufacturing-oriented export strategy means a departure from the import-substitution policy of industrialisation which many developing countries have followed up to a dead end. Though import substitution was designed to save foreign exchange, balance-of-payments difficulties did not diminish. Moreover, import-substitution policy has given too many incentives to capital-intensive lines and methods of production. First, the scope for import replacements is most extensive in capital-intensive branches, and developing countries are less competitive in this field. Secondly, the incentives which have usually been given to encourage industrialisation are concerned mainly with investment. They are consequently more in the nature of a subsidy to capital-intensive than to labour-intensive industry, and more of a subsidy to the use of capital-intensive techniques than to the employment of labour. Thirdly, prestige considerations and the absence of their own technological capacity have led many developing countries to apply production techniques which are as much concerned with labour saving as are those of the developed countries. The counterpart of this over-capitalisation is a lack of jobs in manufacturing which has contributed considerably to mass unemployment.

Export-oriented industrialisation would not only increase the import capacity of developing countries, but would also have a job-creation effect. This is because developing countries would be able to exploit the competitive advantages of low wage rates and a large supply of labour. Developing countries have 'a comparative advantage' in labour-intensive lines of production, especially in activities requiring a relatively large amount of unskilled or low-skilled labour, which constitute the most abundant factors of production in less developed regions. These activities, of course, also require capital, but to a lesser extent than other activites: so that with the same sum invested more jobs can be created.

Such considerations must, however, be regarded as a rule of thumb for an outward-looking design for industrialisation rather than as a guide to action in all circumstances. In concrete investment decisions such factors as demand prospects, the hitherto existing capacities, linkage effects *et al.* have also to be taken into account. Since the early 1960s some countries have been very successfully developed with an export strategy based mainly on labour-intensive products. Examples include Singapore, Hongkong, South Korea, Taiwan, Yugoslavia and Mexico. The outline of developing countries' overall performance in the import markets of the four highly industrialised regions — provided in Table 1 — shows that these countries have gained considerable ground with labour-intensive manufactures in three of those regions. Increasing market shares can also be observed for resource-intensive manufactures, in the case of the European Community and Japan. Even skill-intensive manufactured products achieved a higher market

**TABLE 1  Developing Countries' Export Performance with Five Commodity Groups**

*(Percentage share of total imports)*

| Commodity Group | EEC | | EFTA[f] | | USA | | Japan | |
|---|---|---|---|---|---|---|---|---|
| | 1964 | 1970 | 1964 | 1970 | 1964 | 1970 | 1964 | 1970 |
| Agricultural products[a] | 51.2 | 49.5 | 31.9 | 32.2 | 63.8 | 56.5 | 36.9 | 38.2 |
| Raw materials incl. fuel[b] | 55.0 | 58.2 | 45.8 | 44.3 | 55.6 | 47.4 | 53.7 | 52.0 |
| Raw material-intensive manufacturing[c] | 11.9 | 14.3 | 11.0 | 9.9 | 17.2 | 15.5 | 35.8 | 45.9 |
| Labour-intensive manufacturing[d] | 5.7 | 7.4 | 13.2 | 10.0 | 23.4 | 29.1 | 9.4 | 25.2 |
| Skill-intensive manufacturing[e] | 1.0 | 1.3 | 2.0 | 2.0 | 3.8 | 6.0 | 5.0 | 2.8 |
| Total | 37.7 | 36.6 | 24.5 | 20.4 | 36.0 | 26.3 | 40.3 | 39.7 |

[a] SITC 0+1+4;   [b] SITC 2+3;   [c] SITC 6—65—61—69;   [d] SITC 8—86+65+61+69;   [e] SITC 5+7+86;   [f] Share in extra trade.

share in the Community and the United States, but on a very small scale. Although the export performance of developing countries in the field of manufactured goods has improved rapidly, however, progress is still rather poor and it is shared in by only a few countries.

But apart from misguided policies implemented by the developing countries themselves, this poor performance has a great deal to do with the trade obstacles maintained by developed countries. The tariffs imposed by the latter are often highest in the case of those manufactured products which can be supplied competitively by the developing world. [2] This becomes obvious if one examines the effective tariff rate rather than the nominal rate. While the nominal tariff rate of a commodity refers to its import value, the effective rate of tariff protection is best expressed as the percentage of the value added which is generated by domestic production of the commodity. In calculating this way account can be taken of both tariffs on the final product which work like subsidies to domestic producers and tariffs on imported inputs which have the effect of a production tax. Since tariffs on final products are in general higher than on raw materials and other inputs, domestic value added is in general more protected than the nominal tariff rates indicate. In particular, as can be seen from Table 2, this holds true for lines of production which are under competitive pressure from developing countries. Broadly speaking it seems to be true that the existing tariff structure discriminates against imports from developing countries more than against imports from developed countries. And in addition to tariff protection there also exists a variety of non-tariff barriers to trade — including quotas mainly for imports from some low-wage countries. (The nature of these last is discussed in Chapter 11 above by Peter Lloyd.)

### Preference Schemes in Favour of Developing Countries

Since the early 1960s, in order to facilitate their access to the markets of the developed countries, the developing countries have been claiming preferential treatment for their exports. After the topic was discussed at the 1964 and 1968 sessions of the United Nations Conference on Trade and Development (UNCTAD), the developed and developing countries agreed in 1970 on 'the establishment of generalised, non-discriminatory, non-reciprocal preferential treatment to exports of developing countries in the markets of developed countries'. [3] In the proclamation of the Second Development Decade the United Nations included the adoption of preferential arrangements as an integral part of the proposed Development Strategy. [4] Since 1971 most of the developed countries in Europe including Czechoslovakia and Hungary, and also Japan, have introduced preference schemes, mainly in the form of a part or total cut in tariffs on certain manufactured and semi-manufactured imports from developing countries. The schemes implemented might be considered as an important step towards a better division of labour with the developing countries; and apart from the Soviet Union, the only large developed country which appeared reluctant to grant generalised tariff preferences was the United States, but a scheme was proposed to Congress in 1973.

Nevertheless, the question inevitably arises as to whether the schemes are even approximately adequate for dealing with the vast trade and development problem with which they are concerned. First of all, one has to be aware of a semantic aspect. The term 'preferential treatment' suggests that developing countries have received a competitive advantage *vis-a-vis* suppliers from developed countries. But in truth, nothing more than a moderation of the discriminatory effect against developing countries has occurred. To some extent the starting positions have been made more equal; but even this statement only holds true in narrow limits because the new arrangements contain a variety of exceptions and limitations on duty-free imports.

The exceptions and limitations vary from one preference-giving country to another. Since the specific arrangements are rather complicated only the main features of the schemes can be reviewed.

In the first place, in principle, the commodity-lists only cover manufactures and semi-manufactures. Primary commodities and agricultural products are excluded, with the exception of some selected items. In the field of manufactures there is a negative list which excludes some products — particularly (in the European case) imports of cotton textiles from non-members of the Long-Term Agreement on Cotton Textiles (LTA).

Secondly, the beneficiary developing countries have been selected by the preference-giving countries. In the case of the European Community, the South European developing countries and such important exporters as Israel and Taiwan are totally excluded. In general, the country list covers the members of the Group of 77 and dependent territories and some developed countries have extended this list.

Thirdly, all preference-giving countries combined the schemes with a safeguard mechanism either taking the form of limitation formulas (European Community and Japan), or the form of 'escape clause' measures (United Kingdom and other countries). The Community's limitations consist in ceilings

which are based on the level of imports in 1968 of the commodities in question from countries covered by the scheme;
they are subject to annual increases of 5 per cent in most cases.
No beneficiary country can exceed 50 per cent of these ceilings
and in some cases the maximum is only 30 per cent. The ceilings are of practical importance for a list of products considered sensitive. Here the Community allocated special tariff
quotas among the member countries. On imports which exceed
these quotas, tariffs are imposed according to the most-
favoured-nation (non-discrimination) principle.

Fourthly, now as before, all developed countries employ
quantitative quotas against the import of several 'sensitive'
products from certain developing countries, independent of the
implemented schemes.

Despite these reservations, it seems to be too early to attempt a
comprehensive evaluation of the effects of the preference schemes so
far implemented. In the case of West Germany, according to the
German Government the preferences were exhausted so rapidly that
they had to be withdrawn for sixteen countries and 109 sensitive
positions during the first year of application.[5] Nevertheless, in the
first half of 1972 more than 63 per cent of the imports favoured by
the scheme fell within the field of sensitive commodities. The figures
give evidence that the safeguard mechanism works as it was
intended and it provides a certain degree of security for domestic
producers. But since the list of sensitive products in the main covers
commodities in the production of which developing countries have a
comparative advantage, from the viewpoint of the exporters in
developing countries the safeguard mechanism is not conducive to
encouraging strong efforts. As Richard Cooper, of Yale University,
has pointed out, the limitations have the effect that 'there is no new
incentive where it counts, at the margin'.[6] A similar disadvantage is
associated with the escape clause measures employed by other
countries for they involve a risk element for exporters in developing
countries.

## Priority for Adjustment Assistance

The catalogue of sensitive products can be interpreted as a kind of
social consensus on domestic activites the defence of which must be
recognised as being inconsistent with the export interests of
developing countries. The list reveals the hard core of protection
which is still defended against imports from developing countries.
The question is how to crack this hard core. Adjustment assistance is
designed to do this. It aims at smoothing the adjustment process and

at assisting the rehabilitation or compensation of those who have been put at a disadvantage as a result of increased import competition. In doing so, it involves a shift from the provision of security by actual or potential trade limitations to security by assisting restructuring. (In Chapter 15 below Jan Tumlir discusses adjustment assistance as an integral part of a revised safeguard mechanism providing temporary protection against sudden surges of imports.) Adjustment assistance is a means to overcome the structural frictions and political resistance of those who are afraid to lose from liberalisation. Since the early 1960s assistance measures have been discussed as being complementary to liberalisation or as an alternative to protection in the developed economies. During its 1964 session, UNCTAD recommended assistance arrangements in the developed countries with respect to imports of manufactures from developing countries; at the third UNCTAD conference in 1972 adjustment assistance was one of the major topics of discussion.

A policy which facilitates adaptation to increased imports can be justified in terms of national as well as international welfare. From a cosmopolitical point of view it can be regarded as a pre-condition for further liberalisation, which in turn is an essential for the integration of the developing countries into the world economy. On the other hand, a justification in national terms can be derived from the principles of welfare economics. According to a widely accepted hypothesis, there are net gains from freer trade for the economy as a whole. Therefore, within each developed country, those who gain from increased trade compensate for those who lose from it. The gains are spread among the consumers who benefit from cheaper imports, and among the income earners who participate in the higher overall productivity increase which results from a more efficient allocation of resources. Unfortunately, there are also of course losses: displaced workers and disappointed investors who are not seldom to be found in peripheral regions. However the measures which are available for offsetting these losses cover a close-meshed network of social security, re-training and mobility assistance, as well as special incentives for investment in industries which are not adversely affected by liberalisation.

## Nature of Adjustment Process

Before guidelines can be formulated for the adoption of appropriate adjustment assistance measures, the pattern of the restructuring process has to be analysed. Within each country the adjustment process involves replacements between industries and branches on the one hand and between regions on the other. Assistance arrangements have to be provided at those points where inter-sectoral or

TABLE 2  Selected Characteristics of West German Industries Exposed to the Competitive Pressure of Imports from Less Developed Countries

| Industry | Share of total increase of imports[a] from LDCs 1962-70 | Raw material intensity[a,b] 1964 | Capital intensity[a] 1970 (per employee) | | | Regional concentration[c] 1970 | Share of female employees in total 1968 | Effective rate of tariff protection 1970 | Value added[a] per employee 1970 | Wages and salaries[a] per employee 1970 | Rate of return on physical capital[a] 1970 | Labour saving effect of gross fixed capital formation[d] 1964-70 |
|---|---|---|---|---|---|---|---|---|---|---|---|---|
| | | | Physical capital | Human capital | Total capital | | | | | | | |
| **Raw material-intensive industries** | | | | | | | | | | | | |
| Food, beverages and tobacco industries | 26.1 | 1.8841 | 188.2 | 73.9 | 129.5 | 0.62 | 36.6 | — | 127.6 | 94.6 | 101.9 | 1.04 |
| Woodwork industry | 2.9 | 1.3462 | 130.2 | 57.3 | 92.8 | 0.44 | 13.7 | 11.1 | 107.1 | 86.6 | 108.8 | 1.00 |
| Leather industry | 1.2 | 0.7348 | 113.7 | 88.6 | 100.8 | 0.95 | 27.5 | 10.1 | 101.4 | 86.2 | 114.5 | 4.02 |
| Non-ferrous metal industries | 31.7 | 0.6072 | 132.3 | 91.7 | 111.4 | 0.46 | 17.2 | 26.5 | 137.6 | 105.6 | 167.9 | 0.36 |
| **Labour-intensive Industries** | | | | | | | | | | | | |
| Clothing industry | 8.3 | 0.0989 | 28.9 | 25.5 | 26.7 | 0.43 | 82.2 | 21.5 | 58.4 | 62.5 | 162.9 | 0.77 |
| Leather products industries | 1.2 | 0.0136 | 27.2 | 53.5 | 40.7 | 1.06 | 61.0 | 15.5 | 72.4 | 65.8 | 280.5 | 0.72 |
| Musical instruments, toys, jewellery and sporting goods industries | 3.1 | 0.0135 | 39.4 | 49.1 | 44.4 | 0.85 | 51.9 | 9.3 | 82.5 | 74.0 | 256.0 | 0.79 |
| Footwear industry | 0.9 | 0.0262 | 39.2 | 85.3 | 62.9 | 2.15 | 58.7 | 13.2 | 60.2 | 71.0 | 92.5 | 0.84 |
| Textile industry | 13.7 | 0.2012 | 90.5 | 59.5 | 74.6 | 0.53 | 54.7 | 21.2 | 84.2 | 78.1 | 103.8 | 0.95 |
| Electrical engineering | 2.6 | 0.0214 | 57.3 | 101.4 | 80.0 | 0.67 | 37.3 | 6.7 | 80.0 | 95.5 | 84.9 | 0.43 |
| **Manufacturing total** | 100 | 0.3393 | 100 | 100 | 100 | 0.71[e] | 29.8 | 11.9[f] | 100 | 100 | 100 | 0.57 |

[a]Manufacturing total  100.— [b] Share of Inputs from the primary sector defined according to the German input-output classification (agriculture, hunting and fishing, forestry, mining and quarrying, energy and water works) in total inputs.— [c] Coefficient of Variation for industry shares in manufacturing employment by region.— [d]Ration between the rate of increase in physical capital per employee from 1964 to 1970 and the rate of gross fixed capital formation as given by the ratio between the accumulated capital formation vintages, 1964-1970, and gross fixed capital stock in the base year 1964.— [e]Weighted mean.— [f] Does not include food, beverages, and tobacco.

inter-regional immobility are bottlenecks to re-allocation. While there exist some basic features of adjustment more or less common to all countries with respect to inter-sectoral changes, there are also characteristics which are peculiar to specific countries, such as the endowment of natural resources and the regional distribution of the industries affected by adjustment. In addition to this, the readiness of entrepreneurs and the mobility of labour may differ from each other and from country to country. For instance, in the case of West Germany, entrepreneurs have proved to be highly mobile inter-regionally, but rather immobile inter-sectorally. Workers, on the other hand, do not hestitate to move from one industry to another; but they are very reluctant to change their place of living. This may not hold true for other countries like the United States where the desire to live in the same house for a lifetime is less widespread.

It follows from these considerations that in addition to an analysis of the general adjustment pattern an approach to research which focusses on a specific country is the most appropriate. But country studies of the proposed type are not available on an international scale; and a remedy for this deficiency is far beyond the scope of this paper. Thus with respect to features which might vary from country to country, the analysis is necessarily incomplete, referring only to a study which has been undertaken in the case of West Germany. With respect to other countries, the results quoted from it cannot be rated higher than preliminary hypotheses.

The effects on the developed economies of increasing manufactured exports from the developing world depend largely on the characteristics and the behaviour of the industries primarily affected by increased competition. Table 2 presents some of these features for the ten industries most affected in the case of West Germany. Four points are especially worth noting.

(1) Except for the electrical industry, all the industries chiefly affected require an input of human capital that is beneath the manufacturing average, and they employ more female workers that the average. In other words, a lower share of labour employed consists of engineers, managerial staff and skilled workers, and a higher share of female workers than in other industries.

(2) Six of the ten imports-substituting industries are regionally more evenly distributed than is total manufacturing. The shrinking of these lines, therefore, may lead to a more unequal regional distribution of industry. Moreover, the four industries for which the degree of regional concentration is above average are located mainly in peripheral regions. This reinforces the

regional problems which are likely to arise from increased imports from developing countries.

(3) As regards the factor income of the affected industries, as measured by returns to capital and the wage level, the picture is surprising. While nine of the ten industries have below average wages and salaries, only two of the ten realise below average returns to capital. From this one may presume that, in general, the incentives to move into another line of employment must be higher for entrepreneurs than for employees.

(4) As to the investment behaviour of the competing industries, the main motivation for investment seems to lie in eluding wage pressure. With the exception of the electrical and nonferrous metal industries, the pattern of investment was defensive, in the sense that it was more concerned with labour-saving than is normal.

The key issue for policy makers is the extent of labour displacement which is likely to occur along with adjustment. Though it is impossible to predict the quantitative employment effects exactly, an idea of its magnitude can be obtained by specifying certain assumptions concerning the level of increase of imports, the increase of labour productivity and the reactions of the affected industries. Of course the results are sensitive to the assumptions made and the methods employed. But competition among forecasters might reduce the subjectivity of predictions. Using more or less different assumptions and methods, forecasts have been made by Ian Little, Tibor Scitovsky and Maurice Scott [7] at the University of Oxford, the International Labour Office (ILO),[8] the UNCTAD [9] and the Institut für Weltwirtschaft, Kiel. [10] Despite the differences in the approaches, and despite the fact that most of the studies do not refer to the same countries, all of the studies share a common feature. In each case it is found that the annual rate of total displacements due to increased imports from developing countries amounts to less than one per cent of the manufacturing labour force. As the ILO and the UNCTAD studies pointed out, this is equivalent to only a small fraction of those displacements which are caused by inter-industry differences in labour productivity increases. Thus the threat of unemployment which might result from an increase in the manufacturing exports of developing countries seems to be less dramatic than it is usually described. Two important qualifications have to be made. First, unlike productivity-caused displacements, displacements due to imports are generally not considered unavoidable since it is not believed that foreign trade should be free from interference. Further, displacements of this kind are also often not considered worthwhile, since the benefits from liberalisation are not as obvious as the immediate losses. This attitude is most widespread in those developed countries which suffer from high unemployment for other reasons. Secondly, although the overall rate of import-caused unemployment is rather low, severe problems may arise in certain branches and regions, thus supporting the case for adjustment assistance.

## State of Adjustment Assistance Policy

In a comprehensive study the UNCTAD Secretariat has reviewed the adjustment assistance policies employed in five developed market economies.[11] The principal conclusions derived from this study may be summarised as follows:

(1) There is no programme specifically directed towards alleviating the repercussions of increased imports from developing countries.

(2) Apart from paying lip service to the concept of reallocation, adjustment assistance measures exist primarily in the form of aid to backward regions and in the form of general mobility incentives to investors and workers, including retraining assistance. The purpose of these measures is to facilitate responses to structural change *whatever* its causes are.

(3) Only in the United States and in Canada are adjustment assistance measures available for firms and worker groups suffering from intensified import competition due to liberalisation. These measures were introduced in connection with the tariff reductions arising from the Kennedy Round negotiations. In both countries firms may ask for aid to modernize existing plants as well as for shifting resources to other activities. In the United States' legislation, escape clause relief may be provided instead of adjustment assistance.

(4) Special attention is paid in all five countries to cotton textiles, which are a matter of central interest to many developing countries. The various assistance programmes which have been employed are widely considered to be insufficient. Therefore, in most countries the cotton textile industry presses the government for what may perhaps best be thought of as survival assistance, which can hardly be characterised as adjustment assistance in an anti-protective sense.

In these circumstances the UNCTAD analysis rightly ends on a note of disappointment: 'The continued existence of significant tariff and non-tariff barriers to the exports of developing countries and the exemption by many countries of 'sensitive' items from the generalised system of preferences are *prima facie* evidence that existing adjustment assistance policies and programmes are neither directed nor adequate to lead to greater liberalisation of imports originating in the developing countries'.[12] To sum up, existing tools may be helpful once a crisis has occurred, but they will continue to fail to be an incentive to restructuring and a weapon against protectionism.

## New Restructuring Policies

The lack of adequate adjustment assistance instruments has become a severe impediment to further trade concessions in favour of developing countries. Accordingly a harmonisation of trade policy and internal adjustment policy is needed in order to proceed with liberalisation. Since safeguard mechanisms and quantitative restrictions must be regarded as hindrances to exporters in developing countries, policies should be designed which are able to make them redundant. This objective could be achieved by giving special incentives to motivate entrepreneurs and workers who are producing commodities considered sensitive to move to other non-sensitive production activities. At the same time, assistance to the continuance of sensitive activities must be avoided, in order to avoid defensive investment.

Government aid may take the form of tax allowances including accelerated depreciation and investment premiums in favour of entrepreneurs who wish to invest their profits in non-sensitive activities. Workers should be assisted by grants for retraining and for moving from one place to another. If they are paid less in a new job it would be fair to compensate them for a limited period of time. Older workers who are unsuccessful in attaining new employment should be offered an option of premature retirement. Access to government aid should not be tied to elegibility criteria if an activity is already recognised as sensitive. If restructuring aid is demanded for other activities, elegibility should be checked against criteria, which include comparative advantages in the division of labour with developing countries. Applying such criteria requires a careful analysis of factor intensities, cost structures and demand prospects.

The shift from security by actual or potential trade limitations to security by assistance to restructuring will not be easy for a single country to make. To abolish all trade safeguards, including quantitative restrictions, without having the guarantee that other countries will do the same, may be too much even for the most liberal-minded government. The reason is that a single market which is completely open would attract a more rapid import increase than the best adjustment mechanism can absorb without frictions. Thus a shift towards enforcing adjustment measures would seem to be more easily attainable in proportion to the number of developed countries agreeing upon such measures.

The question arises of whether international trade negotiations should not be concerned with this issue. First, it should be laid down that the existing emergency protection will be removed within a fixed period of time. The second objective must be to achieve a consensus among developed countries that entrepreneurs and workers producing commodities considered sensitive can reasonably expect government aid in order to move into activities not endangered by imports from developing countries. In negotiations it is not as important to agree on the details of the assistance programme which is mainly a matter of national policy, but rather on the removal of the safe-guards which have hitherto been employed.

Independent of the substitution of adjustment assistance for safeguards, each developed country should arrange its regional policy and its domestic and foreign investment policy in ways that make room for more imports from developing countries. In this connection regional policy plays an important role. As analysis of the adjustment process has made evident, peripheral regions and female workers — who are inter-regionally less mobile than male workers — tend to be the most adversely affected by trade adjustment and liberalisation. It is the task of regional programmes to strengthen the attractiveness of peripheral regions for activities which will not be endangered. But at present regional policy in nearly all countries is far from this objective. It aims mainly at simple job creation, thus acting as a hidden subsidy to labour-intensive activities, where further competitive difficulties with developing countries are likely to arise. In order to make regional policy consistent with the adjustment assistance programme outlined above, all sensitive activities should be excluded from regional aid.

Most of the incentives involved in regional programmes, industrial policy and foreign investment are related to the amount of funds invested. Hence the factor of production primarily subsidised is physical capital. But this structure of incentives is not in line with the structure of relative scarcity of factors of production. A common-sense analysis — which of course simplifies — may illustrate the importance of this point. Three main factors of production may be taken into account: physical capital, low-skilled or unskilled labour, and human capital which is a proxy for skilled labour and the capability to develop and apply new productive and organisational techniques. Developed countries have at their disposal a highly educated and well trained labour force and an efficient communication system. Human capital seems therefore to be relatively more abundant than low skilled or unskilled labour. 'Relatively' means here that the scarcity relation is different in developing countries. In those countries there is plenty of unskilled and unemployed labour, but a significant lack of workers and technicians who can operate and manage a modern production process — despite the fact that in some countries people with a formal university degree are also unemployed. Physical capital has to be considered as the factor of production which is the most mobile between developed and developing countries. Thus what matters is to combine physical capital in developed countries primarily with human capital, and in developing countries primarily with low skilled and unskilled labour.

With this rough blueprint of a better international division of production in mind, it might be concluded that the structure of incentives should be redirected along the following lines:

(1) Incentives to direct investment in developing countries based on the number of jobs created would generate more jobs in those countries than the usual practice of tax allowances which vary according to the amount of funds invested. Job-orientated incentives are more conducive to bringing about an efficient reallocation of world resources and an international transfer of industrial activities. Such an international structural transformation is in line with the comparative disadvantages of developed countries and it may mitigate the mass unemployment in developing countries.

(2) Developed countries require a mechanism which diverts capital into those lines in which they can maintain comparative advantages. This mechanism has to work even before the pressure of increased import competition becomes severe. Perhaps such an arrangement could be achieved by domestic investment incentives connected with regional or industrial policies based on the skill-intensity of new projects or upon the research and development investments associated with them. The latter variable, at least, is as easily manageable as the sum of physical investment. In other words, instead of hardware investment we should aim to encourage software investment.

On the basis of these preliminary considerations perhaps the way may be seen more clearly towards an adjustment assistance policy which will operate not only in terms of smoothing and facilitating the adjustment process but also in terms of promoting it.

## NOTES AND REFERENCES

1. Drawing on the work of a major research project on trade barriers and the allocation of resources in West Germany, this paper was first published as 'Exports of the Developing World: the Problem of Adjustment Assistance', *The Round Table*, London, July 1973.

2. Gerhard Fels, 'The Choice of Industry-mix in the Division of Labour between Developed and Developing Countries', *Weltwirtschaftliches Archiv*, Kiel, 1972.

3. *The Generalized System of Preferences*, Report of the UNCTAD Secretariat, TD/124 (Geneva: United Nations, 1971), for the third UNCTAD session in Santiago, Chile.

4. *International Development Strategy for the Second United Nations Development Decade* (New York: United Nations Centre for Economic and Social Information, 1970), para. 30.

5. *Nachrichten für den Aussenhandel*, Frankfurt, 11 October 1972.

6. Richard N. Cooper, 'The EEC Preferences: a Critical Evaluation', *Intereconomics*, Hamburg, April 1972.

7. Ian Little, Tibor Scitovsky and Maurice Scott, *Industry and Trade in Some Developing Countries: a Comparative Study* (London and New York: Oxford University Press, 1970).

8. International Labour Office, 'Some Labour Implications of Increased Participation of Developing Countries in Trade in Manufactures and Semi-manufactures', in *Proceedings of the United Nations Conference on Trade and Development: Second Session*, Vol. IV, Problems and Policies of Trade in Manufactures and Semi-manufactures (New York: United Nations, 1968).

9. *Adjustment Assistant Measures*, Report by the UNCTAD Secretariat, TD/121/Supp. 1 (Geneva: United Nations, 1972) for the third UNCTAD session in Santiago, Chile.

10. Gerhard Fels and Ernst-Jungen Horn, 'Der Wandel der Industriestrukturim Zuge der Weltwirtschaftlichen Integration der Entwicklungsländer', *Die Weltwirtschaft, Kiel*, 1972.

11. *Adjustment Assistant Measures, op. cit.*

12. *Ibid.*

# CHAPTER 15

## Emergency Protection against Sharp Increases in Imports

### JAN TUMLIR

If governments are to be able to commit themselves to a schedule of tariff reductions which will extend over a number of years, it is generally agreed that they need what are termed 'safeguards' — that is, agreed rules according to which (a) tariff cuts might be postponed, (b) previously lowered tariffs might be raised or (c) quantitative restrictions might be imposed on imports whose unrestrained growth exceeds the adjustment capacity of the corresponding domestic industries or at any rate threatens other unacceptable damage.[1] A good number of governments feel strongly that the formulation of a new safeguard mechanism should be an integral, indeed an essential, part of the seventh round of multilateral trade negotiations formally launched in Tokyo in September 1973. Other governments are wary, fearing that such changes as would be demanded in the existing rules might reduce, rather than enhance, the degree of stability in the trading conditions of major markets.

The purpose of this paper is to provide, first, a background to the discussion of the issue, secondly an analysis of what has come to be considered the crucial problem of safeguard action and, thirdly, a possible framework in which that discussion could usefully be conducted. The background consists of an analysis of Article 19 of the General Agreement on Tariffs and Trade (GATT) and of the procedures developed under it, focusing on such aspects of both as might explain the increasingly widespread resort by governments experiencing import 'emergencies' to procedures other than those envisaged in that article. The crucial problem refers to the function of the most-favoured-nation (MFN) clause — expressing the principle of non-discrimination — in the context of emergency protection. Finally, the framework for the discussion of a new safeguard mechanism consists of two simple propositions.

The first proposition is that future needs for emergency protection — for example, those foreseeable in the course of a new phase of trade liberalisation — and all existing non-tariff restrictions[2] are only two aspects of one problem. It cannot be expected that all of the existing restrictions will be eliminated in the Tokyo Round of negotiations. And it is impossible, too, to think of a safeguard mechanism which would be adequate from the exclusive viewpoint of future emergencies, while the control and eventual elimination of

260

the restrictions inherited from the past would be achieved through other clauses and procedures. Clearly, both aspects, the future and the past, can be satisfactorily dealt with only by a procedure derived from a single set of generally accepted principles.

The second proposition grows logically from the first, if the latter is considered against the background of the analysis presented in the first section of this essay. It is that the 'tighter' the safeguard mechanism with respect to future emergencies — the more demanding it is in such matters as 'evidence of injury caused by imports' — the less suited it would be to the purpose of re-establishing multilateral control over, and an eventual elimination of, the existing non-tariff restrictions.

## Existing Multilateral Clause and Procedure

The General Agreement already contains at least nine different safeguard clauses,[3] the most relevant for the present discussion being Article 19[4] on 'emergency action on certain imports'. It authorises emergency import-restricting measures on the conditions that

(a) actual or threatened injury to domestic industries, due to unforeseen developments and to the effect of obligations under the GATT, is shown,

(b) the countries concerned consult each other, and

(c) the import restraints are imposed in a non-discriminatory fashion.

Most of the numerous import restraints imposed in the last decade or so for the purpose for which Article 19 had originally been intended were imposed, however, either under the more permissive Arrangement Regarding International Trade in Cotton Textiles or without any GATT sanction at all. Faced with this reluctance of trading countries to use the existing safeguard clause, apparently because the obligations which it imposes on the import-restraining country are considered too onerous, is it not to be feared that the new mechanism to emerge from multilateral trade negotiations could be so loose as to empty the concurrent tariff agreement of meaning? In this situation Hugh Corbet's observation that 'GATT principles do not need to be reformed as much as they need to be reasserted' seems hard common sense. 'Those (general) principles,' he suggests, 'now appear to be more honoured in the breach than in the observance.'[5]

Yet the observation is, on reflection, rather wistful. It is hard to believe that the GATT could be reasserted by a simple collective decision to return to a situation *quo ante*, and Eden before the fall where rules had been observed, without some old rules being re-written and some additional principles and rules being formally accepted. The economic changes of the last decade (particularly the strong acceleration of world trade in manufactures), and the prospects which they open, make Article 19 even less satisfactory today and to even more countries than it was in the 1950s. In a sense to be specified immediately, the article is too exacting in that the country invoking it risks retaliation (or risks paying too much) for taking emergency action, and, at the same time, it is too lenient in allowing emergency protection to become permanent.

### Article 19: Too Exacting and Too Lenient

In the event that the consultation required by Article 19 does not satisfy a country or countries whose export interest was adversely affected, 'the affected contracting parties (signatory countries) shall then be free, no later than ninety days after such action is taken, to suspend . . . the application to the trade of the contracting party taking such action . . . of such substantially equivalent concessions or other obligations . . . the suspension of which the contracting parties do not disapprove' (Article 19, paragraph 3a). In other words, the country or countries adversely affected can retaliate in a discriminatory fashion, but only to the extent of the injury sustained, the GATT signatory countries (or the Council representing them) seeing to it that the retaliation is not excessive.

To avoid retaliation, countries invoking Article 19 have offered in certain cases compensation in the form of most-favoured-nation concessions on selected products exported by the country adversely affected. It is clear, however, why cases amenable to settlement by a withdrawal or offer of an *equivalent* concession are rare. Since the emergency action itself must conform to the MFN rule, it may adversely affect a number of exporting countries each of which may demand or withdraw a concession on a different product. In most instances, the impossibility of reaching a mutually satisfactory settlement on the basis of reciprocity can be seen *ex ante*, and the country in emergency will then seek a solution to its problem not involving the invocation of Article 19.

On the other hand, Article 19 authorises protective action against imports which 'cause or threaten serious injury' for 'such time as may be necessary to prevent *or* (italics mine) remedy such injury' (Article 19, paragraph 1a). No remedial action being prescribed, protection is in effect sanctioned for so long as the threatening export capacities continue to exist abroad. The consultative procedures developed in practice actually give Article 19 a bias toward making the emergency protection permanent. A retaliatory withdrawal or a compensatory offer settles the account once and for all. And an exporting country which was not offered compensation and which decided against retaliation in the first consultation, is prohibited, by paragraph 3(a) of Article 19, from retaliating after three months following the emergency action.

## Specious Distinction between Legal and Illegal Measures

If these shortcomings are serious enough from the viewpoint of any current emergency, they make Article 19 a wholly inadequate instrument for — indeed, a positive obstacle to — any joint effort to liberalise and dismantle the existing non-tariff restrictions which, in their totality, may well represent a more serious obstacle to international trade than the remaining tariffs. One of the main difficulties in this respect has been the somewhat specious distinction made between legal and illegal restrictions,[6] combined with the strongly held view of certain governments that legal restrictions could be liberalised through reciprocal bargaining, whereas the illegal ones must be either liberalised unilaterally or legalised — that is, submitted to consultation under Article 19. It should be kept in mind that most of the restrictions which are discriminatory in form

. . . including (a) the illegal but formally unassailable 'voluntary' export restraints, as well as (b) discriminatory quotas established under escape clauses of bilateral trade agreements and under Articles 3 and 4 of the Arrangement Regarding International Trade in Cotton Textiles —

were put into effect in this form precisely in order to get around the difficulties inherent in Article 19. For this reason they can hardly be expected to be brought up for consultation, and thus legalised, under that article.

In the case of restrictions imposed on an MFN basis, it can be presumed that all trading partners of the protecting country have an interest in getting the restraint lifted. In the case of discriminatory quotas, however, the interest of a large number of trading countries may be in maintaining the *status quo*. Furthermore, even if it were assumed that the illegal restraints could be legalised, it would not follow that they could afterwards be lifted on the basis of reciprocal bargaining. The preceding discussion has already shown how narrow the basis for reciprocity is in this field, even with respect to restrictions imposed on an MFN basis, and the asymmetry of interests bearing on discriminatory protection erodes the basis for reciprocal bargains still further.

*Need for Generality in Safeguard Clause*

These considerations should be sufficient to establish the need for a new safeguard clause. In the present situation, characterised by a precarious balance of the protectionist and the liberal interest, the clause would have two *equally important* objectives:

> (a) to place all future cases of emergency protection on a legal basis — that is, under truly multilateral surveillance ensuring that such protection would be only temporary; and
> (b) to provide a basis from which an effective attack could be mounted on all non-tariff restrictions already in existence, whether legal or illegal.

The need for generality in such a safeguard clause should be emphasised. Although the cotton textile industry could be regarded, in the early 1960s, as a distinct industry beset by special problems, the Arrangement Regarding International Trade in Cotton Textiles did set a precedent in favour of "sectoral" emergency procedures differing in *principal respects* from industry to industry. The precedent continues to exist and the great acceleration of international trade in recent years, unforseeable in the early 1960s, is making it increasingly dangerous. Indeed, there is no better way of illustrating the danger than by reference to the rates of growth now considered normal in international trade.

> In the decade 1962-72, world trade in manufactures was expanding by some 13 per cent per annum, with exports of manufactures from developing to developed countries growing by 20 per cent per annum and continuing to accelerate. [7]

The only guarantee of order in this dynamic situation lies in the trading countries' acceptance of *general principles* of emergency protection, letting — where necessary — only the modalities vary from industry to industry.

## Central Problem of Safeguard Action

It should be obvious now that the core difficulties with Article 19 are the principles of most-favoured-nation treatment and of reciprocity, the latter including the right to retaliate as its own enforcement mechanism. The principle of reciprocity in particular, however useful or necessary in tariff bargaining, has, in its narrow sense of equating incremental changes in imports and exports, no legitimate function in the regulation of emergency protection. Reciprocity, one recalls, also means mutual dependence, mutual responsibility and co-operation. It appears destructive of the spirit of reciprocity in this sense for a country in an emergency to be obliged to pay for taking *bona fide* temporary action, to negotiate such a payment and to be threatened with retaliation if it does not offer enough. The historical insistence on reciprocity (in the bargaining sense) in Article 19 actions represents an effort by negotiating governments to prevent a balance of concessions achieved in previous negotiations from being upset by a unilateral withdrawal under an emergency clause. One of the reasons for which governments shun invoking Article 19, however, is the domestic political difficulty to which the procedure exposes them. The government taking such action must find it very difficult indeed to explain to the legislature and to the public at large why compensation should be given for what cannot but appear to them a rightful action.

The principle of non-discrimination appears to pose a difficulty in this context only through its conjunction with the principle of reciprocity. But the problem is more complex than that. Article 19 does not explicitly oblige the country taking protective action to compensate its adversely-affected trading partners.[8,9] Instead the practice of compensation developed *ad hoc* in GATT consultations.[10] This indicates that the need for compensation was generated by the MFN requirement, and that the latter would continue to pose a problem even if the right to emergency protection was explicitly recognised.

## MFN Principle in Emergency Protection

In general terms, one of the most important functions of the MFN principle is to ensure a civilised conduct of affairs among sovereign states of unequal strength. Sovereignty implies the right to retaliate against actions adverse to national interest. But only those strong enough in bilateral terms can retaliate effectively. In this sense, by requiring *inter alia* any import restraint to be non-discriminating among all origins, adherence to the MFN rule would protect the interests of the weak countries which cannot retaliate effectively on their own. In the context of emergency protection, the rule was insisted on for the purpose of minimising the frequency of temporary protective actions, and of mobilising the interest of all other trading countries in a speedy termination of such protection.

In this respect, though, the rule proved too effective and, where it clashed with a strong national need, it forced the country pressed for action to solve its problem outside the multilateral framework. When a number of important countries felt the need for emergency protection at the same time, an *ad hoc* arrangement, outside the general rules of the GATT, was arrived at for trade in cotton textiles. Experience has shown that protective measures taken outside the general rules are much more difficult to terminate than actions taken within such a general framework.

In full knowledge of these facts, most governments would probably still be reluctant to waive the rule of non-discrimination in the context of emergency protection, and their motives should be understood. Without the MFN requirements, they can see, there would only be action against imports from the disrupting country or a small group of countries. If the latter was or were strong enough, compensation would no doubt be offered; if it or they were not, however, there are reasons to fear that a 'solution' would be imposed by the importing country, the interest of most others not being involved. These governments are in effect saying: 'With respect to emergency protection, MFN may not be worth much, but it is all we have got.'

### New Principle of Multilaterality

It should not be impossible to provide, in matters of emergency protection, the assurance of civilised conduct, and security for the small and weak, through less rigorous but also less self-defeating rules. The waiver of the MFN rule in this context need not lead to crass bilateralism. It is logically possible to make a distinction between the MFN principle and the principle of multilaterality.

The principle of multilaterality would stand for common responsibilities, joint decisions and international surveillance — the continuous presence of a concerned forum in which a country can complain and seek mediation for its grievance against another country, or even seek adjudication. The experience described in the preceding pages suggests that this principle is more important than non-discrimination pure and simple for ensuring that emergency protection will be limited to real emergencies, where there would be a right to protect and no need to compensate, and that the protective measures will be eventually lifted. If this distinction could be accepted, the pragmatic course would be to seek ways of compromising with the MFN principle without sacrificing multilaterality.

At the outset of this search, it would have to be recognised that in the majority of emergency situations to be expected, it would be impossible anyway to maintain the MFN principle in its purity. It is essentially a principle of tariff policy[11] and, even in this area, it can be easily satisfied in letter but circumvented in intent. The general development of the world economy, the continuing acceleration of international trade and the growing resort in the past decade to protective actions outside the multilateral framework, all suggest that in future emergencies protection will largely rely on non-tariff means. In respect to such policy instruments the notion of 'most-favoured-nation treatment' immediately develops considerable ambiguity.

Assume a situation which is not only plausible but likely to become commonplace in a not too distant future. An important industry in an important trading country is being 'disrupted' by imports. These come from a large number of sources, most of which are mature, industrialised and fully-employed economies whose exports expand along traditional lines of specialisation and at a moderate pace, well within the overall rhythm of development of the mature economies as a group. The dynamic element in the situation, the source of disruption in other words, is exports from a limited number of expanding economies enjoying a comparative cost advantage which is still growing rapidly and unforeseeably, so that the adjustment of the import-competing industry could not be reliably safeguarded by an imposition of emergency duties. If a quantitative restriction seems called for in this situation, the establishment of a global quota within which all exporters would be free to compete would seem to be the only way of satisfying the MFN requirement.

In the case just outlined, though, the limited number of dynamic exporters would be likely to pre-empt the quota for themselves so that, even with provisions for annual growth in the import quota, the large number of the old-established exporters might see their sales to the country-in-emergency decline to zero. In an attempt to protect the established interests, the restraining country might sub-divide the global quota by product varieties. Yet it would still be impossible to know in advance whether the dynamic exporters, having their major export product-variety restrained, might not find it profitable to diversify their production and fill the other specific product-quotas as well.

The only solution offering security to the traditional exporters lies in the establishment of country-quotas. There are two basic alternatives:

(a) All countries could be assured equal growth from a base point volume.

(b) Alternatively, growth of national exports of the products in question could be scaled down proportionately from the recorded national performance in a base period.

Neither solution would conform to the MFN principle strictly speaking, although the second would be closer to it in spirit. The disadvantage of both, however, is in their theoretical nature. The fact is that even within a most narrowly defined industry, different countries export different products. And, obversely, the corresponding import-competing industry has product lines capable of survival and development as well as product lines which are doomed and have to be more or less gently phased out. In a system of quotas that would take account of the structure and relative competitiveness of the industry in the importing country, on the one hand, and of the relative competitiveness of the exporters, on the other, the MFN principle is bound to be ground to dust.

Intensive negotiations would take place to 'take adequate account of special circumstances', and power-politics would again be loosed upon the trading world.[12] In particular, the developing countries as a group could be expected to claim exemption from the emergency restraint.[13] The rapidly growing importance of several developing countries as exporters of manufactures makes it unlikely that this claim would be accepted as a general principle. In this complex situation, a certain degree of uniformity could perhaps be re-established, and a reasonable compromise with the MFN principle achieved, if it were agreed that there was no need to penalise the competitively weak and struggling developing countries, or any other competitively weak country for that matter. It would be both equitable and efficient with respect to the purpose of the safeguard clause if it contained a general exemption, providing that emergency protection measures would not be applied to imports from countries whose export of the product in question towards the country invoking the clause has been growing — for a given number of recent years — at less than the average rate of growth of total imports of the product causing 'disruption'. To take the interest of new exporters into account, the exemption could perhaps contain an additional criterion, according to which the clause could be invoked only against countries whose export of the product in question towards the country invoking the clause exceeded a certain absolute amount in volume or value. Additional criteria, perhaps less rigorous and intended only to guide the discussion of the international committee on emergency protection, or of a panel of experts on whose advice the committee would draw, are easily conceivable.

Related to the distinction made earlier between the principle of MFN treatment and that of multilaterality, criteria of this sort make it possible to separate two aspects (or constituent elements) of discrimination, and to eliminate one of them. The most obvious aspect of discrimination is, of course, that not all trading partners are treated equally. The second and more important one is that it is the importing country which decides what treatment it will mete out to its individual suppliers. It is this second dangerous aspect of sovereign national choice that the proposed criteria would eliminate.

**Range of Alternatives**

In an alternative safeguard clause which would recognise each country's right to emergency protection, that right would have to be balanced by a commitment, and a procedure, giving its trading partners an effective assurance of a continuously growing access to the protected market and of a foreseeable removal of the emergency measures. A balance between a right and an obligation would be achieved if a country experiencing difficulty would be authorised to take protective action on three conditions:

(a) The emergency protection must be degressive on a finite time-scale to be negotiated among the countries concerned, but in no case longer than 'x' years;

(b) It must[14] be accompanied by a demonstrable adjustment effort on the part of the government or the industry seeking emergency protection;[15]

(c) And it must be open to multilateral surveillance from inception to termination.

A procedure based on these principles, it might be noted in passing, would be much easier to defend politically. In the domestic policy debate it would tend to isolate the protectionist interest.

While responding to the most obvious shortcomings of the procedures developed under Article 19, this alternative proposal still has to come to grips with a fundamental objection. It implies that it should not be necessary for the country in difficulty to convince its trading partners, who would be waiving their right to retaliate in the first consultation, that imports from them were causing a serious injury. In any specific case, the balance of rights and obligations might thus not appear to the trading partners to be adequate. The trading community as a whole might consider this new procedure to be too lenient, too readily amenable to abuse and, thereby, too dangerous.[16] Are any further adjustments possible to strengthen the clause against objections of this kind? The scope for variation can best be indicated by sketching out two extreme versions of a procedure based on the recognition of any country's right to emergency protection.

*'Hardest' Version of Proposed Safeguard Clause*

In the 'hardest' version, the country taking action would be required to show serious injury according to the criteria of Article

19,[17] but it would be understood beforehand that where a serious injury was shown to exist, no compensation would be required or relatiation allowed at the moment of implementation of the protective measures. In the first consultation the trading partners would therefore merely discuss the degree of seriousness of the injury, and negotiate (i) about the duration of the required protection, (ii) about the schedule of degressiveness of these protective measures and (iii) about the adjustment measures to be taken in the country invoking the clause. The trading partners would not be permanently waiving their right to retaliation. If the protecting government arrested the phase-out process after a few years, or if its adjustment effort (on which it would have to report annually) were found inadequate, countries adversely affected could then demand compensation or retaliate in a discriminatory fashion.

Even this hard version could be objected to as being too lenient since without the right to retaliate in the first consultation, the trading partners could hardly be said to be in a position to *negotiate* about the duration and modalities of temporary protection. This objection, however, is less serious than it appears since it would also have to be a part of the agreement that emergency protection under this clause cannot last more than 'x' years. The maximum period should be about seven years.[18] In the first negotiation the trading partners would be trying to limit the period of protection to less than the statutory maximum and this might well be possible in some cases, especially if the consultation drew on the advice of, or relied on the mediation by, a panel of independent (or semi-independent) experts. In the long run, the effectiveness of this part of the procedure would depend very much on how early a first precedent — that is, a negotiated period of emergency protection which would be shorter than the statutory maximum — could be created.

To countries vitally dependent on foreign trade, especially to countries forced by the tariff-cutting programme to effect substantial transfers of labour from import-competing to export production,[19] even a period of seven years might seem unduly long. To meet their concern, it should be also understood — and it should not be difficult to agree among countries professing their belief in the beneficial influence of trade on economic efficiency — that in no case should the growth of imports be limited so as to equal, let alone fall below, the rate of growth of the domestic production of comparable goods.[20] Imports produced at competitive prices should continue to increase their share in consumption in the importing market, and so to exert incessant pressure for adjustment. Indeed, for reasons given in the closing part of this paper, it would be advisable to insist that if the invoking country proposed to employ non-tariff means of emergency protection it would have to commit itself in the first consultation to a certain minimum rate of growth of imports of the product under restraint. Finally it has to be pointed out that the phrase 'maximum period of seven years' creates at first sight something of an optical illusion. If it is understood that emergency protection, in whatever form it is given, is progressively declining throughout the period so as to be completely phased out at the end of the last year, it is easy to see that exporters would feel a severe restraint only in the first two or three years.

A more serious shortcoming of the hard alternative lies precisely in its hardness. It must be admitted that a democratic government can come under intense political pressure for protection in situations in which it is difficult if not impossible to show, according to the criteria of Article 19, that a serious injury is being caused by imports. Industries weak in import competition usually suffer from difficulties of domestic origin as well. [21] In this sense the hard alternative might not be sufficiently inviting to induce countries to use it in all cases of need and, consequently, the number of illegal protective measures might continue to grow. By the same token — and this is the most serious shortcoming — the hard alternative appears particularly unpromising as an instrument for coping with the existing illegal measures and with protection sanctioned by more permissive arrangements or imposed under bilateral safeguard clauses and export restraint agreements.

Thus the main, and a not inconsiderable, advantage of the hard alternative is that it would minimise the required changes in the present text of Article 19. All the relatively minor re-interpretations introduced in the preceding paragraphs — the right to retaliate at a later date where the article itself imposes a three months limit, the fixing of the maximum period for which emergency protection would be allowed, the understanding that imports should always, even in the initial year of the period, be allowed to expand somewhat more rapidly than domestic production, and the understanding that adjustment assistance should be arranged for the industry or firms in question — could be converted into commitments through a special protocol of interpretation of Article 19.

### *"Softest" Version of Proposed Safeguard Clause*

The 'softest' alternative, on the other hand, would altogether dispense with the show of injury as a necessary condition for instituting emergency protection. Any country experiencing a difficulty over imports, however 'subjectively' felt, would have the right to institute temporary protection conforming to the principles set out above, without having to fear retaliation at the time it was taking such action. This does not imply that no discussion of the difficulty or injury would take place. In the first consultation the country would have to make a case for protection, to describe the difficulty of the industry in question, in order to show that the adjustment measures it proposes at the same time are adequate in the sense that protection would not longer be necessary after the agreed period. The essential characteristic of the soft alternative is that there would be no right to retaliation at the time the emergency protection measures were introduced, whether the case for them were convincing or not, whereas in the hard alternative initial retaliation would be disallowed only in convincing cases of injury by imports.

The fear that the leniency of this clause would invite abuse can be easily exaggerated. Under both alternatives, retaliation would be authorised against protective measures maintained beyond the agreed or statutory period. The temporariness of the safeguard measures would thus be ensured more strongly than ever before. And, let it be noted, industries do not engage in costly campaigns for protection in order to gain only a temporary respite from imports. Industries clearly prefer protection, which they expect to be permanent, to adjustment; and as long as they can hope to obtain such protection they will deride the available adjustment measures. Post-war European experience shows, though, that industries faced with an irrevocable schedule of trade liberalisation pour all their energy into adjustment and achieve it quite quickly. Following an agreement on a safeguard clause of this type the pressure on governments from their own industries demanding protection would accordingly relent considerably.

Second, the adjustment obligation would not be a light one and this fact, too, would make it difficult if not impossible to use the temporary protection for making political gifts or debt payments. Even the West European governments which operate various kinds of industrial adjustment programmes as a matter of routine would perceive that the commitment to a demonstrable adjustment effort is a burden. The routine industrial adjustment measures are administered by a host of public, semi-public and private institutions, the regular publication of whose accounts does not attract much publicity. There is therefore a certain administrative convenience in the present practice. It would be different, however, in cases where industrial adjustment assistance were being given under an international commitment. In economic theory, subsidies to weak industries are clearly preferable to protection. Governments, on the other hand, consider protection preferable to subsidies because the cost of protection is less visible. Under parliamentary and press scrutiny of public budgets, subsidies to weak industries, seen as transfers of public money to private hands, would clearly be allowed much less frequently than protection.

In short, the 'soft' version amounts to a recommendation to the main trading countries, as a group, to show more trust in the internal democratic process of each of them. It is possible to believe that the examination of the need for emergency protection by a specialised domestic authority, and by the parliament and the press, would be as scrupulous as that performed by an international committee. It should be kept in mind that a discussion of the problem would proceed on the international level virtually at the same time. If an international committee were to discuss the findings of a mediating panel of experts, the international procedure would automatically feed back into, or be anticipated by, the national scrutiny and would thereby make the latter more effective. In this respect, an advantage of the 'soft' version would consist in having at the international level only a discussion of the problem, without the acrimony necessarily accompanying committee fights for approval or rejection of waivers. That bitter part would be unloaded onto the national process.

Even so, the main advantage of the 'soft' option would lie in its suitability to cover all cases of protection afforded to particular lines of production. It would, first of all, considerably reduce the inducement to seek protection outside the multilateral framework; indeed, an agreement on such a safeguard clause could well be accompanied by an explicit standstill agreement as to other emergency actions. More important, it would make it possible to bring under multilateral surveillance all the existing cases of special protection including exporters' 'self-restraints', discriminatory measures allowed under escape clauses of bilateral trade treaties, and even those sanctioned by the Arrangement Regarding International Trade in Cotton Textiles. Two considerations support this conclusion.

First, if the agreement on the rules of the new safeguard clause were considered by the trading community to be a valuable achievement, all countries would feel the need to extend the application of the clause to existing protection for the simple reason that tolerated exceptions inevitably erode the existing rules. There would therefore be a pressure to bring up existing restriction and restraints for consultation under the new procedure. A maximum period for doing this could be agreed. Or perhaps two periods could be agreed: a shorter one for industrial and a longer one for agricultural protection; or one for legal and one for illegal restrictions.

Second, most of the existing special import and export restraints are temporary in form and have to be periodically renewed. Since the new rules of emergency protection would, at the same time, contribute to adjustment in the importing country and strengthen the legal and political position of the exporter, the periodic renewals of such restraints would become less necessary and more difficult to negotiate.

It should be obvious at this stage that between the 'hard' and the 'soft' version there exists practically a continuum of intermediate versions, the degree of hardness depending mainly on the criteria adopted for determining whether an injury is being caused by imports. Whatever the precise form of these criteria, it can be assumed that data on imports on the one hand, and on the corresponding domestic production and employment on the other, would be an essential element of them. From an analytical viewpoint, changes in production, in conjunction with changes in imports, would generally be a more reliable — though still ambiguous — indicator of 'injury by imports' than employment changes. All the same, employment data would have to be considered as well, because both sides could be expected to maintain that harmful effects on employment constituted an important justification of emergency protection.

## Importance of Principles of Procedure

The question of criteria is closely related to that of procedure. If it were possible to agree on a set of precise quantitative criteria to indicate that injury was being caused by a sudden surge of imports, the procedure would be a relatively simple one. A panel of experts would make a finding as to whether these criteria were met in any given situation and, following a positive finding, trade representatives would discuss the nature and duration of the appropriate protective and adjustment measures.

It is, however, unlikely that a uniform set of unambiguous quantitative criteria could be established to diagnose disruption in any and all industries. Industries differ in their health and vigour; indeed, the relative position of an industry varies from economy to economy as well as through time. Where an industry in one country might spontaneously adjust to a given flow of imports, the same industry in a different country might experience a severe difficulty facing an import flow of a similar rate and magnitude. For these reasons, it appears more probable that the determination whether an industry is being injured by imports will have to be made on the basis of a more thorough scrutiny, quantitative as well as qualitative, of all relevant conditons. Ultimately, that is to say, it will have to be based on judgement.

In view of these difficulties, the only way to ensure international equity in the application of the safeguard clause, and therefore its continued effectivness, would be for the trading nations to agree on a set of principles to be observed in the process of arriving at such a judgement; in brief, to agree on a procedure by which an injury would be determined.

Formal procedures to this effect exist in a number of countries and there is also a direct precedent for the signatory countries to the GATT negotiating and accepting a determination procedure conforming to such a common set of principles. This precedent is to be found in the Agreement on the Implementation of Article 6 (the GATT Anti-Dumping Code). Most of the procedural principles specified in that code appear appropriate for safeguard proceedings. The basic ones are three in number and, with slight elaboration, are set out in the following terms:

1. There will be a standing body responsible for the determination of injury. On receiving a complaint, this body — a commission, tribunal, or a panel of experts and officials — will carry out a preliminary investigation of the relevant facts and, having satisfied itself that there is sufficient evidence to justify initiating a full-scale investigation, it will within a prescribed period of time carry out such an enquiry.

2. It will then hold a *public* hearing. Adequate provision will be made for such business information as is by nature confidential not to be revealed. In the hearing, all parties related to, or affected by, the case will have a full opportunity for the defence of their interests. To this end the authorities concerned will provide opportunities for all directly interested parties to meet those parties with adverse interests so that opposing views may be presented and rebuttal arguments offered.

3. The interested parties will normally include: the domestic industry, that is enterprise and labour; the trade, that is foreign exporters, domestic importers and the distributive trade; other industries which may be the user of the product in question; and *the consumer interest*. This last could be taken into account by a requirement that a panel of independent economists presents an estimate of the effect on retail prices of the product in question of various possible forms, extent and duration of emergency protection.

By reviewing the actual practice in countries where such commissions, tribunals or panels are already active, it would be also possible to agree on the more detailed aspects of the procedure, such as the kind of criteria to be used and the mode of their application.[22]

If an international body were to conduct a procedure conforming to these principles it would encounter numerous difficulties. In general, it can be said that a national authority can carry out an enquiry and a hearing of this kind with more thoroughness, expert knowledge and even objectivity than would be attainable at the international level. There is, therefore, a problem of fitting together a national procedure and multilateral surveillance.

The main purpose of multilateral surveillance is, of course, to prevent abuse of the safeguard clause. A commonly accepted national procedure of enquiry and public hearings to determine injury would in itself represent significant progress towards that objective. First of all, a formal requirement would ensure that all interests would be given due consideration, which is not always the case at present. Even more important, the formal body conducting the industrial enquiries and the public hearings would, by having to deal with many industries from the same vantage point, soon develop a view of the needs of the economy as a whole, and such a general view could be relied upon to be on balance favourable to free trade. By contrast, where injury determination is essentially a matter of administrative discretion, the influence of industry specialists — industry 'desks' of the appropriate ministry — is bound to be strong. These specialists are, buy virtue of their closeness to specific industries, generally protection-minded and unlikely to take fully into account the interest of the consumer or the effect of protection on other policies of the government, such as the anti-inflation policy, and thus its possible repercussions on the export sector.

Nonetheless, the trading partners of the country taking safeguard action could feel bound by the findings of such a national authority only if these findings were subject to review and explicit acceptance at the international level. Effective multilateral surveillance thus implies the possibility of the national finding not being accepted internationally, and this poses something of a dilemma since the country initiating the safeguard action would, at this stage of the proceedings, be already bound by the decision of its own legal authority.

A convenient way out of the dilemma would be opened by including in the safeguard clause a provision under which the trading partners would be waiving their right to compensation or retaliation   only in those cases in which the international committee accepted, after its own review,   the finding of injury by a national authority. After such a review the committee of trade representatives would proceed to negotiate the modalities and duration of emergency protection, and to discuss the parallel industrial adjustment plan.

Where the international committee could not accept a national finding of injury, the government in need of safeguard action would still have the possibility of protecting its sensitive industry, but it would have to offer equivalent compensation to, or suffer corresponding retaliation by, its trading partners. In this case it would be the function of the committee to arbitrate possible disputes as to the 'equivalence' of compensatory concessions or retaliatory withdrawals.

## MFN Principle and the Soft Option

This partial return to Article 19 poses the question whether in the second 'soft' alternative safeguard clause, the traditional procedures should not apply in full; that is, whether it should not be required that in cases where there was no international agreement on the existence of injury, emergency protection must be non-discriminatory in nature. It must be admitted that the question has a certain logic. If a country puts up emergency protection where the international body sees no justification for it, multilateral surveillance should be acknowledged to have failed in its main objective of preventing abuse of the safeguard clause. And in this case, the more traditional deterrent to abuse, namely the MFN requirement, should be brought into play as a second line of defence.

A great advantage of this requirement is that it would strengthen the determination procedures of the national authority. Knowing that there were only two alternatives open

—with international concurrence, protection without compensation; without it, non-discriminatory protection with adequate compensation to all adversely affected interests —

the national authority could be expected to be more rigorous in its determination of injury. Positive findings would only be found in those cases in which it could be reasonably sure of international acceptance.

While strong, the case for retaining the MFN requirement with the soft alternative is not overwhelming; in fact, the writer has to admit that in his mind it remains a moot point. It has been shown that in the context of safeguard action, the MFN requirement has not been an ideal deterrent. It has prevented only the abuse of a legal procedure for emergency protection, but not the protection itself, and has therefore led to a proliferation of illegal protective measures.

The danger involved in retaining the MFN rule in the second alternative is that, if the national injury finding were not accepted by the international committee, the country taking action would again have a strong inducement to solve its problem through bilateral arrangements outside the multilateral framework. As a result a situation could emerge in which, in rejecting the finding of the national authority, the international committee would effectively wash its hands of the affair, whereas the general interest in maintaining an open legal procedure, and in narrowing the area in which international problems are being solved by bilateral confrontations, would dictate a continuing preoccupation of the committee with the case, even if it could not agree with the national injury finding.

An important additional consideration in this context is the concern, unerlying virtually all the arguments presented so far, that the new procedure be an all-embracing one; that is, able to accommodate not only all future cases in which a government may be compelled to grant protection to a domestic petitioner, but also all the existing cases of special protection and export retraint.

All these considerations constitute an impressive case for relaxing the insistence on MFN treatment even in the second alternative. It could, for example, be left to the international committee to decide whether a degree of selectivity, conforming to the criteria suggested in the last paragraphs of the section on the 'central problems', might not be allowed in special circumstances.

## Safeguarding the Interests of Small Countries

It has also been shown that in the context of emergency protection one of the main functions of the MFN principle is to protect the weaker members of the international trading community. It is therefore relevant to ask whether a danger exists that the rights of the small countries, possessing inadequate bargaining power, could be infringed if emergency protection were allowed to be selective even in those cases where compensation were required or retaliation allowed. In past cases of discriminatory protective action, a large country could coerce its smaller trading partners into self-restraint or 'voluntary' acceptance of negotiated quotas by threatening to impose, as an alternative, even stricter mandatory quotas. The possibility of exercising this kind of pressure would be significantly reduced by the very act of acceptance by the country seeking emergency protection of the international discipline implied in the safeguard clause.

The main danger inherent in allowing protection to be discriminatory, however, is that the degree of restraint will be negotiated bilaterally, in situations only exceptionally characterised by a symmetry of bargaining power and that, consequently, the notion of 'multilateral surveillance' will be emptied of meaning. Such bilateral bargaining is said to be necessary 'for the special needs of individual exporting countries to be adequately taken into account'. In virtually all cases of past practice, though, it has resulted in strikingly low rates of growth of total imports of the product in question into the restraining country — rates which have been low in comparison with the growth of both similar imports into countries not imposing a special restraint, and of trade in manufactured products in general. Multilateral surveillance is to be provided through an annual meeting of the international committee of trade representatives. But if the discriminatory quotas were set in bilateral negotiations, and thus presumably all special needs were adequately taken into account, how can the committee conclude that the growth of total imports into the restraining country has been restricted unduly?

This risk can be eliminated if the degree of necessary restriction of *total* imports of the product in question is negotiated, prior to the bilateral discussions, in the first multilateral consultation which begins by a review of the finding of the national authority. The restraining country then accepts the negotiated total restriction as a commitment. It should be emphasised that only a commitment of this kind can make multilateral surveillance effective or, indeed, meaningful. It would take the determination of the overall degree of restraint out of the arena of bilateral bargaining. For the small countries this would mean that, with respect to decisions on the orders of magnitude of national quotas, they would not face a large importer one by one but would have the judgement, and the strength, of the concerned trading community on their side. They would consequently have a guarantee that the subsequent bilateral talks would really be only about the accommodation of special needs. The overall commitment would also provide the review committee with an effective criterion by which to judge the performance of the restraining country in the future. Last but not least, it would go a long way towards safeguarding the interest of new exporters which poses a special and most difficult problem in discriminatory arrangements lacking an overall commitment.

Finally, in most past cases of the discriminatory protective action just described there was no question of compensation, whereas in the alternative under discussion there would exist an explicit commitment to compensation, the right to retaliate being held in reserve for situations in which the offered compensation was inadequate and unacceptable. Admittedly a small country is not in a good position to retaliate against a large one. But in this alternative, the risk that it might be forced to accept inadequate compensation would be further narrowed by the possibility open to it of appealing to the international committee for arbitration. In this respect, the position of small countries could be strengthened further by requiring that a panel of independent experts, acting in an advisory capacity to the committee, makes an assessment of the loss caused to an exporting country by the import restraint and of the adequacy of the compensation offered.

## Other Deterrents to Abuse

The main objective of this paper was to explore the possibility, and possible consequences, of relaxing the MFN requirement in the context of emergency protection. Since the main function of the requirement in this context was one of a deterrent to abuse, it might be useful to summarise at this point what other deterrents are present in all the elements and aspects of the safeguard clause that have been discussed.

Possibly the most important one may be found to exist in the reduction of the pressures for protection that would result from the acceptance by the trading countries of the new principles and procedures, and from their embodiment in international rules as well as national legislation.

Second are the deterrents implied in the public national procedure for the determination of injury. In this connection, the experience with international administration of the GATT Anti-dumping Code leads to a reasonable expectation that the discussions and procedures at the international level would in due time come to influence the national procedures in the direction of greater uniformity between countries, and thus greater international equity.

Third is the deterrent implied in multilateral surveillance which can be made effective through an agreement that the overall rate of growth of the imports under restraint will be negotiated multilaterally.

There are, fourthly, the more traditional deterrents implied in the fact that the invocation of the reformed safeguard clause might not be less costly than invocation of Article 19 was in the past. While in certain cases a government might successfully press an industry into adjustment financed from the industry's own resources, in other situations the obligation to effect adjustment might require considerable amounts of public funds. There would also be the provisions for compensation or retaliation in cases where the international committee did not accept a national finding of injury. Even in those cases under this alternative where selective, or discriminatory, emergency protection were allowed, the criteria elaborated at the end of the section in this paper on the 'central problems' would ensure that it would be very rare for the number of exporting countries under restraint to be as small as one, two or three. And since compensation or retaliation are disproportionately costly as the number of restrained exporters increases, the deterrent mainly intended by the MFN requirement would be retained in a somewhat attenuated form.

The procedure would thus contain a whole series of deterrents. Indeed, one could rightly talk of graduated deterrence, corresponding to the similarly graduated arrangements being sought in the reform of the international monetary system. Obviously, the element of graduation could be developed further — for example, by a provision that an additional and proportionately larger compensation could be required, or retaliation allowed, if a country failed to phase out emergency protection in the initially agreed period and had to apply for an extension.

*Two General Considerations*

In closing, two more general considerations should be mentioned briefly. Political developments within the main trading countries have in recent years been indicating the need to limit the degree of bureaucratic discretion in matters of emergency protection. Protectionist pressures from specific industrial interests, with which mankind must expect to live for at least the rest of the century, pose a grave problem for the integrity of the democratic process. Without a procedure of open hearings to establish an injury and a claim to protection, the national administrations, and even the electoral process, would continue to be exposed to finely targeted and increasingly well-financed campaigns, straddling the borders of legality, of which the electorate is generally unaware. Taking the decision-making on protection into the open along the lines suggested here can thus be seen, not merely as a logical development and perfection of the democratic process, but as a necessary defense of its integrity. No less important, the institution of public hearings would improve the democratic process by educating the public to the complexities of the economic issues involved in emergency protection, and away from the still prevalent, crudely xenophobic protectionism.

International policy-planning also has to be based on the expectation that the forces pressing for accelerated transformation of economic structures, against the increasingly widespread vested interest of the new middle class (which now includes most wage-earners) in the fully industrialised countries, will give rise to intensifying protectionist counter pressures, likely to aim at limiting specific imports, not merely from developing countries, but from other developed countries as well. Without an internationally agreed and binding procedure for coping with 'sudden surges' in imports, the governments of the industrialised countries would be in a very weak position against their industries demanding protection. They would have only one ultimate argument for refusing it, namely that the other side would retaliate. While mutual deterrence may be a stable way of life among the great nuclear powers of this world, mutual commercial deterrence of this sort is unthinkable as a long-term arrangement among a much larger group of countries whose professed bond is the principle of the rule of law.

## NOTES AND REFERENCES

1. The writer wishes to emphasise that the opinions expressed in this chapter are his own and not to be interpreted as reflecting the views of the organisation with which he is associated. The paper appeared earlier as Jan Tumlir, *Proposals for Emergency Protection against Sharp Increases in Imports*, Guest Paper No. 1 (London: Trade Policy Research Centre, 1973) and drew on an article published in the *Journal of World Trade Law*, London, July-August 1973.

2. 'Non-tariff restrictions' is a term much narrower than 'non-tariff barriers'. The latter includes all trade-distorting policy devices, even if the distortion is only a by-product of the pursuit of an otherwise legitimate purpose, or results from a misuse of a legitimate device. The former term includes protective devices only; that is, mainly quotas and exporters' 'voluntary' self-restraints.

3. Articles 11(2c), 12, 18(2), 19-21, 25 and 28.

4. Article 12 is a general safeguard clause authorising the imposition of restrictions on all or most imports in times of balance-of-payments difficulties. Other articles mentioned in Footnote 3 authorise restrictions for very specific reasons such as national security. Article 19 authorises restrictions in cases where the flow of imports of a specific product exceeds the adjustment capacity of the corresponding domestic industry.

5. Hugh Corbet, 'Global Challenge to Commercial Diplomacy', *Pacific Community*, Tokyo, October 1971, p. 223.

6. This distinction relates to restrictions maintained with multilateral consent and those imposed without multilateral consultation — the majority of the existing restrictions in the field of manufactures being of the latter type.

7. In both cases 'manufactures' are defined to exclude non-ferrous metals.

8. And it could be argued (a) that the consultation 'in respect of the proposed action' should only be about two questions, whether the criteria of an emergency were met and whether, given the nature of the emergency, the proposed action was not excessive; and (b) that, with agreement on both points, no compensation should be demanded. Other interpretations of the article's language, however, are also possible.

9. The MFN requirement, for that matter, is also not explicit in the text of Article 19, but the view that this was the understanding of the drafters has never been challenged.

10. Twenty out of the sixty-one cases in which Article 19 was invoked involved compensation.

11. Characteristically, the majority (40 out of 61) cases of invocation of Article 19 involved tariff action. Furthermore — in reference to Footnote 10 — compensation was confined to tariff actions only, no case of emergency protection by quantitative restrictions having been compensated.

12. It may be noted that in trade relations power stems from the amounts a country *imports* from another country. Inevitably, considerations of the relative magnitudes of total bilateral exchanges would influence the setting of national quotas for any specific product.

13. A suggestion that developing countries be exempted from measures applied under Article 19 has been under examination in the GATT Committee on Trade and Development for some time.

14. It may not be easy to see at first glance why an obligation to institute an adjustment assistance programme should be a necessary part of the procedure. If the commitment under (a) were sufficiently credible, trading partners might not consider it essential that adjustment assistance be given to the industry enjoying emergency protection. But the commitment under (b) would not only enhance the credibility of the commitment under (a); more importantly, it would constitute a deterrent to an abuse of the procedure.

15. The adjustment assistance programme, too, might be required to terminate with the emergency protection measures, as there is a potential conflict between certain forms of adjustment assistance and competition policy.

16. For a small group of economically homogenous and politically like-minded countries, it may be noted, such as the European Community or the European Free Trade Association (EFTA), the text of a safeguard clause can be brief and maximum reliance placed on consultations, the procedure of which can be developed or amended *ad hoc*. The problem is of a different order of magnitude in a large community of nations among which different interest groups can be distinguished. From this viewpoint, it is important to note that the GATT community contains a group of countries either actually discriminated against or feeling a *de facto* discrimination by finding the barriers facing their particular exports to be higher than the average.

Another characteristic group is formed by the smaller developed economies. In general they are more trade intensive than the large developed economies and the fully industrialised countries of the group also maintain lower tariffs. Their governments are therefore well aware of the gains to be secured through further progress towards free trade yet, since a high proportion of their exports is sold in a few large markets, security of market access must be their primary consideration. Two sub-groups can be distinguished among these economies according to the motive or, perhaps, to the degree of urgency for demanding a safeguard clause in which security of export access would be emphasised.

In the developed economies, such as Canada, whose exports still contain a substantial proportion of primary products, and particularly in the developed but not yet fully industrialised economies, such as those of Australia, New Zealand and South Africa (to be followed soon by a number of countries which are now considered less developed), most of the relatively young manufacturing industries are essentially import-replacing. To this sub-group of developed economies, participation in an agreement substantially to reduce or eliminate industrial tariffs would dictate an extensive shift of manufacturing employment from the import-competing sectors (where they had some power to protect it) to the export sector (where it would depend on the commercial policies of the trading partners). The degree of sovereignty given up by these countries in renouncing their own protection would thus have to be compensated by a strengthening of their ability to influence the commercial policies of their trade partners.

The small and highly developed industrial economies of Western Europe, such as Sweden or Switzerland, on the other hand, have less of a problem on the import side, their import competing industries being highly diversified, efficient and adaptable. These countries are thus well placed to pursue the goal of more secure market access by demanding, and offering, further limitations on freedom of national action under escape clauses.

17. Under these criteria it is necessary to show that: (a) the product in question is being imported in increased quantities; (b) the increased imports are the result of unforeseen developments and of the effect of obligations under the GATT; and (c) the imports enter in such increased quantities as to cause or threaten serious injury to domestic producers of like or directly competitive products.

18. Under the current tax laws, most manufacturing machinery is fully depreciated in seven years or less.

19. It should be emphasised that these transfers need not be of an inter-industry nature. In fact, a large proportion of them might be expected to occur, not merely within the same industry, but within firms.

20. Alternatively, a still more rigorous criterion would be one allowing safeguard action only in cases where domestic production and/or employment can be shown to be stagnating or declining. As long as it continues to expand output, the domestic industry should be presumed to be successfully adjusting to import competition. In these cases the purpose of 'adjustment assistance' in a broader sense would be, not a retraining of workers losing jobs, but the creation of alternative employment opportunities for new entrants in the labour market.

21. In the textile industry, for example, which in most countries is composed of a large number of firms differing in size, efficiency and profitability, profits, unemployment and imports have often been observed to rise together, profits being accumulated by the largest and most efficient firms while the smaller and less-efficient firms have experienced unemployment. It would be impossible to show that workers were being made redundant by imports and not by competition of the large firms. Consequently, a protective action reducing the flow of imports may also, by increasing the profit margin of the large firms and stimulating their expansion, increase unemployment.

22. For example, it could be agreed that, to demonstrate the occurrence of a 'sudden surge' of imports, it would be insufficient to show that the ratio of imports to domestic production or consumption was growing, but a significant acceleration of the growth of that ratio would have to be statistically demonstrated.

23. They would still have the right to compensation or retaliation if the protecting country subsequently failed to comply with the agreed conditions.

24. The international committee would or could be assisted in its own review by a panel of experts. Since the national hearings would be public, members of the expert panel could attend them in an observer capacity and then report to the committee. A further, at the present time probably Utopian, development of this practice would be to allow the members of the international expert panel actively to participate in the national hearing.

# Index

Abu Dhabi, 125-6
American Selling Price (ASP), 41, 206
Andean Group, 61, 66
Anglo-Irish Free Trade Agreement, 179
Anti-Dumping Act, 200
Anti-Dumping Code (GATT), 200, 206, 275, 280
Argentina, 186, 234
Arrangement Regarding International Trade in Cotton Textiles, 100-1, 104, 235-6, 249, 261, 263-4, 273
Arusha Convention, 22, 40, 179
Association of South-East Asian Nations (ASEAN), 61, 66
Atlantic Charter, 37, 51, 55-6, 58-9
Australia, 31n, 40, 52, 61, 135, 137, 180, 186, 200, 204-5, 209n, 211, 218, 221, 225-6, 233, 283n

Belgium, 37, 209n
Benelux countries, 104, 209n
Benelux Economic Alliance Treaty, 103
Bergmann, Denis, 215, 227-8n
Brazil, 52, 62, 234
Bretton Woods Agreement, 17, 38, 51
British Leyland, 135
Brookings Institution, 203-4
Burke-Hartke Bill, 142, 200
'Buy American' Act, 41

Canada, 25, 40, 51, 61, 109, 133-4, 137, 145, 148n, 176, 180, 186-7, 189, 209n, 211, 218, 221, 226, 255, 283n
Canadian-American Committee, 30n, 133
*Census of Manufactures* (Japan), 79, 81, 87, 88
Central American Common Market, 179
Chile, 131
China, 48, 54, 56-7, 62, 115, 123, 134-5
Chung, Dr J.W., 195n, 204, 209n
Churchill, Sir Winston, 55
Colonna Plan, 147, 149
Commerce and Industry Committee, 93

Commission of the European Community, 28, 60, 134, 142, 144, 147, 149n, 174, 177-8, 196n
Committee on Market Disruption (GATT), 101
Committee of Twenty, 114
Committee on Trade in Industrial Products, (GATT), 206
Common Agricultural Policy (CAP), 22, 40, 43-4, 65, 157, 174, 177, 186, 196, 201, 211, 213, 216-17, 221, 226
Common Market, *see* European Economic Community
Cooper, Richard, 30n, 244n, 250, 259n
Corbet, Hugh, 20-1, 29-31n, 45n, 194-5n, 196-7n, 209n, 244n, 261, 282n
Cotton Goods Committee, 104
Council of Ministers, 28-9, 63, 66, 178, 189, 196n, 227n
Council on International Economic Policy, 25, 30-1
Cuba, 134, 237
Culvert Report, 99, 106
Curzon, Gerard, 16, 29n, 31-2n, 44n, 194-8n, 207, 209-10n
Curzon, Victoria, 31-2n, 195-8n, 207, 209-10n
Czechoslovakia, 248

Dahrendorf, Ralf, 16, 25-6, 31n
Declaration of Buenos Aires, 61
de Gaulle, Charles, 48, 59n, 142
Denmark, 31n, 186, 221, 228n, 233
Department of Commerce (USA), 92
Dillon, Douglas, 100
Directorate for Industrial Affairs and Technology, 147
Du Pont, 133

East African Common Market, 39
Eberle, William, 26, 31n, 195n
Egypt, 66
Engels, Friedrich, 49
Euratom, 63
European Coal and Steel Community (ECSC), 63
European Defence Community, 37

*285*